Arguing COMICS

Arguing
COMICS

Literary Masters on a Popular Medium

EDITED BY JEET HEER AND KENT WORCESTER

UNIVERSITY PRESS OF MISSISSIPPI

JACKSON

www.upress.state.ms.us

The University Press of Mississippi is a member of the Association of
American University Presses.

12 11 10 09 08 07 06 05 04 4 3 2 1

Library of Congress Cataloging-in-Publication Data

Arguing comics : literary masters on a popular medium / edited by Jeet Heer and
Kent Worcester.
    p. cm.
  Includes bibliographical references and index.
  ISBN 1-57806-686-7 (cloth : alk. paper)—ISBN 1-57806-687-5 (pbk. : alk. paper)
  1. Comic books, strips, etc.—History and criticism. I. Heer, Jeet. II. Worcester,
Kent, 1959–
  PN6710.A84 2004
  741.5'09—dc22   2004012865

British Library Cataloging-in-Publication Data available

Contents

Introduction

Illustrated storytelling in general, and comic strips and comic books in particular, have long excited fierce controversy. In 1846 the English poet William Wordsworth penned a sonnet, "Illustrated Books and Newspapers," that inveigled against "this vile abuse of pictured page":

> DISCOURSE *was deemed Man's noblest attribute,*
> *And written words the glory of his hand;*
> *Then followed Printing with enlarged command*
> *For thought—dominion vast and absolute*
> *For spreading truth, and making love expand.*
> *Now prose and verse sunk into disrepute*
> *Must lacquey a dumb Art that best can suit*
> *The taste of this once-intellectual Land.*
> *A backward movement surely have we here,*
> *From manhood, —back to childhood; for the age—*
> *Avaunt this vile abuse of pictured page!*
> *Must eyes be all in all, the tongue and ear*
> *Nothing? Heaven keep us from a lower stage! (Wordsworth 16)*

Must eyes be all in all? In the century and a half or so since Wordsworth posed this question, numerous writers and intellectuals have endorsed, amended and contested his claim that illustration and comics are "backward movement" that substitute visual excitement for "the tongue and ear" of conversation and text. In the twentieth century, comic strips and comic books both played starring roles in recurrent cultural conflicts over the pictured page. Individual comic strips, comic books and comics creators and publishers on occasion commanded intense public scrutiny, as did "the comic strip" and "the comic book" as things in themselves. Arguments over specific images, characters and storylines spilled over into larger controversies about the validity of illustration and cartooning in the service of narration, entertainment and social commentary. At different times, political and social figures claiming to speak for children, parents and voters promised to investigate the form and content of comics. But then, so did university and non-university intellectuals, even prior to the "cultural turn" (Bender 41) of the 1970s and 1980s.

This volume seeks to recover the comics writings of influential reviewers and critics—literary masters, if you will—who wrote on comics during the long epoch between the introduction of cheaply printed images and the consolidation of popular culture studies. In the early and mid-twentieth century, the most reflective and provocative comics commentary usually emanated from freelance intellectuals rather than civic activists or academic researchers (psychologists and educationalists were applying behavioralist axioms to comics long before literature and history departments began awarding MAs and PhDs for comics research). As this collection makes clear, a fair number of film critics, art critics, journalists and essayists thoughtfully, if not always sympathetically, paused over comics before returning to their regular preoccupations. Comic strips and comic books attracted not only opponents and disinterested clinicians, but also, occasionally, *critics*. It is this back catalog of compelling commentary and analysis that this volume brings to life for a contemporary readership.[1]

Intellectual responses to comics tend to fall into distinct categories. This volume opens with essays by Sidney Fairfield, Annie Russell Marble and Ralph Bergengren, who viewed *fin de siecle* illustrated material with alarm. Their concerns mirror those expressed by William Wordsworth, whom Marble approvingly cites. (Interestingly, their complaints broadly coincided with the introduction of comic strips in daily and Sunday newspapers, just as Wordsworth's sonnet broadly coincided with the early mechanization of images.) A generation after Fairfield and company issued their elegant salvos, Gilbert Seldes, Dorothy Parker, H.L. Mencken and others revalued the cartoon arts as part of a more generous reappraisal of the American vernacular. Seldes' *The Seven Lively Arts* (1924) became particularly well known for its sympathetic stance toward comic strips and other "popular arts," while Thomas Mann's 1926 introduction to Frans Masereel's "picture novel" identified sequential storytelling with the "spirit of democracy." There is very much the sense of a conscious break with a stereotypically "Victorian" emphasis on cultural standards and canons in these works.

---

1. Thierry Groensteen has observed that an "anthology of what was written about comics between the beginning of the century and the sixties would be extremely boring" (33). If, in developing this project, we had focused on the enormous volume of writings and speeches of politicians, behavioral scientists, and public moralists, then the final project would be dull indeed, if perhaps instructive.

By way of contrast, New York intellectuals like Clement Greenberg, Irving Howe, Harold Rosenberg, Delmore Schwartz and Robert Warshow embraced neither Victorian values nor, for the most part, popular culture. As art historians, Greenberg and Rosenberg wrote insightfully about the few editorial cartoonists they favored, but made it clear that the mass of illustration and comics were not to be taken seriously. Film critic and essayist Robert Warshow warily scrutinized *Krazy Kat* and horror comics, while Irving Howe and Delmore Schwartz located comics within the morass of mass culture. Postwar mavericks like Manny Farber, Leslie Fiedler, Marshall McLuhan, Walter Ong and Donald Phelps read *Partisan Review*, and possibly *Politics* as well, where Irving Howe's tart commentary on mass culture first appeared. Their writings nevertheless offered a conscious departure from the cultural pessimism identified with the metropolitan "little magazines." The early 1950s observations of C. L. R. James, and Umberto Eco's 1962 essay on Superman, which closes the volume, represent a liminal space in comics criticism, marking the terrain between freelance criticism and contemporary cultural studies.

The earliest critics of reproduced images were responding to the greater availability of illustrated material made possible via such processes as lithography, photoengraving and chromolithography. The latter became widely adopted by newspaper and magazine editors and publishers in the 1840s and 1850s. Between the middle and end of the 1800s, the pace of technological innovation in image making accelerated. As Jim Cullen notes, by the end of the century "various means of visual reproduction had proliferated to the point of being woven into the fabric of everyday life" (Cullen 115). While Cullen specifically refers to daguerreotypes (early photographs), postcards, calendars and woodcut photoengravings, comic strips and eventually comic books formed an integral aspect of an expanding universe of visually oriented mass production.

Those who wrote about comics in the tradition of William Wordsworth objected to any effort to place commercial images on an equal footing with text. "The deeds that are conspicuous, the ideas that are garish, the literature that is episodic and pictorial, gain the popular favor," complained essayist Annie Russell Marble in 1903. "Comment is needless upon the supremacy of the pictorial journal, and upon the scanty discrimination, among the mass of readers, as to literary or artistic merits." (297) Ralph Bergengren, writing in the *Atlantic Monthly* in 1906, was even more categorical. Comic strips, he insisted, lacked "respect for property, respect for parents, for law, for decency, for truth, for beauty, for kindliness, for dignity, or for honor. . . . The paucity of invention is hardly less remarkable than the willingness of the inventors to sign their products, or the willingness of editors to publish them" (271). Bergengren commended Winsor McCay's *Little Nemo in Slumberland* for its "charming draught-manship, and an excellent decorative sense of color," but urged that "the average editor of the weekly comic supplement . . . be given a course in art, literature, common sense and Christianity" (273).

Complaints about garish and possibly heathen color Sunday supplements reflected broader anxieties about the emergence of popular visual media that trafficked in entertainment rather than uplift. Pictures were "subversive," notes cultural historian Neil Harris, "because they presented a new and apparently uncontrollable set of sources to the larger public" (Harris 348). In the 1870s, the editor of the *Nation*, Edwin Lawrence Godkin, suggested that newspaper illustrations and reproductions "diffused in the community a kind of smattering of all sorts of knowledge, as taste for 'art'—that is, a desire to see and own pictures—which, taken together, pass with a large body of slenderly equipped persons as 'culture,' and give them unprecedented self-confidence in dealing with the problems of life, and raise them in their own minds to a plane on which they see nothing higher, greater or better than themselves" (qtd. in Cullen 115).

For Sidney Fairfield, modern illustration was untrustworthy. As he pointed out in 1895, the illustrator "takes most outrageous license with the truth as written. He is essentially an exaggerator, a perverter of the facts. He sins on the side of his picture, never on that of the manuscript. He makes effects; he does not inform." In the struggle between words and pictures Sidney Fairfield was prepared to take sides: "Let us have things proportioned to their true value. Let the reading-matter have the most of the space. The written word is the first and the highest expression of thought, and it ever will be" (864). Illustration in any guise was a lesser form, a "lower stage" (Wordsworth 16).

The writings of Fairfield, Marble and Bergengren helped lay the basis for what some historians have identified as a pre-WWI anti-comics campaign. This campaign combined high profile articles (in 1909 the *Ladies' Home Journal* defined comics as "A Crime Against American Children") with sporadic—and occasionally successful—efforts to keep strips out of local newspapers. Elsa Nystrom and Ian Gordon situate this campaign in the years between 1906 and 1912, arguing that it reflected anxieties not only about the circulation of unsavory images, but the stress of urbanization and immigration on national identity and the civic culture (Gordon 38–43; Nystrom chapter five).

The writings of William Crary Brownell (1851–1928) mark the transition between the genteel disciples of Wordsworth and jazz era approaches to comics in particular and popular culture more generally. During his long career as a critic, Brownell upheld Matthew Arnold's ideal of a culture devoted to high seriousness. However, in his last book, *Democratic Distinction in America* (1927), Brownell tried to reconcile Arnoldian standards with a friendlier account of popular culture. "The vitaphone and radio, whatever their imperfections as ersatz, unquestionably educate and, one would think, at worst provide pastime as solidly satisfactory as that to be had at half the theatres," Brownell wrote. "As do the movies, however they perforce leave the cultivation of taste to other agencies. Even the 'comic strip' (could one go beyond that?) is not always 'comic'; at least one syndicate combines text and drawings in the inculcation of historical data and patriotic sentiment" (226–27).

As Brownell's account suggests, comic strips gained some measure of respectability in the 1920s as they catered to a national audience and incorporated a greater number of middle-class characters. Although some readers continued to object to the content of individual strips, the cultural status of newspaper strips stabilized over time, particularly in relation to comic books, which materialized as a mass medium in the late 1930s and 1940s. Adam Gopnik has argued that comic strips, "like the movies, were a public and ceremonial form. They were part of the larger experience of the newspaper, integrated into a ribbon of wars and sports and society. They had a place in a hierarchy," even if that place was lowly and sometimes problematic. In contrast, a comic book "was something you had to walk into a store and buy; it was in its very nature outside parental control—and it had overtones, always, of the secretive, the menacing, and the faintly masturbatory" (1990: 182).

To some extent comic strips benefited from the embrace of the American idiom and the recognition of the vitality of urban life that became an animating theme in early twentieth century intellectual and artistic life. Like jazz, comic strips were something *new*, and like jazz they were associated with, and attractive to, cultural rebels and outsiders. For some, extolling the virtues of a particular strip was an easy means of breaking with outmoded conventionality. The cultivate-good-habits ethic offered by Annie Russell Marble and Sidney Fairfield, not to mention Ralph Bergengren's religion-inflected solemnity, would have struck bohemians and other "moderns" as unnecessarily straight-laced.

The 1920s was also a time of resurgent cultural nationalism. It was a period when the embryonic field of American Studies first canonized homegrown figures like Herman Melville and Edgar Allen Poe. New college courses and programs proposed to examine U.S. history, society and culture as more or less autonomous, self-contained and self-generated areas of study. On a more popular level, disillusionment with the outcome of the First World War led many to question the idea that European culture and politics was necessarily superior to anything that could be produced elsewhere. Comics, despite their European roots, could be claimed as part of a distinctive cultural-national space. What H. L. Mencken described as "the national fancy for the terse, the vivid, and above all the bold and imaginative" (32) played to the comic strip's formal strengths and literary figures as disparate as E. E. Cummings, Dorothy Parker and Mencken all took pleasure in what historian Ann Douglas refers to as the "linguistic explosions" (451) of the comics page.

While some intellectuals were prepared to utter kind words on behalf of individual cartoonists, the essayist Gilbert Seldes was one of the first to consider the comic strip as a creative, expressive medium. Seldes deemed comics "the most despised, and with the exception of the movies" the most popular of the "seven lively arts." The comic strip, he argued, "is an exceptionally supple medium, giving play to a variety of talents, to the use of many methods, and it adapts itself to almost any theme." Admittedly, some comic strips were badly drawn, and monotonous in their "life-of-the-party humor." But "about two dozen good comics now exist," and collectively these strips provide "a changing picture of the average American life—and by compensation . . . the freest American fantasy." Some "twenty million people follow with interest, curiosity and amusement the daily fortunes of five or ten heroes of the comic strip," he mused, "and that they do is this considered by all those who have any pretensions to taste and culture as a symptom of crass vulgarity, of dullness and, for all I know, of defeated and inhibited lives" (213–14).

As both a modernist celebrator of the new and an American cultural nationalist, Seldes was an emblematic figure of the competing cultural tendencies of the 1920s. Through his connections to highbrow magazines like the *Dial* and the *New Republic* (where he reviewed Joyce's *Ulysses*), Seldes developed strong bonds with international modernism in the arts and literature. Characteristically, when Seldes met James Joyce in the mid-1920s, they discussed the *Gasoline Alley* strip that the Irish writer kept on his mantelpiece (Ellmann 577). Yet, for all his ties to international literature, Seldes' defense of art forms like comics and jazz was articulated along nationalist lines. If Seldes did not invent the trope that comics are one of the country's few indigenous art forms, he certainly helped popularize it. As his biographer Michael Kammen notes, Seldes "wanted to say, most of all, that the United States of America had a meaning that needed to be defined, and that the U.S. deserved a national culture that should not be neglected in the schools" (156). This notion of comics as a distinctively American art form slights the medium's lengthy gestation period in the eighteenth and nineteenth centuries, when the iconic language of comics was being developed in Europe. But Seldes' liberal cultural nationalism helped inoculate him against the view that there was nothing new under the artistic sun.

The assimilation of strips into the civic culture was further signaled by the appearance of trade books that peeked "behind the scenes" of cartooning, including Martin Sheridan's *Comics and Their Creators* (1942), Coulton Waugh's *The Comics* (1947), and Stephen Becker's *Comic Art in America* (1959).[2] While Sheridan, Waugh and Becker celebrated the accomplishments of two generations of comic strip creators, George Herriman's *Krazy Kat* attracted the lion's share of favorable, early-to-mid-twentieth-century comics commentary. The love affair between intellectuals and painters, and *Krazy Kat*, is well documented. As the *New Yorker* critic Adam Gopnik noted in 1986, "it's been widely recognized that Herriman had achieved something not only entrancing on its own terms but also uncannily modern, bearing deep affinities to the spirit and form of crucial styles in vanguard art" (19). More than forty years previously, *Art News*, in 1944, had anointed Herriman as a fine artist, referring to him as "one of the first surrealists," and pointed to the fact that "artists and intellectuals" were among Herriman's "most constant readers" (McDonnell, O'Connell and Havenon 26). Among the contributors to this volume, E. E. Cummings, Irving Howe, Gilbert Seldes and Robert Warshow all discuss this single strip, although it would be unfair to describe Howe, unlike the others, as a fan.

The critical success of *Krazy Kat* notwithstanding, Gilbert Seldes' good-natured, open-minded approach did not quite represent the conventional wisdom. The bland dismissal offered by George Babbitt, in the 1922 Sinclair Lewis novel—"He vaguely wanted something more diverting than the newspaper comic strips to read"— probably came closer to the mark (219). Few commentators, even friendly ones, saw comic strips as anything than a diversion from more serious matters. Newspaper columnist Max Lerner, in his best-selling *America as a Civilization* (1956), spoke for many when, after complimenting *Krazy Kat*, *Li'l Abner* and *Pogo* for "deflating the pretentious and mocking the stuffed shirts," nevertheless concluded that the comic

---

2. An early example of the genre is James Parton, *Caricature and Other Comic Art* (1877). Companion twentieth-century volumes include W. A. Murrell's two-volume *A History of American Graphic Humor* (1933), Thomas Craven's *Cartoon Cavalcade* (1943), and Lancelot Hogben, *From Cave Painting to Comic Strip* (1949). An analogous work in animation is E. G. Lutz's *Animated Cartoons: How They Are Made, Their Origin and Development* (1920). See also Martin Sheridan, "A Ghost Remembers: Life in the King Features Bullpen in the 1930s" (1984).

strip "offers recognizable virtue and derring-do on one side and recognizable villainy and skullduggery on the other. It is at once outlandish adventure and a caricatured morality play, in an imagined world in which every emotion is blocked out in stereotyped form" (755–56). Lerner's refusal to speculate about what the comics he liked might say about comics in general is a symptomatic one.

Anti-comics rhetoric often echoed the late nineteenth century battles against penny dreadfuls and dime novels. The moral reformer Anthony Comstock, leader of the New York Society for the Suppression of Vice, devoted an entire book to the perils of the dime novel, *Traps for the Young* (1884), and Comstock, like many critics to come, took particular exception to the exaggerated illustrations that accompanied cheaply printed adventure stories. But Comstockian puritanism constituted only one strand in the DNA of the harsher strains of twentieth century comics criticism. Modernist writers and thinkers were more than capable of favoring words over pictures and lending their support, tacit or otherwise, to logocentric, anti-comics discourse. By the 1940s and early 1950s many left-leaning intellectuals felt beset by a tidal wave of mass culture. Light-hearted sympathy for inconsequential diversions gave way to fears of massification and mind control. The very scale and reach of commercial entertainment unnerved some critics. "We would be the first to acknowledge," wrote the editors of the *Nation* in an unsigned 1949 editorial, "that a generation of Americans has been driven several degrees toward illiteracy by the 'comic' book. And it is appalling that 60 million comic books are sold in this country every month" (319).

In the same period, distinguished journals of opinion, such as *Partisan Review*, *Commentary* and *Politics*, published numerous articles in which essayists agonized as they sifted through one pop cultural artifact after another. Delmore Schwartz did not seem to be enjoying himself when he wrote "Masterpieces as Cartoons," his dissection of the *Classics Illustrated* series, which he described as "the bottom of the pit." Having emerged out of the anti-Stalinist left of the 1930s and 1940s, many New York intellectuals associated mass culture with either the popular front (on the left) or conformist culture (on the right). The prevalence of mass entertainment, from this perspective, was a political problem, or even a crisis, one which helped explain the existence of a "mass man" vulnerable to totalitarian propaganda and control.

In contrast to jazz era intellectuals, the *Partisan Review* circle could find little good to say about cultural material that was tainted by the virus of commerce. What struck one cohort as folkloric or novel came across as mind numbing and time wasting to the next. *PR* writers sought to restore the dividing line between modernism and the mass media that Seldes and others had helped blur. Irving Howe's reference to "the pseudo-cultural amusements that occupy the American people's leisure time" and his respectful invocation of Frankfurt School theorist Theodor Adorno, in his essay on "Notes on Mass Culture," reprinted here, is emblematic of this generational shift in sensibility. As Howe subsequently noted, "a critic who contributes a nuance to Dostoevsky criticism is working within a structured tradition, while one who throws off a clever observation about *Little Orphan Annie* is simply showing that he can do what he has done" ("The New York Intellectuals" 250).

The changing attitude among intellectuals toward popular culture could also be observed in the extended debate that took place between Gilbert Seldes and Dwight Macdonald in the 1950s. In his 1950 book *The Great Audience*, Seldes argued that New York intellectuals such as Macdonald were excessively pessimistic in believing that mass entertainment was fated to be shoddy under contemporary capitalism. Macdonald responded in a 1953 essay, later reprinted in the book *Against the American Grain* (1962), arguing that Seldes was "superficial" and his "democratic-liberal" outlook prevented him from seeing the systemic "mechanism" that had degraded popular taste for several generations (Kammen 326–28).

Even as the New York intellectuals were taking aim at comics, researchers in the behavioral sciences were publishing on comics in peer review journals. Scholarly interest in comics was exceptionally strong in the mid-to-late 1940s.[3] But the bulk of comics-related commentary from this period can be characterized as alarmist. Sterling North, the literary critic, disdained comic books as "a poisonous mush-room growth" foisted on the public by "completely immoral publishers guilty of a cultural slaughter of the innocents" (qtd. in Mitchell "Slaughter of the Innocents, Part One" 30–31). North's "A National Disgrace (And a Challenge to American Parents)" was published in the *Chicago Daily News* in May 1940; within eighteen months it had been reprinted in over forty magazines and newspapers (Nyberg 4).

Anti-comics agitation revived amidst the postwar profusion of horror, crime and adventure-oriented titles on the newsstands. The popularity of specific genres and

---

3. David Manning White and Robert Abel's bibliography lists 184 publications devoted to comics, all in English. It groups these into four categories: books and pamphlets (12 titles), professional and specialized publications (143), general periodicals (22), and theses and special studies (7). The bibliography lists eight publications that appeared in the 1920s, thirty-two in the 1930s, 104 in the 1940s, thirty-five in the 1950s, and one in the 1960s. Volume numbers, but not dates, were given for four titles. Their bibliography is far from complete—it emphasizes scholarly studies and magazine articles, and does not include newspaper articles, nor anything published before the 1920s—but the numbers of articles and studies published in the 1940s in contrast to other decades is striking. See White and Abel (1963): 293–304.

styles set off alarm bells among both moral watchdogs and literary gatekeepers. In a single year—1947—government officials, judges, civic groups and literary types all weighed in against comic books. FBI Director J. Edgar Hoover characterized "crime books, comics, and newspaper stories crammed with anti-social and criminal acts, the glorification of un-American vigilante action and the deification of the criminal" as "extremely dangerous in the hands of the unstable child" (qtd. in Mitchell "Slaughter of the Innocents: Comic-book Controversies Began When Comic Books First Appeared" 32), while the Fraternal Order of Police condemned comic books as "one of the contributing factors to the cause of juvenile delinquency" (qtd. in Mitchell, "Slaughter of the Innocents: Conclusion" 28). In the *New Republic*, former *Vogue* editor Marya Mannes denounced comics as "intellectual marijuana." "Every hour spent in reading comics," Mannes explained, "is an hour in which all inner growth has stopped" (Wright 90–91; Nyberg 11–13). Their shared concerns about violence, delinquency and comics suggested the degree to which anti-comics arguments continued to be framed, disseminated and consumed by intellectuals as well as religious groups and law-and-order traditionalists.

The German-born psychologist Fredric Wertham (1895–1981) came to the study of comics through an interest in the role of social factors in promoting violence and crime. Through his many articles and speeches, as well as his book *The Seduction of the Innocent* (1954), Wertham came to practically embody the mid-century anti-comics crusade. But Wertham was not the only intellectual who was active in the anti-comics cause (Wagner 1955). Gershon Legman, author of the feisty *Love and Death: A Study in Censorship* (1949), part of which is reprinted here, was a featured speaker at a 1948 conference on "The Psychopathology of Comics" that Wertham organized. Legman was no hidebound conservative. A proto-hippy of the 1940s, he believed that American popular culture was both sexually repressed and violence obsessed, leading to dangerous psychological consequences. During World War II, Legman carried on a spirited correspondence with cartoonist Milton Caniff. Legman criticized Caniff for printing wartime propaganda in his comic strip *Terry and the Pirates*, and offering a dehumanized image of the Japanese army. Legman was credited with coining the slogan "make love, not war," which again linked the cause of sexual emancipation with opposition to militarism. While religiously motivated decency crusaders and secular-minded intellectuals like Wertham and Legman started from different places, they joined forces on the comics battlefield.

If the mid-1950s represents a high water mark of anti-comics agitation (which helps contextualize the comics writings of the New York intellectuals), the climate slowly improved thereafter. One source of more receptive forms of analysis was fandom itself. Bill Gaines's EC, which published some of the most notorious titles of the 1950s, attracted some of the medium's most articulate fans, one of whom started an EC fanzine in direct response to Fredric Wertham's stinging claim that "comics were not a valid art form because there was no legitimate ongoing critical discussion of them." (Bernewitz and Geissman 18). Jules Feiffer's *The Great Comic Book Heroes* (1965) used disarming wit to suggest the multiple layers of meaning underneath the superhero surface. It also foreshadowed the catalytic role that artist-intellectuals have played in the recent development of comics theory, history, and criticism.[4] David Manning White, a professor of journalism at Boston University, helped stimulate critical interest in comic strips, via *Mass Culture: The Popular Arts in America* (1957), which was a more sophisticated and diverse collection than standard accounts of 1950s cultural awareness would permit, and *The Funnies: An American Idiom* (1963). Interest in comics among art historians was sparked by the work of E. H. Gombrich, an influential student of the iconic language of visual culture. In *Art and Illusion* (1960), Gombrich argued that iconic art achieved its power by appealing to cognitive skills that transcended particular cultures. Gombrich found comics, with their linkage of narrative meaning and visual shorthand, an especially useful example. He studied such pioneering cartoonists as Rodolphe Topffer (1799–1846), encouraging his students to do the same. By 1971, a small bookshelf worth of English-language titles had appeared that examined the development of the comic strip and the comic book.[5]

A more positive view of comics and popular culture could also be gleaned from certain intellectuals who were likely to read than contribute to *Partisan Review*. Catholic writers like Marshall McLuhan, Hugh Kenner and Walter Ong, who helped form a maverick but non-leftist circle of public intellectuals in the 1950s and 1960s, were respectful of *PR* but felt no obligation to follow its lead. (While McLuhan and Kenner were Canadian, Ong was a U.S. citizen but maintained close ties to these Toronto-based intellectuals.) For these writers, mass culture offered a way of rebuilding a communal culture that could heal the wounds of individualism. While

---

4. Relevant sources include Will Eisner, *Comics and Sequential Art* (1985); Scott McCloud, *Understanding Comics* (1993) and *Rethinking Comics* (2000); Trina Robbins, *The Great Women Cartoonists* (2001); and Art Spiegelman and Chip Kidd, *Jack Cole and Plastic Man: Forms Stretched to Their Limits* (2001).

5. Examples include Les Daniel's *Comix: A History of Comic Books in America* (1971), Dick Lupoff and Don Thompson's *All in Color for a Dime* (1970), Russel Nye's *The Unembarrassed Muse* (1970), Judith O'Sullivan's *The Art of the Comic Strip* (1971), and James Steranko's *History of Comics* (1970).

McLuhan insisted that technology changes culture, he also believed that new developments could be restorative rather than disruptive. If technological change was a powerful, even determinative social force, this did not mean the future was necessarily bleak, or the present unbearable (Heer 1995 and 2002).

The essayists Donald Phelps and C. L. R. James were familiar with the ideas of the New York intellectuals, and read their work, but arrived at a more positive assessment of popular culture. For an outsider like C. L. R. James, who relocated to the United States at the end of the 1930s to play a leadership role in the non-Communist far left, popular culture provided an increasingly useful road map for decoding American civilization (Worcester 2002). Meanwhile, Donald Phelps looked back in fondness to comic strips of the 1920s and 1930s, when cartoonists displayed "the capacity for originality of form and invention" within the framework of a "routine situation" (Alpert 110). Phelps was influenced by the painter and movie critic Manny Farber, who was careful to respond to the textural and formal qualities of the visual arts. Both Farber and Phelps reacted in part against what they perceived as the excesses of the New York intellectuals, who they saw as being overly moralistic and sociological in their treatment of the popular arts. Phelps was also sympathetic to experimental poets like LeRoi Jones/Amira Baraka and Fielding Dawson, who sometimes incorporated pop culture into their poetry.

Leslie Fiedler and Umberto Eco offer perhaps the best known examples of intellectuals who turned their backs on the "elitist" impulse to reject and abstain from popular culture. Their lively essays challenged the moralists, scientists and cultural declinists who feared popular culture or saw nothing meaningful in it, thereby helping to lay the groundwork for contemporary cultural studies. The writings of critics like Eco, Fiedler and of course McLuhan soon turned up in the burgeoning humanities literature on comics.

Despite their many differences, the contributors to this anthology wrote on comics in ways that should command the attention of anyone concerned with the art of comics and its cultural context. While the bulk of what was published on comics before, say, 1965, holds a mainly historical or antiquarian interest, some essays still retain their vital spark. As this collection shows, some of the richest writings on comics were by people who wrote about culture with a magpie general intelligence. At their best, these writers managed to remain theoretically challenging without being excessively abstract, sensitive to aesthetic questions of line and form but also concerned with social and political content and addressed to a non-specialized audience while avoiding snapshot journalism.

A comparison with the larger and more established field of film criticism might help clarify this point. An anthology that brought together film reviews from the *New York Times* or *Variety* from the 1940s would hold a certain documentary interest. Such a volume would shed light on how people in the past interpreted film and the evolving vocabulary of movie criticism. By contrast, collections reprinting the film reviews of James Agee and Manny Farber (and Robert Warshow, for that matter) engage readers not just as historical documents but also as perennially valuable essays, which can help sharpen our ability to see and read films. The pieces collected here can teach us about the aesthetics, history and form of comics in the same way that Agee and Farber can still instruct us about film. Farber actually moonlighted as a comic strip reviewer, bringing the same attentiveness to the comic strip's visual surface that characterizes his film writing. Robert Warshow also ventured into comics criticism, prompted in part by his son's passion for EC comics.

In preparing this anthology, we noticed certain recurring commonalities. Because they wrote as public intellectuals, the disparate authors gathered here took part in, and helped promote, a common cultural discourse. A few thread-lines can help map out the territory. Certainly, Gilbert Seldes' essays were widely read and cited, and helped set the terms whereby comics would be discussed in the coming decades. As a citadel of high modernist criticism, *Partisan Review* was both admired and reviled by those outside its gates. Writers like C. L. R. James and Marshall McLuhan, very much mavericks, wrote in part to redress what they saw as deficiencies in the *PR* worldview. Donald Phelps was capacious in reading almost everything that preceded him (from Seldes to Farber to Warshow to Legman) and in trying to synthesize a bricolage aesthetic. Gershon Legman, a somewhat obscure figure in recent decades, was a lighting rod of controversy in the late 1940s: Warshow reviewed Legman's *Love and Death* unfavorably in *Partisan Review* while in the *New Republic* Manny Farber alluded to Legman's work. Marshall McLuhan was inspired by his insights and published in Legman's journal *Neurotica*, Leslie Fiedler both respected Legman (paying tribute in the title of his 1960 book, *Love and Death in the American Novel*) but also kept a distance from him. Rather than writing in isolation, these authors participated in a lively, and often contentious, conversation about comics, intellectuals, and popular culture that spanned the twentieth century.

JH
KW

Works Cited

Alpert, Barry. "Donald Phelps: An Interview." *Vort* 6 (1974): 97–113.

Barker, Martin. *A Haunt of Fears: The Strange History of the British Horror Comics Campaign*. London: Pluto Press, 1984.

———. *Comics: Ideology, Power and the Critics*. Manchester: Manchester University Press, 1989.

Bataille, Georges. "Les Pieds nickelés." *Documents* 4 (1930).

Becker, Stephen. *Comic Art in America: A Social History of the Funnies, the Political Cartoons, Magazine Humor, Sporting Cartoons, and Animated Cartoons*. New York: Simon and Schuster, 1959.

Bender, Thomas. "Politics, Intellect, and the American University." *American Academic Culture in Transformation: Fifty Years, Four Disciplines*. Eds. Thomas Bender and Carl Schorske. Princeton: Princeton University Press, 1998. 17–56.

Bergengren, Ralph. "The Humor of the Colored Supplement." *Atlantic Monthly* Aug. 1906: 269–73.

Berger, Arthur Asa. *The Comic-Stripped American: What Dick Tracy, Blondie, Daddy Warbucks, and Charlie Brown Tell Us About Ourselves*. New York: Walker and Company, 1973.

———. *Li'l Abner: A Study in American Satire*. New York: Twayne, 1970.

Bernewitz, Fred von and Grant Geissman, eds. *Tales of Terror! The EC Companion*. Seattle: Fantagraphics, 2000.

Brownell, William Crary. *Democratic Distinction in America*. New York: Charles Scribner, 1927.

Couperie, Pierre. *A History of the Comic Strip*. New York: Crown Publishers, 1968.

Cohen, Lizabeth. *Making a New Deal*. Cambridge: Cambridge University Press, 1990.

Comstock, Anthony. *Traps for the Young*. New York: Funk, 1883.

Craven, Thomas. *Cartoon Cavalcade*. New York: Simon and Schuster, 1943.

Cullen, Jim. *The Art of Democracy: A Concise History of Popular Culture in the United States*. New York: Monthly Review Press, 1996.

Daniels, Les. *Comix: A History of Comic Books in America*. New York: Outerbridge and Dienstrey, 1971.

Davenport, Guy. "Transcendental Satyr," in *Every Force Evolves a Form: Twenty Essays*. San Francisco: North Point Press, 1987.

Dorfman, Ariel and Armand Mattelart, *How to Read Donald Duck: Imperialist Ideology in the Disney Comic*. New York: International General, 1976.

Douglas, Ann. *Terrible Honesty: Mongrel Manhattan in the 1920s*. New York: Noonday Press, 1995.

Ellmann, Richard. *James Joyce*. New York: Oxford University Press, 1982. Second ed.

Eisner, Will. *Comics and Sequential Art*. Tamarac, FL: Poorhouse Press, 1985.

Estren, Mark James. *A History of Underground Comics*. San Francisco: Straight Arrow, 1974.

Fairfield, Sidney. "The Tyranny of the Pictorial." *Lippincott's Monthly Magazine* June 1895: 861–64.

Feiffer, Jules. *The Great Comic Book Heroes*. New York: Dial Press, 1965.

Fiedler, Leslie. *The Collected Essays of Leslie Fiedler, Vol. 2*. New York: Stein and Day, 1971.

———. *Love and Death in the American Novel*. New York: Criterion, 1960.

Gilbert, James. *A Cycle of Outrage: America's Reaction to the Juvenile Delinquent in the 1950s*. New York: Oxford University Press, 1986.

Gombrich, E. H. *Art and Illusion: A Study in the Psychology of Pictorial Representation*. New York: Pantheon, 1960.

Gopnik, Adam. "Comics." *High and Low: Modern Art and Popular Culture*. Eds. Kirk Varnedoe and Adam Gopnik. New York: The Museum of Modern Art, 1990. 153–228.

———. "The Genius of George Herriman." *New York Review of Books* 18 Dec 1986: 19–28.

Gordon, Ian. *Comic Strips and Consumer Culture, 1890–1945*. Washington, DC: Smithsonian Institution Press, 1998.

Greenberg, Clement. *Art and Culture: Critical Essays*. Boston: Beacon Press, 1961.

———. *The Collected Essays and Criticism: Vol. 2. Arrogant Purpose, 1945–1949*. Ed. John O'Brian. Chicago: University of Chicago Press, 1986.

Groensteen, Thierry. "Why Are Comics Still in Search of Cultural Legitimation?" *Comics and Culture: Analytical and Theoretical Approaches to Comics.* Eds. Anne Magnussen and Hans-Christian Christiansen. Copenhagen: Museum Tusculanum Press, 2000. 29–41.

Harris, Neil. *Cultural Excursions: Marketing Appetites and Cultural Tastes in Modern America.* Chicago: University of Chicago Press, 1990.

Heer, Jeet. "Catholicism, Mass Culture, Technology and Literary Modernism: The Intellectual Parameters of the McLuhan Circle." Unpublished manuscript, 2002.

———. "McLuhan's Hare." *Literary Review of Canada* 4.1 (1995): 10–11.

Hess, Thomas B. "The Art Comics of Ad Reinhardt." *Artforum.* 12.8 (1974): 46–51.

Hess, Thomas B. and John Ashbery, eds. *Narrative Art.* New York: Macmillan, 1970.

Hogben, Lancelot. *From Cave Painting to Comic Strip.* New York: Chanticleer Press, 1949.

Horn, Maurice, ed. *The World Encyclopedia of Comics.* New York: Chelsea House, 1976.

Howe, Irving. "The New York Intellectuals." *Selected Writings, 1950–1990.* New York: Harvest, 1992. 240–80.

James, C. L. R. "Letter to Bell." *The C. L. R. James Reader.* Ed. Anna Grimshaw. Oxford: Blackwell, 1992: 220–31.

Kammen, Michael. *The Lively Arts: Gilbert Seldes and the Transformation of Cultural Criticism in the United States.* New York: Oxford University Press, 1996.

Kunzle, David. *History of the Comic Strip, Vol. 1: The Early Comic Strip.* Berkeley: University of California Press, 1973.

———. *History of the Comic Strip, Vol. II: The Nineteenth Century.* Berkeley: University of California Press, 1990.

Legman, Gershon. *Love and Death: A Study in Censorship.* New York: Breaking Point, 1949.

Lent, John, ed. "Pioneers of Comic Art Scholarship." *International Journal of Comic Art* 4.1 (Spring 2002): 5–96.

Lent, John, ed. "Pioneers of Comic Art Scholarship." *International Journal of Comic Art* 5.1 (Spring 2003): 3–73.

Lent, John, ed. "Pioneers of Comic Art Scholarship." *International Journal of Comic Art* 5.2 (Fall 2003): 205–60.

———. ed. *Pulp Demons: International Dimensions of the Postwar Anti-Comics Campaign.* Teaneck, NJ: Fairleigh Dickinson University Press, 1999.

Lerner, Max. *America as a Civilization: Life and Thought in the United States Today.* New York: Henry Holt, 1987 [1957].

Lewis, Sinclair. *Babbitt.* New York: New American Library, 1961 [1922].

Lupoff, Richard A. and Don Thompson, eds. *All in Color for a Dime.* New Rochelle: Arlington House, 1970.

———. eds. *The Comic-Book Book.* New Rochelle: Arlington House, 1973.

Lutz, E. G. *Animated Cartoons: How They are Made, Their Origin and Development.* New York: Charles Scribner's Sons, 1920.

Macdonald, Dwight. *Against the American Grain.* New York: Random House, 1962.

Marble, Annie Russell. "The Reign of the Spectacular." *The Dial* 1 Nov. 1903: 297–99.

Marchand, Philip. *Marshall McLuhan: The Medium and the Messenger.* Toronto: Vintage, 1998.

McCloud, Scott. *Reinventing Comics.* New York: Paradox Press, 2000.

———. *Understanding Comics.* Northampton: Tundra, 1993.

McDonnell, Patrick, Karen O'Connell and Georgia Riley de Havenon. *Krazy Kat: The Comic Art of George Herriman.* New York: Harry N. Abrams, 1986.

McLuhan, Marshall. *The Mechanical Bride: Folklore of Industrial Man.* New York: The Vanguard Press, 1951.

———. *Understanding Media: The Extensions of Man.* New York: McGraw Hill, 1964.

Mencken, H. L. *The American Language.* New York: Alfred A. Knopf, 1919.

Mitchell, Steven E. "Slaughter of the Innocents: Comic-book Controversies Began When Comic Books First Appeared." *Comics Buyers' Guide* 4 July 2003: 32.
———. "Slaughter of the Innocents: Part One: Comic-book Controversy Long Before Wertham." *Comics Buyers' Guide* 26 Sept. 2003: 30–31.
———. "Slaughter of the Innocents: Part Three: Comic-book Controversy Long Before Wertham." *Comics Buyers' Guide* 10 Oct. 2003: 30.
Murrell, W. A. *A History of American Graphic Humor.* New York: Macmillan, 1933 and 1938.
The Nation. Unsigned editorial. 19 March 1949. 319.
Nyberg, Amy Kiste. *Seal of Approval: The History of the Comics Code.* Jackson, MS: University Press of Mississippi, 1998.
Nystrom, Elsa. *A Rejection of Order: The Development of the Newspaper Comic Strip in America, 1830–1920.* PhD dissertation, Loyola University of Chicago, 1989.
Nye, Russel. *The Unembarrassed Muse: The Popular Arts in America.* New York: Dial Press, 1970.
O'Sullivan, Judith. *The Art of the Comic Strip.* College Park: University of Maryland Press, 1971.
Parker, Dorothy. "A Mash Note to Crockett Johnson." *PM,* 3 Oct 1943.
Parton, James. *Caricature and Other Comic Art.* New York: Harper and Bros, 1877.
Perry, George and Alan Aldridge, ed. *The Penguin Book of Comics.* London: Penguin, 1967.
Phelps, Donald. *Covering Ground: Essays for Now.* New York: Croton Press, 1969.
———. *Reading the Funnies.* Seattle: Fantagraphics, 2001.
Reitberger, Reinhold and Wolfgang Fuchs, *Comics: Anatomy of a Mass Medium.* Boston: Little, Brown, 1972.
Robinson, Jerry. *The Comics: An Illustrated History of Comic Strip Art.* New York: G. P. Putnam, 1974.
Robbins, Trina. 2001. *The Great Women Cartoonists.* New York: Watson-Guptill, 2001.
Rose, Barbara, ed. *Art as Art: The Selected Writings of Ad Reinhardt.* Berkeley: University of California Press, 1975.
Rosenberg, Bernard and David Manning White, ed. *Mass Culture: The Popular Arts in America.* Glencoe, IL: Free Press, 1957.
Rosenberg, Harold. *The Anxious Object: Art Today and Its Audience.* New York: Horizon Press, 1964.
———. *The Tradition of the New.* New York: Horizon Press, 1959.
Seldes, Gilbert, *The Great Audience.* New York: Viking, 1950.
———. *The Seven Lively Arts.* New York: Harpers, 1924.
Shelton, William Henry. "The Comic Paper in America." *Critic* Sept 1901: 227–34.
Sheridan, Martin. "A Ghost Remembers: Life in the King Features Bullpen in the 1930s." *Nemo: The Classic Comics Library,* Oct. 1984: 53–55.
———. *Comics and Their Creators: Life Stories of American Cartoonists.* Boston: Hale, Cushman and Flint, 1942.
A Smithsonian Book of Comic-Book Comics. Eds. Michael Barrier and Martin Williams. Washington, DC: Smithsonian Institution Press, 1981.
A Smithsonian Collection of Newspaper Comics. Eds. Bill Blackbeard and Martin Williams. Washington, DC: Smithsonian Institution Press, 1977.
Spiegelman, Art and Chip Kidd. *Jack Cole and Plastic Man: Forms Stretched to Their Limits.* San Francisco: Chronicle Books, 2001.
Steranko, James. *History of Comics.* Reading, PA: Supergraphics, 1970.
Sternberg, Jacques and Michel Caen, eds. *Les Chefs-d'oeuvre de la Bande Dessinee.* Paris: Editions Planete, 1967.
Wagner, Geoffrey. *Parade of Pleasure: A Study of Popular Iconography in the United States.* New York: Library Publishers, 1955.
Warshow, Robert. *The Immediate Experience.* Cambridge: Harvard University Press, 2001 [1962].
Waugh, Coulton. *The Comics.* New York: Macmillan, 1947.
Wertham, Fredric. *Seduction of the Innocent.* New York: Holt, Rinehart and Winston, 1954.

White, David Manning and Robert H. Abel, eds. *The Funnies: An American Idiom. The Role of Comic Strips in American Life, Thoroughly Explored by Critics, Creators, and Scholars.* New York: Free Press, 1963.

Worcester, Kent. "C. L. R. James, Mid-Century Marxism, and the Popular Arts." *Reconstruction: An Interdisciplinary Cultural Studies Community* 2.4 (2002): <www.reconstruction.ws>

Wordsworth, William. "Illustrated Books and Newspapers." 1846. *The Victorians: An Anthology of Poetry and Poetics.* Ed. Valentine Cunningham. Oxford: Blackwell, 1999. 16.

Wright, Bradford W. *Comic Book Nation: The Transformation of Youth Culture in America.* Baltimore: Johns Hopkins University Press, 2001.

PART ONE

Early Twentieth-Century Voices

The high-toned intellectual magazines of early twentieth century America featured acres of text, rarely adorned by pictures. Within this austere, print-dense environment, perhaps the main cultural battle was between the established defenders of the genteel tradition and the insurgent forces of literary modernism. The two sides of this battle had a very different attitude towards comics. For adherents to the genteel tradition, illustrated magazines and comics were symptomatic of much that was going wrong in the contemporary world: the newfound preference for visual stimulations rather than time-honored literary values; the growing strength of disorderly immigrant cultures in the United States which threatened to overturn Anglo-Saxon supremacy; the increasing acceptance of roughhouse slang which endangered norms of proper grammar and refined diction.

The cluster of essays by Sidney Fairfield, Annie Russell Marble, and Ralph Bergengren, here offered in excerpted form, give voice to these complaints. In subsequent decades, the themes sounded by the genteel tradition would be periodically repeated by waves of parental and educational reformers, who would particularly emphasize the dangers of children imitating what they read in comics. However, the lofty and ornately literary tone of the genteel tradition would be replaced by tracts written either in neutral-voiced social-scientific jargon or blunt journalistic anger.

The critic and historian Annie Russell Marble (1864–1936) is nicely emblematic of the cultural profile of the genteel tradition. In her studies of the women of the Mayflower and writers of revolutionary era America, Marble sought to shore up the Anglo-Saxon ascendancy in the age of mass immigration. Naturally, Marble was distressed that otherwise "refined" parents were allowing their children ("the traditional if not the lineal descendants of the Puritans") to read the Sunday "picture section." A similar undercurrent of anxiety over the loss of traditional WASP cultural authority peeps through in the article by Ralph Bergenren, who continually notes that the most popular comic strip characters are "German-Americans" or issue from "the slums."

The genteel tradition would be strongly opposed by the advocates of literary modernism, who emerged just prior to World War I and gathered strength in the 1920s. Just as Annie Russell Marble was a quintessential genteel writer, Gilbert Seldes (1893–1970) embodied the spirit of modernism. As managing editor of the *Dial* in the 1920s, Seldes was instrumental in publishing some of the early master-works of literary modernism, including T. S. Eliot's *The Waste Land* (1922) and Thomas Mann's *Death in Venice* (1924). For the *Nation*, Seldes wrote one of the very first positive reviews of Joyces's *Ulysses*. As critic Edmund Wilson once noted, Seldes played a major role in "the liquidation of genteel culture in America."

Seldes became the central figure of early comics criticism when he wrote his most famous and influential book, *The Seven Lively Arts* (1924). In this pioneering text, Seldes championed popular art forms such as jazz and slap-stick comedy films, as well as the early comic strips. *Krazy Kat* creator George Herriman was, along with Charlie Chaplin, one of the key popular artists celebrated by Seldes.

Throughout the book, Seldes cleverly upturned the genteel tradition by show-ing that what earlier critics had regarded as vices were in fact virtues. As against the genteel tradition's fear of comics as an alien immigrant incursion against the purity of American culture, Seldes argued that comics were in fact an indigenous art form. While the genteel tradition claimed that print was intrinsically superior (more rational and thoughtful) to visual art forms, Seldes stressed that each art should be judged by its own internal criteria. Rather than decrying the slang of comic strip dialogue as evidence of bad grammar and diction, Seldes praised car-toonists for their vernacular vigor. If the genteel tradition gave priority to tradition, Seldes responded by stressing the modernist value of novelty.

The more positive approach to comics can also be seen in other writers closely associated with literary modernism. Writing from Germany, Thomas Mann found in the woodcut novels of Frans Masereel a promising new art form that captured the raw urban reality of modernity. For Mann, part of the excitement of Masereel's graphic work is precisely its mass appeal—being wordless, the woodcuts promised to transcend traditional cultural boundaries. Once again, a quality that horrified cultural traditionalists was been re-valued as a virtue.

Like other modernist poets, E. E. Cummings enjoyed with language: he adopted phonetic spellings ("lil Oinis" for "little Ernest") and played games with typography (spelling his name in lower case). Cummings found a kindred spirit in George Herriman, whose *Krazy Kat* comic strip was also a riot of language. As the critic Guy Davenport once suggested, we can "appreciate a lot of Cummings by remembering that at any moment in his poems he is likely to be ventriloquizing the elate Krazy." Cumming's tribute to *Krazy Kat* is written in an appropriately high-spirited style.

The short story writer and poet Dorothy Parker, famous for her stiletto wit, had little patience with sentimental children's literature: in the 1920s, she regularly trashed Winnie the Pooh creator A. A. Milne in the pages of *The New Yorker*. Therefore, when Parker started championing Crockett Johnson's *Barnaby* comic strip in the 1940s, her praise carried real weight. Only a notable work could please such a waspish critic. Yet Parker's acclaim is offset by some remarks that point to the continued low status of comics as a whole: "For a bulky segment of a century, I have been an avid follower of comic strips—all comic strips," Parker notes; "this is a statement made with approximately the same amount of pride with which one would say, 'I've been shooting cocaine into my arm for the past 25 years.' "

Sidney Fairfield

From "The Tyranny of the Pictorial"

Lippincott's Monthly Magazine, June 1895, pp. 861–64.

Certain aspects of the illustration of newspapers and periodicals are interesting just now as indicative of modern tendencies and as marking the difference between the standard of what is worth publishing to-day and the standard that prevailed a decade or two ago. The editor of a prominent weekly says that his paper wants no literary matter beyond a very small amount,—about enough to fill three columns. What he does want and gives all his energies to secure is illustrations; the reading matter to carry them is easy enough to get, probably without calling upon outside help. In other words, the purely pictorial element is the controlling end and be-all of this enterprising publisher.

While this may be an extreme instance of the craze for pictures, it cannot be denied that the same spirit, if in a less degree, actuates the entire secular weekly press and, in larger measure than ever before, the daily press. It has also invaded the large and important field of trade publication, so that to-day no trade paper that claims to be up to date is without the inevitable half-tone.

Of the latter feature of the reign of the pictorial I do not desire to say more, but rather to call attention to the almost unlimited field that has been opened in the literary and journalistic world to the man who is skilled as a draughtsman and who can put into his drawings the quality which stamps them as art. Precious few of these young fellows have this quality, it is true, and more's the pity for it, for if there is any department of American publication that should be improved, it is that of illustration. The trouble is not that there are too many artists, but that there are too few good ones. There are almost as many men drawing pictures, good, bad, and indifferent, as there are writers. And it is far easier for an artist of ability, as newspaper artists go, to get profitable work, than it is for the equally good writer.

[. . .]

Coincident with this ascendancy of the art pictorial is the peculiar character of the illustration itself. If the average picture-paper is a criterion of the public taste, the race has developed a predominant curiosity regarding the female adorned and unadorned. Woman is the *summum bonum* and the sine qua non of the art of the modern illustrator. The clever ones do her adequate justice and show her to us in satisfactory poses and correct costumes, although we tire of their weekly or monthly iteration of the same subject with a new joke or dialogue as its only excuse for existence.

[. . .]

With all this space in our publications pre-empted by the pictorial, the gentry who live by selling what they write must take metaphorically to the woods, for the reading public has suddenly become picture-mad. The highest thought, the deepest truth, the most exquisite bit of sustained description, poetry, dialogue, love, tragedy, humor, realism of any kind, all are subjected by the weeklies and monthlies to the tyranny of the pictorial, until everything a writer writes, and too often, alas, that which he doesn't write, is seized upon and illustrated as if in the endeavor to help him make himself understood.

And does the illustrator really help the writer? Not necessarily. Often he takes most outrageous license with the truth as written. He is essentially an exaggerator, a perverter of the facts. He sins on the side of his picture, never on that of the man-uscript. He makes effects; he does not inform. If his picture is not an attractive one, we are apt not to read what accompanies it, and in such a case he does the writer an absolute injury. If the picture *is* an attractive one, the reader's curiosity is often satisfied by the picture alone, and he doesn't care to read what has been written. And it is very frequently true that the pictorial attractiveness of a publication is such that the mere contemplation of its pictures suffices, and the purchaser tosses it aside without reading a line.

Let it not be supposed that I would do away entirely with the illustrator. Far from it. What I object to is over-illustration, the picture-on-every-other-page idea. Let us have things proportioned to their true value. Let the reading-matter have the most of the space. The written word is the first and the highest expression of thought, and it ever will be. To illustrate the perfect literary production does not necessarily improve it artistically. To assume that it does improve it implies that the writer has produced an unfinished work. Are the works of the best modern literary artists improved by illustration? Can an artist with his brush or pen add anything to the well-developed characterizations of our successful novelists? In other words, is not the literary art of a master amply sufficient to portray to the appreciative, intelligent reader all in his book that is charming or thrilling or pathetic or humorous? I believe that it is, and also that it is a literary crime for the average illustrator to inject an unsympathetic personality into the pages of a great work of fiction, of whose creative forces he can know no more than the reader. Some of this sort of illustration is amazingly clever, but most of it is just the opposite. To distinguish the pictorial opportunity in a book-manuscript is a work requiring rare discretion, and too many of our illustrators, with the approval of the publishers, take their cure for a picture from some such inadequate and puerile suggestion as that conveyed in the familiar climax of love-stories: "And she fell on his breast and wept tears of unutterable joy."

Annie Russell Marble

From "The Reign of the Spectacular"

The Dial, November 1, 1903, pp. 297–99.

In the varied phases of modern thought and activity, the obvious holds unchallenged sway. The deeds that are conspicuous, the ideas that are garish, the literature that is episodic and pictorial, gain the popular favor. The eye of the senses is regnant,—often a substitute for ear, imagination, and reason. Surface-impressions satisfy; "the eyes of our understanding" are dimly enlightened. In the vernacular of the American youth, every entertainment is a "show," whether at the theatre or the church, at home or at school. With all possible tribute to the progress and appreciation of art during the last quarter-century, one must admit that there is a craze for pictures and pageants apart from their essential or even relative value.

[. . .]

Comment is needless upon the supremacy of the pictorial journal, and upon the scanty discrimination, among the mass of readers, as to literary or artistic merits. Only experience could make credible the fact that in homes, refined in other ways, the "picture section" of the Sunday newspaper is given to the children as amusement,—lofty pabulum for the traditional if not lineal descendants of the Puritans! Lowell's words are relevant: "Good taste may not be necessary to salvation or to success in life, but it is one of the most powerful factors of civilization."

The alliance of picture and text dates back even to the crude wood-cuts of Caxton's "Game and Play of the Chesse" in 1476, and the early broadsides down to Bewick and his successors. Pictorial and literary art have been reciprocally stimulating. Hiram Powers's "Greek Slave" evoked one of Mrs. Browning's most tender sonnets. Giotto's portrait of Dante inspired Lowell to rare verse. The Cenci gave incentive to Shelley's drama and Hawthorn's romance. Many an artist of a later generation has infused fresh vitality into a hackneyed literary model. Millais visualized Effie Deans. Mr. Abbey's character-interpretations have reveals anew the creative genius of both poet and painter. Miss Austen and Mrs. Gaskell have been rejuvenated by Mr. Hugh Thomson's delineations. "Lewis Carroll" could not have foreseen the revival of popularity which would greet his wonderland-child when Mr. Peter Newell should portray the droll fancies of his creation.

Because of the usefulness of such commingled art of a high grade, one must the more deplore the bizarre in text and illustration. Perhaps with prevision of this danger, Wordsworth wrote his sonnet on "Illustrated Books and Magazines," with its warning,—

Avaunt this vile abuse of pictured page!
Must eyes be all in all, the tongue and ear
Nothing? Heaven keep us from a lower stage!

As a natural means of educating the starved imaginations of children, victims of the lifeless, statistical text-books of the past, as a road to forming word-concepts and moral ideas, picture-studies have been of inestimable value. A few far-seeing students of pedagogy, however, have sounded the alarm against excess of picture-teaching, lest it defeat its end and leave inert both mind and fancy. To cultivate individual ideas, to educe subjective interpretations of life and letters, is the desideratum of all education; such results are often hindered by excess of scenic material.

[. . .]

The student of history is not depressed by the flaunting symptoms of current life and literature. Under different aspects, in varied ages, there have been like excesses of fashion. After the reign of euphuism and the later age of poetic artifice, there came reactions, renewed devotion to simple fundamental truths. Satiated with the spectacular, there are indications to-day of a tendency toward a saner life. In many communities, nobler standards already rebuke mere affluence and gaud. There is a general recognition of Nature's restorative for the strain of city life,—a life melodramatic in its seething streets by daylight not less than in its illusive forms around the foot-lights. Surviving the artificial and the sensational rises the Excelsior of the true artist,—the creation and illumination of the vital. Elements of such endeavor are cemented in Mr. Garland's ideal for individual and universal service: "Life is the model, truth is the master, the heart of the man himself is the motive-power."

Ralph Bergengren

From "The Humor of the Colored Supplement"

Atlantic Monthly, August 1906, pp. 269–73.

Ten or a dozen years ago—the exact date is here immaterial—an enterprising newspaper publisher conceived the idea of appealing to what is known as the American "sense of humor" by printing a so-called comic supplement in colors. He chose Sunday as of all days the most lacking in popular amusements, carefully restricted himself to pictures without human and color without beauty, and presently inaugurated a new era in American journalism. The colored supplement became an institution. No Sunday is complete without it,—not because its pages invariably delight, but because, like flies in summer, there is no screen that will altogether exclude them. A newspaper without a color press hardly considers itself a newspaper, and the smaller journals are utterly unmindful of the kindness of Providence in putting the guardian angel, Poverty, outsider their portals. Sometimes, indeed, they think to outwit this kindly interference by printing a syndicated comic page without color; and mercy is thus served in a half portion, for, uncolored, the pictures are inevitably about twice as attractive. Some print them without color, but on pink paper. Others rejoice, as best they may, in a press that will reproduce at least a fraction of the original discord. One and all they unite vigorously, as if driven by a perverse and cynical intention, to prove the American sense of humor a thing of national shame and degradation. Fortunately the public has so little to say about its reading matter than one may fairly suspend judgment.

[. . .]

At no period in the world's history has there been a steadier output of so-called humor,—especially in this country. The simple idea of printing a page of comic pictures has produced families. The very element of variety has been obliterated by the creation of types,—a confusing medley of impossible countrymen, mules, goats, German-Americans and their irreverent progeny, specialized children with a genius for annoying their elders, white-whiskered elders with a genius for playing practical jokes on their grandchildren, policemen, Chinamen, Irishmen, negroes, inhuman conceptions of the genus tramp, boy inventors whose inventions invariably end in causing somebody to be mirthfully spattered with paint or joyously torn to pieces by machinery, bright boys with a talent for deceit, laziness, or cruelty, and even the beasts of the jungle dehumanized to the point of practical joking. *Mirabile dictu!*— some of these things have even been dramatized.

With each type the reader is expected to become personally acquainted—to watch for its coming on Sunday mornings, happily wondering with what form of inhumanity the author will have been able to endow his brainless manikins. And the authors are often men of intelligence, capable here and there of a bit of adequate drawing and an idea that is honestly and self-respectingly provocative of laughter. Doubtless they are often ashamed of their product; but the demand of the hour is imperative. The presses are waiting. They, too, are both quick and heavy. And the cry of the publisher is for "fun" that no intellect in all his heterogeneous public shall be too dull to appreciate. We see, indeed, the outward manifestation of a curious paradox: humor prepared and printed for the extremely dull, and—what is still more remarkable—excused by grown men, capable of editing newspapers, on the ground that it gives pleasure to children.

Reduced to first principles, therefore, it is not humor, but simply a supply created in answer to a demand, hastily produced by machine methods and hastily accepted by editors too busy with other editorial duties to examine it intelligently. Under these conditions "humor" is naturally conceived as something preeminently quick; and so quickness predominates. Somebody is always hitting somebody else with a club; somebody is always falling downstairs, or out of a balloon, or over a cliff, or into a river, a barrel of paint, a basket of eggs, a convenient cistern, or a tub of hot water. The comic cartoonists have already exhausted every available substance into which one can fall, and are compelled to fall themselves into a veritable ocean of vain repetition. They have exhausted everything by which one can be blown up. They have exhausted everything by which one can be knocked down or run over. And if the victim is never actually killed in these mirthful experiments, it is obviously because he would then cease to be funny,—which is very much the point of view of the Spanish Inquisition, the cat with a mouse, or the American Indian with a captive. But respect for property, respect for parents, for law, for decency, for truth, for beauty, for kindliness, for dignity, or for honor, are killed, without mercy. Morality alone, in its restricted sense of sexual relations, is treated with courtesy, although we find throughout the accepted theory that marriage is a union of uncongenial spirits, and the chart of petty marital deceit is carefully laid out and marked for whoever is likely to respond to endless unconscious suggestions.

[. . .]

In these days of syndicated ideas a comparatively small body of men produce the greater part of it. Physical pain is the most glaringly omnipresent of these *motifs*; it is counted upon invariably to amuse the average humanity of our so-called Christian civilization.

[. . .]

Deceit is another universal concept of humor, that combine easily with the physical pain "motif"; and mistaken identity, in which the juvenile idiot disguises himself and deceives his parents in various days, is another favorite resort of the humorists. The paucity of invention is hardly less remarkable than the willingness of the inventors to sign their products, or the willingness of editors to publish them. But the age is notoriously one in which editors underrate and insult the public intelligence.

[. . .]

In all this noisy, explosive, garrulous pandemonium one finds here and there a moment of rest and refreshment,—the work of the few pioneers of decency and decorum brave enough to bring their wares to the noisome market and lucky enough to infuse the spirit of refinement, art, and genuine humor into its otherwise hopeless atmosphere. Preeminent among them stands the inventor of *Little Nemo in Slumberland*, a man of genuine pantomimic humor, charming draughtmanship, and an excellent decorative sense of color, who has apparently studied his medium and makes the best of it. And with him come Peter Newell, Grace G. Weiderseim, and Conde,—now illustrating *Uncle Remus* for a Sunday audience,—whose pictures in some of the Sunday papers are a delightful and self-respecting proof of the possibilities of this type of journalism. Out of the noisy streets, the cheap restaurants with their unsteady-footed waiters and avalanches of soup and crockery, out of the slums, the quarreling families, the prisons and the lunatic asylums, we step for a moment into the world of childish fantasy, closing the iron door behind us and trying to shut out the clamor of hooting mobs, the laughter of imbeciles, and the crash of explosives. After all, there is no reason why children should not have their innocent amusement on Sunday morning; but there seems to be every reason why the average editor of the weekly comic supplement should be given a course in art, literature, common sense, and Christianity.

Thomas Mann

Introduction to Frans Masereel, *Passionate Journey: A Novel Told in 165 Woodcuts*

This essay originally appeared as the introduction to *Passionate Journey: A Novel Told in 165 Woodcuts*, by Frans Masereel, published in 1948 by Lear Publishers, Inc. Translation by Joseph M. Bernstein.

I should like first of all to say a few words about the two quotations which Masereel has chosen as epigraphs for his *Passionate Journey*.[1] Not everyone who picks up this book of pictures may be "cultured" enough to read these passages in the original. For you do not have to be as multilingual as a Riviera hotel-waiter or a nineteenth-century boarding-school miss to enjoy and appreciate the work of this great artist—especially in the volume before us. You may, for example, be a worker, a taxi-driver, or a young telephone-operator without any gift for languages, and yet be intellectually curious enough, close enough to the spirit of democracy, to know Frans Masereel, to have read him and wondered about him; whereas your Mr. Employer is not "cultured" enough to understand him and does not even want to, because unfortunately he considers Masereel "subversive," synonymous with Bolshevism.

This Flemish-European art is so genuinely human, it relies so little on a culture which is not purely inward or a product of ordinary democratic education in our time, that a knowledge of foreign languages is no prerequisite to understanding the epigraphs in this book. We are dealing here with a creative work of such simplicity that you do not even have to know how to read or write to see it: it is a novel in pictures, a kind of movie which, except for two introductory quotations, needs no other words, captions, or sub-titles to explain it. It appeals directly to the eye. Nevertheless, it is decidedly helpful if you do understand the rather simple statements which the artist has quoted in order to make clear his own intentions: they immediately give you the "feel" of the pictures.

The excerpt from the American, Walt Whitman, runs: "Behold! I do not give lectures, or a little charity: When I give, I give myself." And the words of the Frenchman,

---

1. The original title in German was *Mein Stundenbuch*; in French *Mon Livre d'Heures*.

Romain Rolland, read: ". . . pleasures and pain, pranks and jests, experiences and follies, straw and hay, figs and grapes, green fruit and ripe fruit, roses and skyscrapers, things I have seen, read, known, had, and lived!"

I said above that these are simple statements. In them an artist explains, in words of foreign languages he loves, that he has no intention of teaching or exhorting; he wishes to depict not just a carefully chosen part of himself but all of himself. He means to show himself as he is. His life is a dedicated life, the life of an individual—in a sense, man's life. And this marvelous adventure is rich in faces and experiences, invaluable in its mingling of pleasure and pain, happiness and sorrow, joy and bitterness—a life into which we are driven, we know not why, and from which we will one day be taken, again probably without knowing why. Here is no moralist, no pedagogue, no guardian of souls, no zealot with a one-track mind. Here we are in the presence of a good companion—a kind, sincere, naive fellow who lives life to the full and, if he criticizes it for its distortions, does so not out of bitter disillusionment but with natural, unaffected feeling . . . Does that not inspire unusual confidence as a beginning?

It is only a beginning. Here confidence is in order as it rarely is in this time of confusion, in which prophets shout each other down and hucksters cry their wares on both right and left. Confidence—what a virtue that is today! What an opportunity! What an unusual possibility! In the presence of a work of art that offers it, one should give precedence to this deeply reassuring word, this rare quality, this fortunate avenue to emotion—in short, to the human-moral side of art.

I feel this as I write my introduction. I find it terribly difficult and even ridiculous to play the connoisseur and pontifically direct the attention of my readers to linear charms and God knows what other aesthetic "values." In this world it is no longer a question of such "values": it is a question of genuine values, human worth, trustworthiness. And a good book should be introduced by telling why it is good, why the human being from whom it springs deserves our confidence.

In this connection, I have generally observed the following: people find it hard to have faith in a way of life that is only old or only young and new, only traditional or only modern, only aristocratic or exclusively the opposite. The one, sincerely but stubbornly turned toward the past, despises the present as vulgar; the other, quite free and untrammeled, basically arrogant, without roots or traditions, is solely concerned with the present and future. Both factors must be present if there is to be confidence—nobility and freedom, history and actuality. And it is just this fusion that is most happily expressed in the art of Frans Masereel.

He is a wood-engraver. He practices that old, noble, pious German handicraft, handed down from the Middle Ages through Lucas van Leyden and Albrecht Duerer, through the Nuremberg Chronicler and the Latin *Biblia Pauperum* (Bible of the Poor). It is a conservative art, primitive in material, old-fashioned in technique. Today as five hundred years ago, it requires nothing but a piece of peartree-wood, a small knife—and man's genius. Could such a worthy calling and occupation—in our period of raucous street-noises and shrieking factory-whistles—fail to influence the moods and attitudes of a man who is fundamentally modern and democratic-minded? In his *Passionate Journey*, Masereel depicts himself. Before the giant factories of modern industry, their belching smokestacks, their derricks, blast furnaces, and forges, he scratches the back of his head, leans his chin on his hand and finally, seized by some mysterious panic, takes to his heels with his arms outstretched.

At the very outset, in a title-picture, he shows himself at work. Peering through his glasses and seated at a simple table, he engages in his pious task of creation. Before him are bits of wood and tiny tools for cutting and piercing. Thus he spends hours every day, with the passionate patience of a handicraftsman. He progresses slowly and deliberately, sincerely and creatively, in exactly the same way as those medieval masters who were his forebears. I have been told that he is no artist of moods, dallying for weeks and then producing his works of genius with a sudden burst of explosive fury. He prefers consistent daily work; to him, diligence is the highest form of passion. He is now only thirty-seven years old[2] but has long since produced his first thousand woodcuts, not to speak of the thousands of his drawings. What concentration!—the concentration of genius, without which such a passion for work is inconceivable. And what self-possession! It is of course wrong to say that genius is diligence, that diligence creates genius. But the idea that the two are somehow bound up with each other is quite valid—the order, however, should be reversed. Genius creates diligence, demands and compels it. At least this is so in the case of masterworks and here we are in the living presence of mastery over form. The form itself is traditional, conservative, age-old; it is romantic and turned toward the past. Hence it would not arouse complete confidence were the content not imbued with such immediacy and such sustained modernity that the old and the new, the traditional and the dynamic fuse to inspire human confidence.

Seldom has raciness so blended with conviction as here in the contrast between a fundamentally old and traditional technique and the sharpness and contemporary

---

2. In 1926.

boldness of the things it expresses. Masereel has produced a volume of woodcuts called *The City*—in its hundred illustrations he has mirrored our entire civilization as seen by his penetrating and pitying eye. He has depicted the brutal fantasy of modern life, grotesque and horrible in its inexorable vulgarity. It is crowded with contradictions, contradictions of the diabolical and the damned. As you thumb through this German-Flemish "block-book" brought up-to-date, you pass in review all the coarsest aspects of the present. It is a present that has been tried and convicted by a graphic artist who is himself so much a part of the present that in the impact of his art he is closely akin to one of the most characteristic products of our times. For is not the play of black-and-white on a movie screen a democratic pleasure? Has it not succeeded in charming even the most exacting intellectual aristocrat?

I have already alluded to the movies, as does every one who discusses this artist. Darken the room! Sit down with this book next to your reading-lamp and concentrate on its pictures as you turn page after page. Don't deliberate too long! It is no tragedy if you fail to grasp every picture at once, just as it does not matter if you miss one or two shots in a movie. Look at these powerful black-and-white figures, their features etched in light and shadow. You will be captivated from beginning to end: from the first picture showing the train plunging through dense smoke and bearing the hero toward life, to the very last picture showing the skeleton-faced figure wandering among the stars. And where are you? Has not this passionate journey had an incomparably deeper and purer impact on you than you have ever felt before?

Recently, a film magazine published abroad asked me if I thought that something artistically creative could come out of the cinema. I answered: "Indeed I do!" Then I was asked which movie, of all I had seen, had stirred me most. I replied: Masereel's *Passionate Journey*. That may seem an evasive answer, since it is not a case of art conquering the cinema but of cinema influencing art. At any rate, it involves a meeting and fusing of two arts—the infusion of the aristocratic spirit of art into the democratic spirit of the cinema. What has hitherto been purely a pleasure of the senses is here intellectualized and spiritualized. And if movies are usually nothing but pure sensation, without art, here we have an artistically produced film of life, a human life lived in art and the spirit, a dedicated life, if you will. The pious "block-book" of olden days has here developed into a stimulating and entertaining movie. As a matter of fact, Masereel is very fond of the cinema and has even written a scenario himself. He calls his books "Romans en images"—novels in pictures. Is that not an accurate description of motion pictures? The wood-block in which this Fleming silhouettes his plastically drawn figures against broad surfaces of light is akin to the small white screen of the cinema. We expect so little of that narrow screen as we sit down in front of it; yet when pictures flicker on it before our eyes, we marvel at the way in which life seems to open out.

These picture-novels, mute but eloquent creations, bear such titles as *A Man's Path of Sorrow*, *The Sun*, *The Idea*, *The City*, and they are all so strangely compelling, so deeply felt, so rich in ideas, that one never tires of looking at them. But the most personal, the most intimate, the warmest, the most human, and most candid of them all is this *Passionate Journey*. It is such a popular work that it is quite natural and fitting for a publisher to want to take it out of the realm of the esoteric and make it available to the worker, the taxi-driver, and the young telephone-operator. It belongs much more to the common people than to the snobs; and I am happy to do my part in making it better known to the democratic-minded public.

Franz Masereel was born in 1889 in Blankenberghe (Belgium), the son of well-to-do parents, and grew up in Ghent. The young etcher, woodcutter, and illustrator was twenty-five when World War I came. He had illustrated many books: volumes of Emile Verhaeren, Pierre Jean Jouve, Romain Rolland, Georges Duhamel, and especially Charles-Louis Philippe, before he found his own specific direction. The war marked a turning-point in everyone's life. It changed Masereel from a Flemish realist into an European artist. He has said so himself. Speaking to his compatriot, Henri van de Velde, he declared: "Before the war, I delighted in crude, genuinely Flemish realism: carnivals, open-air dances, whores and sailors . . . I have whole piles of sketches of life—on the street, in courtyards, in shabby taverns. I have always worked hard . . . But the deepest meaning of all these things eluded me, and I feel that the war did much to make me understand them." In sum, he had been national-minded and a realist; the war europeanized and spiritualized him. That is a typical and familiar process: the search for ideals under the impact of war, the spiritual drive, the revaluation of all values, which war imposes. But rarely has that experience brought about such an artistic heightening and intensification, such an increase in human and world insight as in the case of Masereel. He had been a run-of-the-mill sensuous talent, making sketches in Belgian alehouses. War made of him a spiritual figure, a voice of the people's conscience.

Is he then a revolutionary? I trust that the slight hesitation with which I answer that question in the affirmative is not misunderstood, for of course it has to be answered affirmatively. I said above that Masereel's art accuses and condemns our civilization; I also said that if it criticizes the distortions of life and society, it does so on the basis of the freest and most natural human emotions. In other words, it criticizes artistically and not because of disillusionment over shattered ideals. I feel that he lacks something in order to be a pure and true revolutionary. The prophet of political salvation is necessarily a man of a single idea, a man of doctrine and power who knows exactly what he wants and strives to accomplish it without counting the cost. I do not think that Masereel possesses that knack or even that he feels it is his business to acquire it. To be sure, he tells in symbolic pictures the tragic-comic story of an idea—but what idea does he invoke if not that of an honest and free humanity? As you leaf through his book, you see that it is inconceivable for such a man, whose very being breathes sympathy for the things of this world, to interpret that idea as fanaticism, dictatorship, or spiritual enslavement. As I express this incredulity, I find myself thinking over and over again of the psychology of confidence to which I have referred earlier. I should like to complete my thought by venturing to assert, on the basis of experience, that today men's confidence is not placed in power-drunk fanatics. Men refuse to pin their faith on those who are prepared to wallow in blood for the sake of the omnipotent state, who are all too ready to make a clean slate of the past and sacrifice two-thirds of humanity so that the last third may be totalitarian. Masereel has taken one of his epigraphs from Romain Rolland—nor is this accidental, for his case is similar. Rolland's authority and renown, heightened during the disgraceful spectacle of World War I, sprang from his fundamentally human attitude and his sense of conscience. Rolland loved ideas more than The Idea. He was a man of goodwill—and his good will liberated rather than enslaved.

You may even find in Masereel the creative artist that worldliness, pure delight in the adventure of life, takes the form of a certain playfulness, a certain irresponsibility, so that his revolutionary side remains just an episode. It is included among the many other adventures he has genuinely lived through, among his other "experiences and follies," without receiving any undue emphasis. In his *Passionate Journey* there are eight pictures portraying the hero simply as a friend and lover of children, as a "big brother" to the young, standing on his head for them, telling them stories, playing games with them. More than a dozen woodcuts deal with women, the raptures of the body, disappointments in love. No less than ten express the majesty of the sea. Thirteen tell of distant journeys to the land of the Moors and of the Chinese. Then there are those in which he does everyday, inconsequential things boxing, dancing, playing an accordion, folk-dancing at a picnic, climbing and shooting, eating well, drinking and sleeping, skating and bicycling, strolling and lolling in the fields, occasionally even saving somebody's life . . . All this is really too planless to be considered a virtuous life, the life of a revolutionary.

It does not involve principles. So it is not incongruous to see our hero burst with laughter at the sight of a bejewelled priest and then, one day when his anguish and disgust are great, to encounter him in a church, bowing his head and kneeling in the mystic atmosphere of muted sorrow. Experiences and follies . . . Four of the one hundred sixty-five pictures present him listening to a speaker at a mass meeting, studying social problems in a library, even making a revolutionary speech himself and stirring a crowd of men to revolt. Then come other adventures, showing that he has also sown his Socialist wild oats.

That, I say, is the outward appearance. On the surface, fun, trial and error, playing the game of life. But there is one picture—look at it, it is the richest of all. Its meaning is clearly conveyed: the catharsis of human suffering. The Eternal has cast him down. Amid legendary flowers he extends his arms and lies as if dead in the foliage, behind which the evening sun sets. Then a storm begins to rage. Stamping and clenching his fists, he tramples on his heart, his sensitive human heart. And now, quite free and nonchalant, his face a skull, one hand in his trouser pocket, the other jauntily upturned, he begins his cosmic journey and trades jokes with the stars . . . Do you understand? Going through life, sharing its sorrows, was not such a callous journey. It involved the heart; it took a very heavy toll of the heart. Release, a free and easy life without sorrow or love, only came afterwards. It was his heart, his accursed human heart, that forced him to live, profoundly affecting the course of his life, causing him to love and to suffer, making him laugh and curse at the false, the shoddy, the vulgar, and the unfeeling. His heart, not Socialism, made a revolutionary of him, even when he indulged in pranks and follies. For the true revolution is not "in principle," not in "The Idea"—but in the human heart.

The psychology of confidence is a willful and capricious psychology! If I have analyzed it, I have done so because of its bearing on the problem of artistic creation—a problem that is still crucial, more crucial now perhaps than ever before, whatever may be said about it. For there are those who assert that art is finished, its role played out. They claim that in our period of history nothing more is expected of the artist or his "aesthetic" life, that the artist has nothing more to say. Nowadays, so much is investigated, tracked down, and proclaimed as dogma that the bloodhounds and dogmatists often go right past the truth and hand down judgments which deserve simply to be tossed aside. Thus for example, this notion of the untimeliness or untrustworthiness of the artist. But how easy it is to prove that today artistic creation alone enjoys and merits human confidence. One can prove it by this book with its woodcuts, with its autobiography in pictures of a man who sits in a train and rushes toward life. Yet he cannot really be fitted into this life. He does not really belong to any of its forms. He sees nothing reasonable about it and insists only on living with his heart.

Look at him in one of the very first pictures: he stands on the steps of the train in the midst of travelers rushing to and fro. What is he? How is one to place him? What manner of man is he? What is his occupation? To what social class does he belong? One cannot tell. To no class, apparently. He is not of the middle class; he does not even wear a hat, as all respectable citizens do. In a later picture this hatlessness is amusingly exploited. We see a well-fed burgher lose his hat in a storm. Our hero, with turned-up collar, stands there and roars with laughter at the sight of the panicky Philistine lunging after his careening hat. Nor does he seem to be a worker either, certainly not a class-conscious one. His clothing is nondescript; his attitude is neither arrogant nor vulgar, just comfortable, natural, relaxed—human. There is something pure, strange, free, unattached in his bearing as he remains there on the train-step alone in the crowd. As you follow him, you get the impression that he is on earth like a visitor to a strange land whose customs and spectacles he appreciates and in whose life he participates with a feeling, all-too-feeling heart. Yet to him, the foreigner, all this merely adds up to "experiences and follies." Eventually too, the hatless man makes a clean break with this world of philistinism in which he finds himself completely out of place. There are a few pictures in which he exhibits his contempt for this philistinism in such a violently Flemish way that he has to flee an irate mob of the "right-minded." The world has had enough of him and he enough of the world. He has even had enough of love, judging from the gesture with which he exits through the door. Then his life-journey comes to an end. A mystical *denouement* begins. And he tramples on his heart . . .

Gazing at him, you wonder what can he "be"—this tall hatless fellow who almost always keeps his hands in his trouser pockets in a nonchalant fashion that contrasts sharply with the passion with which he goes through life and which endears him to children all over the world? Moorish children as well as white children love him and climb up on his knees when he visits them. Occasionally, you see him working cooking, washing, tilling the fields. But it is clear that these acts too are merely "experiences and follies," brief parts he plays to, tolerated out of naïve love of mankind. Surely, however, his humanity must fit into some category of class and occupation. Yet it does not fit into any. It is classless. So he is probably an artist; that is the only supposition possible. For only the artist is classless, declassed from birth. If he is born a worker, his intellect and *noblesse* bring him close to the middle class. If, as almost all artists today, he is a product of the middle class, again his intellect, freeing him of social ties, alienates him from his class, makes him suspicious of middle-class interests, and carries him much closer in spirit to the worker, even though he is likewise mistrustful of the latter's class interest. His classlessness is not utopian; it is a natural result of fate and genuine at all times. It is this that surrounds him with an aura of purity, strangeness, detachment, something which in former times would have been called "saintliness"; and it is this too which, in a world shattered and torn asunder by implacable class conflicts, makes him, the outsider, the uninterested, the pure guest, the only one secretly enjoying the confidence of humanity, despite all the suspicions the "practical" man inevitably feels toward the intellectual and imaginative man.

Take his work—this old-new, aristocratic and free, traditional and contemporary product of his diligent hands, the pictorial masterpiece of an artist's life! Mingle with the hero in this marvelous and many-faceted world of human beings; be amazed, laugh, and let yourself be carried away! Share in his ecstasy when for the first time he finds happiness with a woman, the carnal and metaphysical happiness of love. He is so blissful that he drapes his arm around the neck of an old coachhorse. Yes, live with him! He feels the beauty of helping man and beast, the sacred value of the simplest gifts of God: sleeping next to an open window, awakening refreshed in the early morning, swimming in the vast ocean. He will take you with him to distant lands of wonder, to dark-skinned and yellow-skinned human companions. Then see what happens: see how he plays upon your tenderness and wins you entirely. Let worry and disgust bring bitter intoxication, until the streets reel about you. Follow the exquisite story in eleven pictures, in which our hero takes in a victimized young girl and is happy with her, only to see his beloved waste away and die, and in the despair of his last agonizing sorrow bury his head on her deathbed. Sob with him behind her poor coffin, and turn again—since it must be so—to a new life, new beatings of the heart. As you go through these pages, immerse yourself in the great riddle of this dream of life here on earth. It is as nothing since it ends and dissolves into nothingness. Yet everywhere in this nothingness, quickening it to life, the infinite is at hand! Look and enjoy and let your joy in contemplation be deepened by brotherly confidence.

(Translated from German by Joseph M. Bernstein)

Gilbert Seldes

"The Krazy Kat That Walks by Himself"

From *The Seven Lively Arts* (1924), p. 231–45. Reprinted by the permission of Russell & Volkening as agents for the author. Copyright © 1924 by Gilbert Seldes, renewed in 1952 by Gilbert Seldes.

Krazy Kat, the daily comic strip of George Herriman is, to me, the most amusing and fantastic and satisfactory work of art produced in America to-day. With those who hold that a comic strip cannot be a work of art I shall not traffic. The qualities of *Krazy Kat* are irony and fantasy—exactly the same, it would appear, as distinguish *The Revolt of the Angels*; it is wholly beside the point to indicate a preference for the work of Anatole France, which is in the great line, in the major arts. It happens that in America irony and fantasy are practiced in the major arts by only one or two men, producing high-class trash; and Mr. Herriman, working in a despised medium, without an atom of pretentiousness, is day after day producing something essentially fine. It is the result of a naïve sensibility rather like that of the *douanier* Rousseau; it does not lack intelligence, because it is a thought-out, a constructed piece of work. In the second order of the world's art it is superbly first rate—and a delight! For ten years, daily and frequently on Sunday, *Krazy Kat* has appeared in America; in that time we have accepted and praised a hundred fakes from Europe and Asia—silly and trashy plays, bad paintings, woeful operas, iniquitous religions, everything paste and brummagem, has had its vogue with us; and a genuine, honest native product has gone unnoticed until in the year of grace 1922 a ballet brought it a tardy and grudging acclaim.

Herriman is our great master of the fantastic and his early career throws a faint light on the invincible creation which is his present masterpiece. For all of his other things were comparative failures. He could not find, in the realistic framework he choose, an appropriate medium for his imaginings, or even for the strange draughtsmanship which is his natural mode of expression. *The Family Upstairs* seemed to the realist reader simply incredible; it failed to give him the pleasure of recognizing his neighbors in their more ludicrous moments. *The Dingbats*, hapless wretches, had the same defect. Another strip came nearer to providing the right tone: *Don Koyote and Sancho Pansy*; Herriman's mind has always been preoccupied with the mad knight of La Mancha, who reappears transfigured in *Krazy Kat*. And—although the inspirations are *never* literary—when it isn't Cervantes it is Dickens to whom he has the greatest affinity. The Dickens mode operated in *Baron Bean*—a figure half Micawber, half Charlie Chaplin as man of the world. I have noted, in the writing of Chaplin, Mr. Herriman's acute and sympathetic appreciation of the first few moments of *The Kid.* It is only fair to say here that he had himself done the same thing in his medium. Baron Bean was always in rags, penniless, hungry; but he kept his man Grimes, and Grimes did his dirty work, Grimes was the Baron's outlet, and Grimes, faithful retainer, held by the bonds of admiration and respect, helped the Baron in his one great love affair. Like all of Herriman's people, they lived on the enchanted mesa (pronounced: macey) by Coconino, near the town of Yorba Linda. The Baron was inventive; lacking the money to finance the purchase of a postage stamp, he entrusted a love letter to a carrier pigeon; and his "Go, my paloma," on that occasion is immortal.

Some of these characters are reappearing in Herriman's latest work: *Stumble Inn.* Of this I have not seen enough to be sure. It is a mixture of fancy and realism; Mr. Stumble himself is the Dickens character again—the sentimental, endearing, innkeeper who would rather lose his only patron than kill a favorite turkey cock for Thanksgiving. I have heard that recently a litter of pups has been found in the cellar of the inn; so I should judge that fantasy has won the day. For it is Herriman's bent to disguise what he has to say in the creations of the animal worlds which are neither human nor animal, but each *sui generis.*

This is how the Kat started. The thought of a friendship between a cat and a mouse amused Herriman and one day he wrote them in as a footnote to the *The Family Upstairs.* On their first appearance they played marbles while the family quarreled; and in the last picture the marble dropped through a hole in the bottom line. An office boy named Willie was the first to recognize the strange virtues of *Krazy Kat.* As surely as he was the greatest of office boys, so the greatest of editors, Arthur Brisbane, was the next to praise. He urged Herriman to keep the two characters in action; within a week they began a semi-independent existence in a strip an inch wide under the older strip. Slowly they were detached, were placed at one side, and naturally stepped into the full character of a strip when the *Family* departed. In time the Sundays appeared— three quarters of a page, involving the whole Krazy Kat and Ignatz families[1] and the

---

1. I must hasten to correct an erroneous impression which may have caused pain to many of Krazy's admirers. The three children, Milton, Marshall, and Irving, are of Ignatz, not, as Mr. Stark Young says, of Krazy. Krazy is not an unmarried mother. For the sake of the record, I may as well note here the names of the other principals: Offisa Bull Pupp; Mrs. Ignatz Mice; Kritofer Kamel; Joe Bark the moon hater; Don Kiyoti, that inconsequential heterodox; Joe Stork, alias Jose Cigueno; Mock Duk; Kolin Kelly the brick merchant; Walter Cephus Austridge; and the Kat Klan: Aunt Tabby, Uncle Tom, Krazy Katbird, Osker Wildcat, Alec Kat, and the Krazy Katfish.

flourishing town of Coconino—the flora and the fauna of the enchanted region which Herriman created out of his memories of the Arizona desert he so dearly loves.

In one of his most metaphysical pictures Herriman present Krazy as saying to Ignatz: "I ain't a Kat . . . and I ain't Krazy" (I put dots to indicate the lunatic shifting of background which goes on while these remarks are made; although the action is continuous and the characters motionless, it is in keeping with Herriman's method to have the backdrop in a continual state of agitation; you never know when a shrub will become a redwood, or a hut a church) . . . "it's wot's behind me that I am . . . it's the idea behind me, 'Ignatz' and that's wot I am." In an attitude of a contortionist Krazy points to the blank space behind him, and it is there that we must look for the "Idea." It is not far to seek. There is a plot and there is a theme—and considering that since 1913 or so there have been some three thousand strips, one may guess that the variations are infinite. The plot is that Krazy (androgynous, but according to his creator willing to be either) is in love with Ignatz Mouse; Ignatz, who is married, but vagrant, despises the Kat, and his one joy in life is to "Krease the Kat's bean with a brick" from the brickyard of Kolin Kelly. The fatuous Kat (Stark Young has found the perfect word for him: he is crack-brained) takes the brick, by a logic and a cosmic memory presently to be explained, as a symbol of love; he cannot, therefore, appreciate the efforts of Offisa B. Pupp to guard him and to entrammel the activities of Ignatz Mouse (or better, Mice). A deadly war is waged between Ignatz and Offisa Pupp—the latter is himself romantically in love with Krazy; and one often sees pictures in which Krazy and Ignatz conspire together to outwit the officer, both wanting the same thing, but with motives all at cross-purposes. This is the major plot; it is clear that the brick has little to do with the violent endings of other strips, for it is surcharged with emotions. It frequently comes not at the end, but the beginning of an action; sometimes it does not arrive. It is a symbol.

The theme is greater than the plot. John Alden Carpenter has pointed out in the brilliant little forward to his ballet, that *Krazy Kat* is a combination of Parsifal and Don Quixote, the perfect fool and the perfect knight. Ignatz is Sancho Panza and, I should say, Lucifer. He loathes the sentimental excursions, the philosophic ramblings of Krazy; he interrupts with a well-directed brick the romantic excesses of his companion. For example: Krazy blindfolded and with the scales of Justice in his hand declares: "things is all out of perpotion, 'Igntaz,' " "In what way, fool?" enquires the Mice as the scene shifts to the edge of a pool in the middle of the desert. "In the way of 'ocean' for a instinct." "Well?" asks Ignatz. They are plunging head down into midsea, and only their hind legs, tails, and words are visible: "The ocean is so innikwilly distribitted." They appear, each prone on a mountain peak, above the clouds, and the Kat says casually across the chasm to Ignatz: "Take 'Denva, Kollorado' and 'Tulsa, Okrahoma' they ain't got no ocean a tall—" (they are tossed by a vast sea, together in a packing-case) "while Sem Frencisco, Kellafornia, and Bostin, Messachoosit, has got more ocean than they can possibly use"—whereon Ignatz properly distributes a brick evenly on Krazy's noodle. Ignatz "has no time" for foolishness; he is a realist who and Sees Things as They ARE. "I don't believe in Santa Claus," says he. "I'm too broad-minded and advanced for such nonsense."

But Mr. Herriman, who is a great ironist, understands pity. It is the destiny of Ignatz never to know what his brick means to Krazy. He does not enter into the racial memories of the Kat which go back to the days of Cleopatra, of the Bubastes, when Kats were held sacred. Then, on a beautiful day, a mouse fell in love with Krazy, the beautiful daughter of Kleopatra Kat; bashful, advised by a soothsayer to write his love, he carved a declaration on a brick and, tossing the "missive," was accepted, although it had nearly killed the Kat. "when the Egyptian day is done it has become the Romeonian custom to crease his lady's bean with a brick laden with tender sentiments . . . through the tide of dusty years" . . . the tradition continues. But only Krazy knows this. So at the end it is the incurable romanticist, the victim of of acute Bovaryisme, who triumphs; for Krazy faints daily in full possession of his illusion, and Ignatz, stupidly hurling his brick thinking to injure, fosters the illusion and keeps Krazy "heppy."

Not always, to be sure. Recently we beheld Krazy smoking an "eligint Hawanna cigar" and sighing for Ignatz; the smoke screen he produced hid him from view when Igntaz passed, and before the Mice could turn back, Krazy had handed over the cigar to Offisa Pupp and departed, saying "Looking at 'Offisa Pupp' smoke himself like a chimly is werra werra intrisking, but it is more wital that I find 'Ignatiz' "—wherefore Ignatz, thinking the smoke screen a ruse, hurls his brick, blacks the officer's eye, and is promptly chased by the limb of the law. Up to this point you have the usual techniques of the comic strip, as old as Shakespeare. But note the final picture of Krazy beholding the pursuit, himself disconsolate, unbricked, alone, muttering. "Ah, there him is—playing tag with 'Offisa Pupp'— just like the boom compenions wot they is." It is this touch of irony and pity which transforms all of Herriman's work, which relates it, for all that the material is pre-posterous, to something profoundly true and moving. It isn't possible to retell these pictures; but that is the only way, until they are collected and published, that I can give the impression of Herriman's gentle irony, of his understanding of tragedy, of the *sancta simplicitas*, the innocent loveliness in the heart of a creature more like Pan than any other creation of our time.

Given the general theme, the variations are innumerable, the ingenuity never flags. I use haphazard examples from 1918 to 1923, for though the Kat has changed somewhat since the days when he was even occasionally feline, the essence is the same. Like Charlot, he was always living in a world of his own, and subjecting the commonplaces of actual life to the test of his higher logic. Does Igrnatz say that "the bird is on the wing," Krazy suspects an error and after a careful scrutiny of bird life says that "from rissint obserwation I should say that the wing is on the bird." Or Ignatz observes that Don Kiyoti is still running. Wrong, says the magnificent Kat: "he is either still or either running, but not both still and both running." Ignatz passes with a bag containing, he says, bird-seed. "Not that I doubt your word, Ignatz," says Krazy, "but could I give a look?" And he is astonished to find that it is bird-seed, after all, for he had all the time been thinking that birds grew from eggs. It is Ignatz who is impressed by a falling star; for Krazy "them that don't fall" are the miracle. I recommend Krazy to Mr. Chesterton, who, in his best moments, will understand. His mind is occupied with eternal oddities, with simple things to which his nature leaves unreconciled. See him entering a bank and loftily writing a check for thirty million dollars. "You haven't that much money in the bank," says the cashier. "I know it," replies Krazy; "have you?" There is a drastic simplicity about Krazy's movements; he is childlike, regarding with grave eyes the efforts older people to be solemn, to pretend that things are what they seem; and like children he frightens us because none of our pretensions escapes him. A king to him is a "royal cootie." "Golla," says he, "I always had a ida they was grend, and megnifishint, and wondafil, and majestic . . . but my goodniss! It ain't so!" He should he given to the *enfant terrible* of Hans Andersen who knew the truth about kings.

He is, of course, blinded by love. Wandering alone in springtime, he suffers the sight of all things pairing off; the solitude a lonesome pine worries him and when he finds a second lonesome pine he comes in the dead of night and transplants one to the side of the other, "so that in due course, Nature has her way." But there are moments when the fierce pang of an unrequited passion dies down. "In these blissful hours my soul will know no strife," he confides to Mr. Bum Bill Bee, who while the conversation goes on, catches sight Ignatz with a brick, flies off, stings Ignatz from the field, and returns to hear: "In my Kosmis there will be no feeva . . . all my immotions will function in hominy and kind feelings." Or we see him at peace with Ignatz himself. He has bought a pair of spectacles, and seeing that

Ignatz has none, cuts them in two, so that each may have a monocle. He is gentle, and gentlemanly, and dear; and these divagations of his are among his loveliest moments; for when irony plays about him he is as helpless—as we are.

To put such a character into music was a fine thought, but Mr. Carpenter must have known that he was foredoomed to failure. It was a notable effort, for no other of our composers had seen the possibilities; most, I fear, did not care to "lower themselves" by the association. Mr. Carpenter caught much of the fantasy; it was exactly right for him to make the opening a parody—The Afternoon Nap of a Faun. The "Class A Fit," the Katnip Blues were also good. (There exists a Sunday Krazy of this very scene—it is 1919, I think, and shows hundreds of Krazy Kats in a wild abandoned revel in the Katnip field—a rout, a bacchanale, a satyr-dance, an erotic festival, with our own Krazy playing the viola in the corner, and Ignatz, who ha been drinking, going to sign the pledge). Mr. Carpenter almost missed one essential thing: the ecstasy of Krazy when the brick arrives at the end; certainly, as Mr. Bolm danced it one felt only the triumph of Ignatz, one did not feel the grand leaping of Krazy's heart, the fulfillment of desire, as the brick fell upon him. The irony was missing. And it was a mistake for Bolm to try it, since it isn't Russian ballet Krazy requires; it is American dance. One man, one man only can do it right, and I publicly appeal to him to absent him from felicity awhile, and though he do it but once, though but a small number of people may see it, to pay tribute to his one compeer in America, to the one creation equaling his own—I mean, of course, Charlie Chaplin. He has been urged to do many things hostile to his nature; here is one thing he is destined to do. Until then the ballet ought to have Johnny and Ray Dooley for its creators. And I hope that Mr. Carpenter hasn't driven other composers off the subject. There is enough there for Irving Berlin and Deems Taylor to take up. Why don't they? The music it requires is a jazzed tenderness—as Mr. Carpenter knew. In their various ways Berlin and Taylor could accomplish it.

They may not be able to write profoundly in the private idiom of Krazy. I have preserved his spelling and the quotations have given some sense of his style. The accent is partly Dickens and partly Yiddish—and the rest is not to be identified, for it is Krazy. It was odd that in Vanity Fair's notorious "rankings," Krazy tied with Doctor Johnson, to whom he owes much of his vocabulary. There is a real sense of the color of words and a high imagination in such passages as "the echoing cliffs of Kaibito" and "on the north side of 'wild-cat peak' the 'snow squaw' shake their winter blankets and bring forth a chill which rides the wind with goad and spur, hurling with an icy hand rime, and frost upon a dreamy land musing in the lap of

Spring"; and there is the rhythm of wonder and excitement in "Ooy, 'Ignatz' it's awfil; he's got his legs cut off above his elbows, and he's wearing shoes, and he's standing on top of the water."

Nor, even with Mr. Herriman's help, will a ballet get quite the sense of his shifting backgrounds. He is alone in his freedom of movement; in his large pictures and small, the scene changes at will—it is actually our one work in the expressionistic mode. While Krazy and Ignatz talk they move from mountain to sea; or a tree, stunted and flattened with odd ornaments of spots or design, grows suddenly long and thin; or a house changes into a church. The trees in this enchanted mesa are almost always set in flower pots with Coptic and Egyptian designs in the foliage as often as on the pot. There are adobe walls, fantastic cactus plants, strange fungus and growths. And they *compose designs*. For whether he be a primitive or an expressionist, Herriman is an artist; his works are built up; there is a definite relation between his theme and his structure, and between his lines, masses, and his page. His masterpieces in color show a new delight, for he is as naive and as assured with color as with line or black and white. The little figure of Krazy built around the navel, is amazingly adaptable, and Herriman economically makes him express all the emotions with a turn of the hand, a bending of that extraordinary starched bow he wears around the neck, or with a twist of his tail.

And he has had much to express, for he has suffered much. I return to the vast enterprises of the Sunday pictures. There is one constructed entirely on the bias. Ignatz orders Krazy to push a huge rock off its base, then to follow it downhill. Down they go, crashing through houses, uprooting trees, tearing tunnels through mountains, the boulder first, Krazy so intently after that he nearly crashes into it when it stops. He tolls painfully back uphill. "Did it gather any moss?" asks Ignatz. "No." "That's what I thought." "L'il fillossiffa" comments Krazy, "always he seeks the truth, and always he finds it." There is the great day in which Krazy hears a lecture on the ectoplasm, how "it soars out into the limitless ether, to roam willy-nilly, unleashed, unfettered, and unbound" which becomes for him: "Just imegine having your 'ectospasm' running around, William and Nilliam, among the unlimitliss etha—golla, it imbillivibil—" until a toy balloon, which looks like Ignatz precipitates a heroic gesture and a tragedy. And there is the greatest of all, the epic, the Odyssean wanderings of the door:

Krazy beholds a dormouse, a little mouse with a huge door. It impresses him as being terrible that "a mice so small, so dellikit" should carry around a door so heavy with weight. (At this point their Odyssey begins; they use the door to cross a chasm.) "A door is so useless without a house is hitched to it." (It changes into a raft and they go down stream.) "It has no ikkinomikil value." (They dine off the door.) "It lecks the werra werra essentials of helpfilniss." (It shelters them from a hailstorm.) "Historically it is all wrong and misleading." (It fends the lightning.) "As a thing of beauty it fails in every rispeck." (It shelters them from the sun and while Krazy goes on to deliver a lecture: "You never see Mr. Steve Door, or Mr. Torra Door, or Mr. Kuspa Door doing it, do you?" and "Can you imagine my li'l friends Ignatz Mice boddering himself with a door?") His li'l friend Ignatz has appeared with the brick; unseen by Krazy he hurls it; it is intercepted by the door, rebounds, and strikes Ignatz down. Krazy continues his adwice until the dormouse sheers off, and then Krazy sits down to "concentrate his mind on Ignatz and wonda where he is at."

Such is our Krazy. Such is the work which America can pride itself on having produced, and can hastily set about to appreciate. It is rich with something we have too little of—fantasy. It is wise with pitying irony; it has delicacy, sensitiveness, and an unearthly beauty. The strange, unnerving, distorted trees, the language inhuman, un-animal, the events so logical, so wild, are all magic carpets and faery foam—all charged with unreality. Through them wanders Krazy, the most foolish of creatures, a gentle monster of our new mythology.

E. E. Cummings

"A Foreword to Krazy"

Originally published in *The Sewanee Review*, Spring 1946 and in George Herriman's *Krazy Kat* (New York: Henry Holt, 1946. Copyright © 1946, 1974 by the Trustees for the E. E. Cummings Trust, from *A Miscellany Revised* by E. E. Cummings, edited by George J. Firmage. Used by permission of Liveright Publishing Corporation.

Twenty years ago, a celebration happened—the celebration of Krazy Kat by Gilbert Seldes. It happened in a book called *The Seven Lively Arts*; and it happened so wisely, so lovingly, so joyously, that recelebrating Krazy would be like teaching penguins to fly. Penguins (as a lot of people don't realize) do fly not through the sea of the sky but through the sky of the sea—and my present ambition is merely, with our celebrated friend's assistance, to show how their flying affects every non-penguin.

What concerns me fundamentally is a meteoric burlesk melodrama, born of the immemorial adage *love will find a way*. This frank frenzy (encouraged by a strictly irrational landscape in perpetual metamorphosis) generates three protagonists and a plot. Two of the protagonists are easily recognized as a cynical brick-throwing mouse and a sentimental policeman-dog. The third protagonist—whose ambiguous gender doesn't disguise the good news that here comes our heroine—may be described as a humbly poetic, gently clownlike, supremely innocent, and illimitably affectionate creature (slightly resembling a child's drawing of a cat, but gifted with the secret grace and obvious clumsiness of a penguin on terra firma) who is never so happy as when egoist mouse, thwarting altruist-dog, hits her in the head with a brick. Dog hates mouse and worships "cat," mouse despises "cat" and hates dog, "cat" hates no one and loves mouse.

Ignatz Mouse and Offissa Pupp are opposite sides of the same coin. Is Offissa Pupp kind? Only in so far as Ignatz Mouse is cruel. If you're a twofisted, spineless progressive (a mighty fashionable stance nowadays) Offissa Pupp, who forcefully asserts the will of socalled society, becomes a cosmic angel; while Ignatz Mouse, who forcefully defies society's socalled will by asserting his authentic own, becomes a demon of anarchy and a fiend of chaos. But if—whisper it—you're a 100% hidebound reactionary, the foot's in the other shoe. Ignatz Mouse then stands forth as a hero, pluckily struggling to keep the flag of free-will flying; while Offissa Pupp assumes the monstrous mien of a Goliath, satanically bullying a tiny but indomitable David. Well, let's flip the coin—so: and lo! Offissa Pupp comes up. That makes Ignatz Mouse "tails." Now we have a hero whose heart has gone to his head and a villain whose head has gone to his heart.

This hero and this villain no more understand Krazy Kat than the mythical denizens of a twodimensional realm understand some threedimensional intruder. The world of Offissa Pupp and Ignatz Mouse is a knowledgeable power-world, in terms of which our unknowledgeable heroine is powerlessness personified. The sensical law of this world is *might makes right*; the nonsensical law of our heroine is *love conquers all*. To put the oak in the acorn: Ignatz Mouse and Offissa Pupp (each completely convinced that his own particular brand of might makes right) are simple-minded—Krazy isn't—therefore, to Offisa Pupp and Ignatz Mouse, Krazy is. But if both our hero and our villain don't and can't understand our heroine, each of them can and each of them does misunderstand her differently. To our softheaded altruist, she is the adorably helpless incarnation of saintliness. To our hardhearted egoist, she is the puzzlingly indestructible embodiment of idiocy. The benevolent overdog sees her as an inspired weakling. The malevolent undermouse views her as a born target. Meanwhile Krazy Kat, through this double misunderstanding, fulfills her joyous destiny.

Let's make no mistake about Krazy. A lot of people "love" because, and a lot of people "love" although, and a few individuals love. Love is something illimitable; and a lot of people spend their limited lives trying to prevent anything illimitable from happening to them. Krazy, however, is not a lot of people. Krazy is herself. Krazy is illimitable—she loves. She loves in the only way anyone can love: illimitably. She isn't morbid and she isn't longsuffering; she doesn't "love" someone because he hurts her and she doesn't "love" someone although he hurts her. She doesn't, moreover, "love" someone who hurts her. Quite the contrary: she loves someone who gives her unmitigated joy. How? By always trying his limited worst to make her unlove him, and always failing—not that our heroine is insensitive (for a more sensitive heroine never existed) but that our villain's every effort to limit her love with his unlove ends by a transforming of his limitation into her illimitability. If you're going to pity anyone, the last anyone to pity is our loving heroine, Krazy Kat. You might better pity that doggedly idolatrous imbecile, our hero; who policemanfully strives to protect his idol from catastrophic desecration at the paws of our iconoclastic villain—never suspecting that this very desecration becomes, through our transcending heroine, a consecration; and that this consecration reveals the ultimate meaning of existence. But the person to really pity (if really pity you must) is Ignatz. Poor villain! All his malevolence turns to beneficence at contact with Krazy's head. By profaning the temple of altruism, alias law and order, he worships (entirely against his will) at the shrine of love.

I repeat: let's make no mistake about Krazy. Her helplessness, as we have just seen, is merely sensical—nonsensically she's a triumphant, not to say invincible, phenomenon. As for this invincible phenomenon's supposed idiocy, it doesn't even begin to fool nonsensical you and me. Life, to a lot of people, means either the triumph of mind over matter or the triumph of matter over mind; but you and I aren't a lot of people. We understand that just as there is something—love—infinitely more significant than brute force, there is something—wisdom—infinitely more significant than mental prowess. A remarkably developed intelligence impresses us about as much as a sixteen inch bicep. If we know anything, we know that a lot of people can learn knowledge (which is the same thing as unlearning ignorance) but that none can learn wisdom. Wisdom, like love, is a spiritual gift. And Krazy happens to be extraordinarily gifted. She has not only the gift of love, but the gift of wisdom as well. Her unknowledgeable wisdom blossoms in almost every episode of our meteoric burlesk melodrama; the supreme blossom, perhaps, being a tribute to Offissa Pupp and Ignatz Mouse—who (as she observes) are playing a little game together. Right! The game they're playing, willy nilly, is the exciting democratic game of *cat loves mouse*; the game which a lot of highly moral people all over the socalled world consider uncivilized. I refer (of course) to those red-brown-and-blackshirted Puritans who want us all to scrap democracy and adopt their modernized version of *follow the leader*—a strictly ultraprogressive and super-benevolent affair which begins with the liquidation of Ignatz Mouse by Offissa Pupp. But (objects Krazy, in her innocent democratic way) Ignatz Mouse and Offissa Pupp are having fun. Right again! And—from the Puritan point of view—nothing could be worse. Fun, to Puritans, is something wicked: an invention of The Devil Himself. That's why all these superbenevolent collectivists are so hyperspinelessly keen on having us play their ultraprogressive game. The first superbenevolent rule of their ultaprogressive game is *thou shalt not play*.

If only the devilish game of democracy were exclusively concerned with such mindful matters as ignorance and knowledge, crime and punishment, cruelty and kindness, collectivists would really have something on the ball. But it so happens that democracy involves the spiritual values of wisdom, love, and joy. Democracy isn't democracy because or although Ignatz Mouse and Offissa Pupp are fighting a peaceful war. Democracy is democracy in so far as our villain and our hero—by having their fun, by playing their brutal little game—happen (despite their worst and best efforts) to be fulfilling our heroine's immeasurable destiny. Joy is her destiny: and joy comes through Ignatz—via Offissa Pupp; since it's our villain's loathing for law which gives him the strength of ten when he hurls his blissyielding brick. Let's not forget that. And let's be perfectly sure about something else. Even if Offissa Pupp should go crazy and start chasing Krazy, and even if Krazy should go crazy and start chasing Ignatz, and even if crazy Krazy should swallow crazy Ignatz and crazy Offissa Pupp should swallow crazy Krazy and it was the millennium—there'd still be the brick. And (having nothing else to swallow) Offissa Pupp would then swallow the brick. Whereupon, as the brick hit Krazy, Krazy would be happy.

Alas for sensical reformers! Never can they realize that penguins do fly; that Krazy's idiocy and helplessness in terms of a world—any world—are as nothing to the Nth power, by comparison with a world's—any world's—helplessness and idiocy in terms of Krazy. Yet the truth of truths lies here and nowhere else. Always (no matter what's real) Krazy is no mere reality. She is a living ideal. She is a spiritual force, inhabiting a merely real world—and the realer a merely real world happens to be, the more this living ideal becomes herself. Hence—needless to add—the brick. Only if, and whenever, that kind reality (cruelly wielded by our heroic villain, Ignatz Mouse, in despite of our villainous hero, Offissa Pupp) smites Krazy—fairly and squarely—does the joyous symbol of Love Fulfilled appear above our triumphantly unknowledgeable heroine. And now do we understand the meaning of democracy? If we don't, a poet-painter called George Herriman most certainly cannot be blamed. Democracy, he tells us again and again and again, isn't some ultraprogressive myth of a superbenevolent World As Should Be. The meteoric burlesk melodrama of democracy is a struggle between society (Offissa Pupp) and the individual (Ignatz Mouse) over an ideal (our heroine)—a struggle from which, again and again and again, emerges one stupendous fact; namely, that the ideal of democracy fulfills herself only if, and whenever, society fails to suppress the individual.

Could anything possibly be clearer?

Nothing—unless it's the kindred fact that our illimitably affectionate Krazy has no connection with the oldfashioned heroine of common or garden melodrama. That prosaically "virtuous" puppet couldn't bat a decorously "innocent" eyelash without immediately provoking some utterly estimable Mr. Righto to liquidate some perfectly wicked Mr. Wrongo. In her hyperspineless puritanical simplicity, she desired nothing quite so much as an ultraprogressive and superbenevolent substitute for human nature. Democracy's merciful leading lady, on the other hand, is a fundamentally complex being who demands the whole mystery of life. Krazy Kat—who, with every mangled word and murdered gesture, translates a mangling and murdering world into Peace And Good Will—is the only original and authentic revolutionary protagonist. All blood-and-thunder Worlds As Should Be cannot comprise this immeasurably generous heroine of the strictly unmitigated future.

She has no fear—even of a mouse.

Dorothy Parker

"A Mash Note to Crockett Johnson"

PM, October 3, 1943. The publisher wishes to thank the National Association for the Advancement of Colored People for authorizing the use of Dorothy Parker's work.

I cannot write a review of Crockett Johnson's book of *Barnaby*. I have tried and tried, but it never comes out a book review. It is always a valentine for Mr. Johnson.

For a bulky segment of a century, I have been an avid follower of comic strips—all comic strips; this is a statement made with approximately the same amount of pride with which one would say, "I've been shooting cocaine into my arm for the past twenty-five years." I cannot remember how the habit started, and I am presently unable to explain why it persists. I know only that I'm hooked, by now, that's all. I can't stop. I even take a certain unspeakable tabloid for its strips, though, when I am caught with it on my doorstep, I still have shame enough left to try to laugh matters off by explaining that you really ought to know what your enemies are up to. When I tell you that I am in daily touch with the horrible, sightless, Orphan Annie—who, I am convinced, is Westbrook Pegler's adopted child—that I keep up with the particular nasty experiences of Dick Tracy, that even, for heaven's sake, I was the one who strung along with Deathless Deer until her mercy killing, you will know that Mother is a gone pigeon. When cornered, I try to make rather doggy excuses. I say that comic strips are important pieces of Americana. But it doesn't hold, you know. You cannot class the relationship between Flash Gordon and Dale as something peculiarly American. I flatly do not know why I do as I do. For I do not enjoy the strips. I read them solemnly and sourly, and there is no delight in me because of them.

That is, I had no delight and no enjoyment and no love until *Barnaby* came. I suppose you must do it this way; I suppose you must file *Barnaby* under comic strips, because his biography runs along in strip form in a newspaper. I bow to convention in the matter. But, privately, if the adventures of *Barnaby* constitute a comic strip, then so do those of *Huckleberry Finn*.

I think, and I am trying to talk calmly, that Barnaby and his friends and oppressors are the most important additions to American arts and letters in Lord knows how many years. I know that they are the most important additions to my heart.

I love Barnaby, I love little Jane, I love Gus, the Ghost, I hate and admire and envy Mr. O'Malley, above all I love Gorgon, the dog.

I think the conception of a dog who talks—"Didn't know I could do it; never tried it before, I guess"—and then turns out to be such a crashing bore that they have to lock him away so they won't be obliged to listen to him, is—well, it's only glorious, that's all. You have to love dogs before you can go on to the step of taking them down, understandingly. I think Mr. Johnson must love dogs. I think Mr. Johnson must love people. I know darned well I must love Mr. Johnson.

Barnaby is fine to have in book form—you can't go on, you know, cutting strips out of *PM* and meaning to paste them in an album the next rainy day. The book will be invaluable to those who must read aloud a while every evening. I am told, by those fortunates who own them, that children love *Barnaby*; which information has appreciably raised my estimation of children. While for adults—I can only say *Barnaby*, the book, costs $2. If you have $5, save out three for the landlord and spend the remainder to feed your soul.

Well. I told you I couldn't write anything but a valentine, didn't I?

PART TWO

The New York Intellectuals

The New York Intellectuals were an amorphous and contentious group of mid-century cultural critics and thinkers associated with *Partisan Review* magazine, City College and Columbia University. Emerging as a coherent group in the late 1930s, the New York intellectuals inherited a dual tradition. The centrality of modernism had been established by Jazz Age writers and the importance of political engagement by the radicalized generation of the early 1930s. Uniquely, the writers gathered around *Partisan Review* and a few allied magazines would try to link this double tradition of cultural and political radicalism.

In attempting to create a fusion between modernism and Marxism, the *Partisan Review* group set itself against the dominant cultural tendencies of the American left in the 1930s and 40s which involved a romantic celebration of populist political art and folk art (for example, John Steinbeck's *The Grapes of Wrath* and the songs of Woody Guthrie). Indeed, one of the main reasons *Partisan Review* was created in 1937 was to challenge the "proletarian realism" aesthetic promulgated by the American Communist Party.

Yet in rejecting the didactic and simple minded art of the popular front, the New York intellectuals still distinguished themselves from the opposite tendency of liberals and conservatives to disengage art from its social and political context. Thus, the New York writers tended to dismiss the New Criticism, a formalist tendency in literary criticism that was gaining increasing academic respectability in the 1940s, as aridly ahistorical. Giving the darkening political climate of the Great Depression and the Second World War, the New York writers also inclined to give short shrift to the optimism of Jazz Age writers like Gilbert Seldes, Although admired as a pioneer, Seldes was also condescendingly regarded as a naïve liberal too confident about the possibility of finding a common ground between astringent modernism and mass-produced popular culture.

In writing about comics and other popular art forms, the New York writers tended to strike a pessimistic note, especially during the Second World War and early years of the Cold War. Instead of the "lively arts" or "popular culture" they wrote about "mass culture," usually defined as an impediment to the development of a genuinely autonomous and democratic culture. This bleak vision was, of course, widely shared. Especially after witnessing the success of Joseph Goebbels as propaganda minister for the Nazi regime, many intellectuals came to see the general population as being easily manipulated by those who controlled the mass media. Two famous dystopian novels of the era, Brave New World (1932) and 1984 (1948), both give vivid expression to this fear. Also contributing to this dark view of contemporary life was the formidable critique of the cultural industries developed by Frankfurt School writers such as T. W. Adorno and Max Horkheimer, then in exile from the Nazi regime.

Irving Howe's "Notes on Mass culture" registers the postwar mood. In his thoughtful (if overly defensive) retrospective essay "The New York Intellectuals" (1968), Howe would later note that the writers of this group started using cultural criticism as a substitute for politics during the Cold War. Seen in this light, cultural criticism served as a refuge during a politically barren era. While there is a grain of truth to this theory, especially in describing the career of a writer such as Dwight Macdonald, it would be more accurate to say that for the New York intellectuals politics was always intermixed with culture, including popular culture.

Even a writer like Clement Greenberg, who is often facilely described as a purely formalist critic, was always careful to situate a work of art within a social context. In his brief and pointed articles on William Steig and David Low, Greenberg examines how these successful artists relied on the expectations and assumptions of their audiences. In a parallel move, Harold Rosenberg, Greenberg's great rival as an analyst of modern art, writes about Saul Steinberg by describing the cartoonist as an artist alert to ideas about representation. What interests Rosenberg is the way Steinberg plays with the mind of his reader/viewer.

A serious effort to grapple with the audience response to mass culture can also be seen in the essays of Delmore Schwartz and Robert Warshow, although these writers are noticeably out of sympathy with both comics and their readers. "A man watches a movie, and the critic must acknowledge that he is that man," was

Warshow's credo as a film critic. In a handful of classic essays he wrote during his brief life, Warshow demonstrated that he was unusually gifted in registering the emotional impact of such genres as the western and the gangster film. Yet this emotional empathy for the film-going experience doesn't extend to comics-reading. Although he has a few sharp sentences on daily habits of comic strip readers and the brand-loyalty of comic book fans (thereby documenting the birth of organized fan culture), Warshow's essays are marked by a chilly distance from their subjects, including even Herriman's beloved *Krazy Kat* strips.

Whether they were sympathetic to comics or not, the lasting legacy of the New York intellectuals is their attempt to link aesthetic experience with social context. Even as they contested the ideas of their Jazz age predecessors, the New York writers furthered the project of examining mass culture as a product of contemporary realities.

Clement Greenberg

"Steig's Cartoons: Review of *All Embarrassed* by William Steig"

The Nation, 3 March 1945. Reprinted in Clement Greenberg, *The Collected Essays and Criticism: Vol. 2, Arrogant Purpose, 1945–1949*, pp. 10–11. Ed. John O'Brian. Chicago: University of Chicago Press, 1986. © 1986 by Clement Greenberg and John O'Brian.

The mating of drawing with caption has produced a new but very dependent and transitory pictorial genre. The future will be more informed than delighted by it. We can still relish the brush-drawing on a Greek vase for its own sake as a drawing—whether fitted happily or unhappily to the shape of the vessel. But to appreciate William Steig's cartoons you have to get their point, and to get their point you have to be intimately acquainted with the contemporary American literate middle classes. And yet in spite of all this, Steig's cartoons push and strain against the social and psychological limitations of the cartoon form and strive to become self-sufficient, time-transcending art. The quasi-abstract drawings in *All Embarrassed* are, though not necessarily the best, those which most visibly embody Steig's aesthetic yearning. A good deal of automatism has gone into them as well as a full acquaintance with Klee, Picasso, and particularly Miró, yet they do not manage to escape the neatness and the formularization of the cartoon—nor will they until Steig forces himself to leave his forms more open and to take into greater account the shape of the page. It is no accident that the cartoon called *Organism and Environment* is the best in the book as a matter of drawing and picture composition.

Once in a while Steig's wit makes all the above irrelevant. I submit the cartoons called *The Conversation Lags I*, *Misunderstanding*, and *Intrusion*. If, however, Steig were somewhat more susceptible himself to those dangers of middle-class existence he too triumphantly points out, he would score much more frequently.

Clement Greenberg

"Limits of Common Sense: Review of *Years of Wrath: A Cartoon History, 1931–1945* by David Low"

Commentary, December 1946. Reprinted in Clement Greenberg, *The Collected Essays and Criticism: Vol. 2, Arrogant Purpose, 1945–1949*, pp. 115–16. Ed. John O'Brian. Chicago: University of Chicago Press, 1986. © 1986 by Clement Greenberg and John O'Brian.

The success of Low's cartoons with the newspaper public would suggest that the public is more sensitive to art for its own sake than its members themselves realize.

Despite the claims made on the jacket of this latest collection of his cartoons to the effect that Low "combines technical mastery of his medium with a political intelligence that puts many of our contemporary statesmen to shame"—his insight into world affairs turns out to be only what might have been expected from any liberal with decent instincts and a large endowment of common-sense humor. Low has never, in reality, seen beyond the headlines, and his penetration of events is rarely superior to that of his readers. Altogether without any positive political ideas, and equally devoid of political imagination, he has manifested political intelligence only by being more afraid of fascism than Stanley Baldwin and Chamberlain were.

In my opinion the attraction of Low's cartoons consists in some part in the vividness with which they mirror, to the mind raised on Anglo-Saxon common-sense liberalism, the exact quality of its own attempts to make sense out of contemporary history. But I doubt whether this reflection of futility would have gone down so smoothly with newspaper readers had it not been embodied in, and thus transcended by, art. For Low is at least a remarkable draftsman, a worthy continuator of the great but still largely unrecognized nineteenth-century English tradition of popular graphic art.

Examine almost any one of his cartoons and you will see how little its effect depends on its "idea" and how much on the drawing and design. Franco, at the end of the war, trying to buy a ticket for the "Victory Bus" from a ticket-seller who happens to be Stalin; Franco carrying a stick of confetti labeled "War on Japan" (perhaps) and a tag on his ship saying "Hooray for Liberty"—anybody could have thought of that. What is funny and even illuminating in an inexplicable way is the frowzy, wistful, pint-sized figure of Franco (in 1937 Low drew him much larger) standing in his silly uniform in the gray penumbra of the left foreground, while in the blank white background anonymous civilians crowd aboard a bus. Linear definition, composition, and the distribution of darks and lights drive home something that is more satisfying to the emotional requirements of the occasion than any possible real insight could be. Like every first-rate journalist, Low provides us with a proper state of mind, not with truth or information; and in the day-to-day struggle, the right emotion is a more urgent necessity to the newspaper reader than right understanding.

Since the beginning, Low's art has developed steadily toward greater crispness, economy, and broad, dramatic effect. In the early '30s there was still something about it of the jiggly-jerkiness of British bourgeois cartooning in its post-Edwardian decline. That style had a tendency to bog down in the narrative detail and in human-all-too-human sentiment. Low escaped from it quickly, but retained its concern for the likeness, and for that which is instantaneously, incandescently characteristic. By 1931 his squat little Japanese soldiers are depicted with such an infallible eye for the right detail, whether of anatomy or uniform, that they become more Japanese and more soldier than the reality itself.

In dealing with public personalities, Low is usually most telling when they happen to be British—naturally he understands his own kind best. Now and then, however, he manages to nail Roosevelt, Goebbels, Mussolini. And he always gets those he can see around and behind—Franco, for instance, or any other small, shabby potentate. But he is completely taken in by the fellow travelers' version of Stalin as a benign tomcat; and while he can get the Germans and the German situation, he is incapable of seeing Hitler as anything more than a popinjay, a mincing hotel clerk. Perhaps it is too much to ask of common sense that it comprehend the lumpy, fermented, "soulful" vulgarity which seems to have been the Fuehrer's most personal and most German quality. And perhaps the failure to get Hitler marks the limit of Low's talent. After all, he is no Daumier.

Irving Howe

"Notes on Mass Culture"

Politics, vol. 5, Spring 1948, pp. 120–23. Reprinted by permission.

When we glance at the pseudo-cultural amusements that occupy the American people's leisure time, we soon wonder: what happens to the anonymous audience while
it consumes the products of mass culture?[1] It is a question that can hardly be
answered systematically or definitively, for there is no way of knowing precisely what
the subterranean reactions of an audience are—and it will certainly not do merely to
ask it. We can only speculate, and the answer to our question, if one is to be had at all,
can be found only within ourselves.

Here we meet our first difficulty: the only people who can analyze the effects of
mass culture on an audience are those who reject its uncritical acceptance of mass
culture. "Contaminated" by art standards, the intellectual must necessarily hesitate
when he tries to decide which of his reactions to mass culture are similar to those
of the audience and which are the product of his private cultivation. He may overcome this difficulty by frankly admitting to himself that, like it or not, he is part of
the mass audience and is influenced by mass culture. If he is to speculate fruitfully,
he must reach that precarious condition where he can identify himself with the
audience's reactions while yet retaining his critical distance.

To some extent the intellectual can dispense with mass culture, though far less
than he knows or is willing to admit. So long as we live in a class society, mass culture will remain indispensable even to those who have learned to scorn it; we cannot
escape what is so much a part of the atmosphere in which we live. Nor would such
an attempted escape be particularly desirable: the price of public experience may he
a kind of contamination, but in view of the alternative it is not too high a price to pay.

---

1. As used in recent discussions, "mass culture" refers to the production of synthetic, easily accessible amusements
for mass audiences, as well as to the products themselves. In mass culture the materials of art are exploited,
although art works, except very rarely and that by accident, are not created. Mass culture allows art neither to thrive
nor to perish, since art is at once its most dangerous competitor and its one indispensable source of "ideas."

I: The Unconscious Urge to Self-Obliteraton

Mass culture is an urban product. Confined to the close spaces of a city, members of an industrial society must always face the disturbing problem of what to do with their leisure time, how to organize it in relation to their work day.

One thing seems certain: except during brief revolutionary intervals, the quality of leisure time activity cannot vary too sharply from that of the work day. If it did, the office or factory worker would be exposed to those terrible dualities of feeling that make it so difficult for the intellectual to adjust his job to himself. But the worker wants no part of such difficulties, he has enough already. Following the dictum of industrial society that anonymity is a key to safety, he seeks the least troublesome solution: mass culture.

Whatever its manifest content, mass culture must therefore not subvert the basic patterns of industrial life. Leisure time must be so organized as to bear a factitious relationship to working time: apparently different, actually the same. It must provide relief from work monotony without making the return to work too unbearable; it must provide amusement without insight and pleasure without disturbance—distinct from art which gives pleasure through disturbance.

Mass culture is thus oriented towards a central aspect of industrial society: the depersonalization of the individual. On the one hand, it diverts the worker from his disturbing reduction to semi-robot status by arranging "relaxing" amusements for him. The need for such amusements explains the ceaseless and hectic quest for novelty in the mass culture industries (e.g., the "twist" in popular songs, the melodic phrase the audience remembers.) On the other hand, mass culture reinforces those emotional attitudes that seem inseparable from existence in modern society—passivity and boredom. Precisely the frenetic chase after novelty, after something new that might rise above routine experience becomes the means of molding leisure time activity according to work time patterns. What is supposed to deflect us from the reduction of our personalities actually reinforces it.

In a fascinating study, "On Popular Music,"[2] T. Adorno makes some remarks on the standardization of popular music that seem a specific working-out of the views expressed here:

"... the heroic cornerstone of each hit—the beginning and the end of each part—must beat out the standard scheme. Complications have no consequences ... regardless of what

---

2. Studies in Philosophy and Social Science, vol. IX, 1941

aberrations occur, the hit will lead back to the familiar experience, and nothing funda-
mentally novel will be introduced. . . . The composition hears for the listener. This is how
popular music divests the listener of his spontaneity.

"Boredom has become so great that only the brightest colors have any chance of
being lifted out of the general drabness. Yet it is just those violent colors which bear witness
to the omnipotence of mechanical, industrial production . . . the means used to overcome
reality are more humdrum than reality itself.

"To escape boredom and avoid effort is incompatible. . . . They seek novelty but the
strain and boredom associated with actual work lead to avoidance of effort in leisure
time. . . . That means boredom again. . . ."

What is true for popular music is also true for the movies. The movie theatre is like a dark cavern, a neutral womb, into whose soothing and dissolving blackness we can escape from our frayed selves. In a nonreligious age, the movie is one of the few places that provides a poor man with a kind of retreat, a place where he can throw off the shackles of his social responsibility, relationships and personality. Here, at least, he does not have to acknowledge his irritating self.

It is interesting to compare the movie theatre with the baseball park. In the theatre one ceases, in a sense, to exist. One seldom talks, one is seldom brought to those heights of consciousness that a genuine work of dramatic art can arouse. (Even the adolescents necking in the back rows do so with a kind of grim anonymity.) The movie house is a psychological cloakroom where one checks one's personality. But baseball, one of the few mass urban activities that seems to retain some folk spontaneity, is different. The game is so paced that one usually has enough time to return to oneself, and the entire atmosphere of the ball park allows for some spontaneity: the audience argues, eats, shouts, participates as an *independent* group that is reacting to the events on the field. As a result, one encounters a kind of rough and pleasing wit in the ball park, as well as an easy-going camaraderie. The ball park, I find, is one of the few public places where one can converse uninhibitedly with total strangers.

If only because it must conform to the psychological patterns of industrial society, mass culture is inseparably related to common experience. The notion that it concocts a never-never world of irrelevant fantasy is nonsense spread by the kind of people whose only complaint about Hollywood is that it isn't "realistic" enough. In actuality, the audience accepts both mass culture and daily experience precisely to the degree that the two blend. By now neither can be maintained without the other, which is one reason why there prevails in this country such a blurred notion of what human experience is and such an inadequate notion of what it should be.

But, it may be objected, don't the movies create atmospheres and situations totally removed from the experience the audience? How many people are in a position to lead the kind of lives Van Johnson and Bette Davis, Ronald Colman and Ingrid Bergman portray on the screen? Precious few, of course; and if the comparison the life of an audience and that portrayed on the screen is made simply in such formal terms, it will yield us nothing. Furthermore, there are obviously many films whose major purpose is to construct an atmosphere or environment characterized precisely by its complete irrelevance to the audience's life. But I think that the majority of films do have strong psychological contact with our lives. From the tough guy films we find so exciting because they rouse our unexpended sadism to the sophisticated comedies that play on our yearning for charm and grace, from the musical comedies that make taffy of our tensions to the socially conscious films that seek to exorcise our guilts—more movies than we know are comments on our experience and help us to "adjust" to it, that is to acquiesce in it. They may not be truthful or authentic or profound comments, but they do touch on essential aspects of our relationship both to society and ourselves. The movies help us remain at peace with ourselves by helping us to suppress ourselves.

By now daily experience and mass culture are so interlaced that it would be futile to seek causal relation slips between them. Does Gregory Peck model himself after the American Lover or does the American Lover model himself after Gregory Peck? It would be hard, and unnecessary, to say. All we need know is that the relationship between mass culture and daily experience is so intimate that millions of people seem hardly able or willing to distinguish between the two. They send letters of advice to comic strip and radio characters. Little Orphan Annie has for years been receiving letters from readers that tell her how to get out of her endless difficulties. (She never seems to follow the advice.) Some years ago when the creator of *Terry and the Pirates* was rash enough to kill a favorite character, the *New York Daily News* was besieged with letters of complaint. And the movie magazines establish relationships between millions of American women and idealized versions of movie stars in which it is impossible to distinguish between reality and fantasy, so closely are they interwoven.

Mass culture elicits the most conservative responses from the audience. So long as the audience feels that it must continue to live as it does; it has little desire to see its passivity and deep-seated though hardly conscious boredom upset;

it wants to be titillated and amused but not disturbed. For those molded in the image of contemporary society, art has many dangers: its effects are unpredictable and its demands tremendous. Art demands effort, a creative response from the audience. Joyce makes it hard for us, but he offers us the tempting possibility of reaching his heights of sensibility. But mass culture makes things "easy" and does not "upset" us; mass culture is safe, for its end is already present in its beginning.

A common item of experience tends to confirm these observations. When we feel vaguely upset and dissatisfied with ourselves, we "take in" a movie. If we are somewhat intellectualized, we know the movie will not provide us with the fundamental satisfactions that, say, a Dostoevsky novel might, but because of our attachment to our disturbance we are unable to summon the effort a work of art would demand. In an act of self-destructive bravado we even deliberately look for a "bad" movie; we punish ourselves for "feeling bad" by doing something that must ultimately make us feel worse. The analogy with neurosis in which the sufferer clings to the source of his disturbance, is obvious.

2: The Dissociation of Personality

Mass culture seems always to involve a pact between medium and audience to suppress the free play of the unconscious. Where art stirs a free and rich passage of materials from dream to experience and from experience to dream, mass culture tries to cage the unconscious. It cannot of course succeed; but it does often manage to dissociate conscious from unconscious life. The audience therefore responds on two unintegrated levels: surface unconsciousness ("having a good time") and suppressed unconscious (the distorted evocation of experience by popular culture themes). On the surface the Donald Duck and Mickey Mouse cartoons seem merely pleasant little fictions, but they are actually overladen with the most competitive, aggressive and sadistic themes. Often on the verge of hysteria, Donald Duck is a frustrated little monster who has something of the SS man in him and whom we, also having something of the SS man in us, naturally find quite charming. . . .

This discrepancy between conscious and unconscious reactions to mass culture seems inseparable from the audience's need for social approval. Whoever has attended a jam session or gone to the Paramount Theatre when a favorite bandleader is featured, knows how compulsive the seemingly spontaneous audience responses can be. No doubt the audience believes it is "enjoying," itself, but a central component of that enjoyment is the very powerful pressures towards social conformism. How can a bobby-soxer admit to not enjoying Vaughn Monroe?

(In fairness, it should be admitted that there is probably nothing more conformist about the mass audience's feeling that the famous bandleader or the all-star picture must be entertaining than the intellectual's analogous feeling that the great writer must be profound.)

In the comics, this dissociation of personality is taken for granted. Comic characterization consists of persistent identification of each name with an outstanding personality trait: Tillie is always the toiler, Joe Jinks always worries, Little Orphan Annie always suffers and Maggie always wants to break into society. Dissociation of personality has been institutionalized in the "balanced comic section" of the McCormick-Patterson chain:

"*The Gumps* (represent) gossip, realistic family life; *Harold Teen*, youth; *Smitty*, cute-kid stuff; *Winnie Winkle*, girls; *Moon Mullins*, burly laughter; *Orphan Annie*, sentiment. . . *Dick Tracy*, adventure and the most up-to-date sophisticated type; *Smilin' Jack*, flying and sex." (This rather naive list is taken from a naive but useful book, *The Comics* by Coulton Waugh.)

The comics further dissociate personality by erasing the distinctions between adulthood and childhood. (Popular songs revert to baby-talk to relieve adult tension.) The first comic strip in this country was *The Yellow Kid*, a creature half-man and half-child, full of premature and malicious wisdom. Little Orphan Annie and Kayo are both of uncertain age, neither children nor adults, and show no sign of growing older (or younger, for that matter) in the next few decades. Harold Teen is blessed with the secret of eternal adolescence, than which his readers find little more desirable. Such strips allow adults to sink, for the moment, into the uncomplicated ways of childhood. On the other hand, the numerous comics that are little more than schematized abstractions of violence and sadism quickly push children into premature adulthood.[3]

Like comic strips, though seldom so simply, movie stars also tend to become identified in the mass mind with one personality strand. Their status as stars is seldom secure unless they have developed one dominant emotional characteristic which serves the audience as an identifying sign. It is this characteristic that determines the emotional essence of a movie, as distinct from the surface subject.

---

3. The idea for this paragraph has been developed from a note on the comics by Dwight Macdonald; *Politics*, April 1945.

Although *The Hucksters* was presumably a satire on advertising, it was actually about Clark Gable, the irresistible male. Every Gable film has sexual aggression as its dominant inner theme no matter what its ostensible plot. Similarly, no matter which role he plays Ronald Colman is always the man of the world. In no picture has the divergence between inner theme and apparent subject been so wide as in the film *Crossfire*, which while ostensibly an attack on anti-Semitism, was actually about a tough guy who violates social convention and in passing accidentally kills a Jew.

At most, Hollywood allows several characters in a movie to represent conflicting emotional strands. Like all mass culture media, it is neither able nor interested in grouping conflicting emotions within one character. From its point of view, that would he dangerous.

3: The Unpunished Violation of Law

"Mit dose kids, society iss nix," says the Inspector about his juvenile tormentors, the Katzenjammer Kids. The adult-baiting that is the main theme of this comic strip seems never to weary its audience, since children and adults are always at war and adults often secretly sympathize with children. To children the strip appeals directly and for obvious reasons, and to adults it offers the possibility of vicariously rejecting their own adulthood and of safely breaking the laws of social life. While perpetuating passivity and shredding personality, mass culture yet allows the audience the limited freedom of vicariously breaking social law which, in turn, satisfies "a perpetual latent craving in the American psyche for physical expression, for a type of energy that humdrum factory and office jobs have no way of releasing." (Parker Tyler, *The Hollywood Hallucination*.) But even this safe violation of social law in the audience's reactions to mass culture serves ultimately to reinforce real life adherence to social law.

Krazy Kat, the one comic strip intellectuals have admitted to liking, won wide favor with mass audiences simply because Herriman satisfied this deep craving for safe violations of traditional orders. He obeyed neither the conventions of social life nor the internal requirements of his medium, he simply did what he pleased. To the audience there was something immensely gratifying when for no apparent reason the background of the strip moved while its characters remained still. The knowledge that no matter what else happened Ignatz would for no discernible reason always throw his brick was both reassuring and consoling. For once, when straphangers glanced each evening at *Krazy Kat*, they could escape from the tyranny of causality. In a world too cluttered with reasons, there seemed no reason for what happened to Officer Pup, Ignatz and Krazy—and this very lack of order helped the audience reestablish order in its own life.

What happens when a mass culture product does not conform to this pattern of safely violating social law I learned in a rather terrifying incident several years ago. I was then stationed at an army reception center where new recruits were prepared for military life. After they exchanged civilian for army clothes, their behavior often took a sharp turn to a kind of lawlessness, a break from old patterns. Feeling that they had to live up to a new role they indulged in a fantastic amount of profanity and wild sexual boasting. They had to show they were men.

One evening at a showing of the film *The Ox-Bow Incident* I could not help noticing that most of the new soldiers were volubly identifying themselves with the film's lynch mob as it tracked down and murdered three innocent men. The feelings they had about their new status in life were apparently projected into sympathy for the lynchers, *also men of violence*. And they assumed that this film would allow them, as might most Hollywood products, to cheat out of the consequences of their vicarious violence.

When, however, at the end of the film the lynching was sharply condemned—not merely in formal terms but in psychic and visual images the audience could not escape—the soldiers openly jeered. They were as perplexed and disoriented as the lynchers in the movie. For once, they discovered, they could not identify themselves with the law-breakers without suffering emotionally. And they felt that in this way the movie was "cheating" them, as in a sense it was.

The motif of unpunished violation of social law is strongly emphasized in the most important recent development in mass culture—the "tough guy" movies. When we go to see the old-fashioned detective (Sherlock Holmes, Ellery Queen) and western films, we are hardly involved emotionally; such films are put together along strictly stereotyped patterns that permit us the pleasure of relapsing into passive spectators. Their crimes and their punishments provoke no violent reactions since they concern relationships to law that no longer count. In fact, their major source of pleasure is their frank irrelevance.

But we react both violently and with some complexity to the tough guy films. (The detective film is concerned with patterns of deduction, the tough guy film with situations of existence, even if distorted ones.) When we project ourselves into the position of the tough guy who is often not quite clearly on either side of the law, our enjoyment in this identification is deep since it is so close—for does not modern life force all of us to be at least part-time tough guys? And our pleasure in the inevitable denouement is equally deep, since the greater the evil by which we have been tempted the greater our relief at escaping it. Like the Christian who views the Jew as both murderer and murdered, the spectator can gain from the tough guy film the symbiotic pleasure of being both hunter and hunted.

I think this can best be illustrated by going back to a movie made several years ago, *Double Indemnity*. In this film an insurance agent named Neff is attracted by a woman, Phyllis, who lures him into a plot to kill her husband and share his insurance. In the end they are trapped by Keyes, the insurance company's claims investigator. As played by Barbara Stanwyck, Phyllis is a remarkable sexual woman: frank, aggressive, bitchy. To the spectator's mind she therefore represents lawlessness, the violation of traditional sex mores. She is what the audience might like to be or like to possess, but she is too much so to allow us readily to identify ourselves with her. Keyes, on the other hand, is a creature of sheer intelligence: the supervisory mind that investigates and punishes us for our hidden transgressions. With neither can we fully identify ourselves.

But Neff, the hapless victim in the middle, is just another little guy, as bumbling as you, I or Fred MacMurray. We could fall for Phyllis and we could be trapped by Keyes. Neff is a passive transmission belt through which runs the conflict between Phyllis and Keyes—lawless instinct versus lawful conduct. Since Neff's feelings about that conflict are as ambiguous as those of the audience itself, he is, in a sense, the audience brought directly into the film, the modern anonymous moviegoer torn between what he takes for lawless sexual desire and intelligent lawful suppression. Farther in the violation of social law, mass culture cannot go. And this, too, is the deepest identification we can feel towards a mass culture hero—an identification that, unlike a genuine work of art which brings into play—a variety of emotions and character components, rests largely on the least individualized and most anonymous aspects of ourselves. The identification is ultimately with our role of social anonymity.

But this is as far as mass culture can go in the direction of art—much farther incidentally than the more pretentious or "socially significant" products of Hollywood. The next step is the crucial step, and Hollywood, like all other mass culture industries, cannot take it. Here it has reached the great divide.

Delmore Schwartz

"Masterpieces as Cartoons"

Partisan Review, vol. 19, July–August, 1952, pp. 461–71. Reprinted by permission.

Recently I have been trying hard to watch television and read comic books. I do not know whether this is an effort to keep in touch with the rest of the American population or an attempt to win the esteem and keep up with my brother-in-law, aged twelve, who regards me as a hideous highbrow and thinks that I am probably a defrocked high school English teacher. The effort is, at any rate, one which permits me moments of self-congratulation. I feel that no one can say that I have not tried my best to keep open the lines of communication between myself and others, and to share the intellectual interests of the entire community.

The bottom of the pit has been reached, I think, in the cartoon books which are called *Classics Illustrated*, a series of picture-and-text versions of the masterpieces of literature. Seventy-eight of them have been published, but so far I have only been able to obtain six of them, and they have been so exciting and fascinating and distracting that I have only been able to read three of them with any care: Dostoevsky's *Crime and Punishment*, Shakespeare's *A Midsummer Night's Dream*, and *Gulliver's Travels*. The intentions of the publishers and the editors of these illustrated classics are either good, or they feel guilty, or perhaps both, since at the end of *A Midsummer Night's Dream* there is a striking and entirely capitalized sentence: "NOW THAT YOU HAVE READ THE CLASSICS ILLUSTRATED EDITION, DON'T MISS THE ADDED ENJOYMENT OF READING THE ORIGINAL, OBTAINABLE AT YOUR SCHOOL OR PUBLIC LIBRARY." Notice how it is assumed that the reader has not read the original version of these works and it is taken for granted that he will not buy, he will only borrow, the original version from school or the public library. An interesting and significant fact to discover would be: just how many readers who first encounter Shakespeare, Dostoevsky, or Jonathan Swift in their comics garb are moved by this encounter to read the original. It would take a good detective or a good pollster to find out. When one feels optimistic, it seems possible that some quality of the masterpiece may bring some readers to the original; but when one feels pessimistic, one remembers an analogous phenomenon: even when a reader goes from James M. Cain to William Faulkner and James Joyce because they are all available in pocket book form for twenty-five cents, most readers who come to Faulkner and Joyce by means of pocket books do not know the difference between James M. Cain and James Joyce or Dashiell Hammett and William Faulkner; and some of the time they do not remember the names of the authors, no matter how many of their works they read.

The good intentions, or the guilty conscience, of the publishers of *Classics Illustrated* show clearly at the end of the cartoon version of *Crime and Punishment*, where again, as with Shakespeare, they write sentences of bold apology and excellent advice: "BECAUSE OF SPACE LIMITATIONS, WE REGRETFULLY OMITTED SOME OF THE ORIGINAL CHARACTERS AND SUB-PLOTS OF THIS BRILLIANTLY WRITTEN NOVEL. NEVERTHELESS, WE HAVE RETAINED ITS MAIN THEME AND MOOD. WE STRONGLY URGE YOU TO READ THE ORIGINAL." This explanation is more interesting and more inaccurate, the more one thinks about it and the more one remembers the novel which Dostoevsky wrote. For one of the characters who is omitted is Sonia, the heroine. She may have been omitted because of space limitations but it is just as likely that her prostitution had something to do with her absence from the illustrated version. What remains after the deletion of some of the original characters and sub-plots is the thin line of a detective story in which a murderer is tracked down; as the publishers explain, at the end of the last slot in which Raskolnikov confesses his crime: "This then was the story of the intelligent young man who committed a premeditated 'perfect crime.' His conscience and the efforts of a brilliant police attorney brought about the dramatic confession and a just punishment. Raskolnikov was sentenced to serve a long term at hard labor in a Siberian prison." Not much is left of the profound affirmation of Christianity with which the original work concludes, although there are cartoon book versions of the Old and New Testaments.

The miracle, or perhaps one should say the triumph of Dostoevsky's genius, is that despite all the cuts and mutilations of the original, there are gleams and glitters throughout the illustrated version of the psychological insight which Dostoevsky possessed to so powerful a degree and which made so stern a judge as Freud declare that only Shakespeare surpassed him as an author and as a literary psychologist. The brilliance and the originality of Dostoevsky's psychologizing comes through mainly in the exchanges between Raskolnikov and Porfiry the detective as the latter gradually traps the murderer into confessing his crime. There are also numerous moments in the illustrated edition which are unknowingly comic and probably the expression of deep unconscious attitudes upon the part of the illustrator and the editor. For example, Raskolnikov at times looks very much like a Russian delegate to the UN who is afraid that the NKVD is after him. At other times Raskolnikov has an unquestionable resemblance to Peter Lorre the film star who has so often been a villain. At other moments the illustrations but not the text—suggest a detestation of all intellectuals, not only Raskolnikov and in general there is the sharp implication throughout that most Russians are either criminals or police agents and all Russians are somehow fundamentally evil.

I tried to check on this impression which seemed possibly an over-interpretation by examining another cartoon series called *Crime Does NOT Pay* (an immortal aphorism which is not going to hold much weight when the readers and the children find out about Frank Costello); a series about true crimes in the United States. The results of the comparison are incontestable: American crimes and criminals do not resemble Russia's or Dostoevsky's in the least.

The illustrated "edition" of *A Midsummer Night's Dream* is much less of a distortion of the original work. There are none of the serious cuts and omissions which virtually reduce the cartoon version of *Crime and Punishment* to a trite detective story. And the reason is clear enough: Shakespeare's play was intended for an audience which was very much like the juvenile readers of *Classics Illustrated*, and *A Midsummer Night's Dream* is one of the most playful and child-like of plays. Nevertheless here too the medium of the cartoon tends to make this version misleading. For one thing, the title page presents the (juvenile) reader with boxed and oval portraits of four of the leading characters. Under them is a landscape—a lake, a grove of trees, a distant temple, and Puck flying through the air in front of an enormous rising moon—and at the foot of the page there is a scroll-like band of words which announces the leading elements of the plot: "A dark forest. . . . An angry fairy king. . . . His mischievous messenger. . . . A magic flower. . . . Four thwarted lovers. . . . And a troupe of wretched actors make a merry mix-up on a midsummer night . . . ," all of which is fair enough as a brief overture. The illustrated edition begins at the very beginning of the play (something which is certainly far from being the case in all cartoon versions of the classics) and it is at this point that the most important kind of distortion takes place. For first, there is a slot which explains to the youthful reader the purpose of the scene: "In his palace, Theseus, Duke of Athens, and Hippolyta, Queen of the Amazons, discuss their coming wedding . . . ," an explanation which interferes with the natural dramatic unfolding, although the intention,

I suppose, is to help the reader as much as possible and keep him from being in the least perplexed or from feeling that he has to make any serious exertion beyond keeping his eyes open.

Second, and more important by far, the opening speeches, which are in blank verse, are printed as if they were prose. This occurs from beginning to end. There is no conceivable way in which the juvenile reader can find out from the illustrated edition itself that he is reading poetry and not prose, although one would guess that some sense of the movement of language in blank verse rhythms certainly must impinge upon every reader. This failure to make it clear that the speeches are often poetry and not prose may not seem as serious, at first glance, as in actuality it is. For the speeches are bound to be read incorrectly; and worse still, when the juvenile reader does at some later date encounter poetry printed as poetry he is likely to be annoyed, if not irritated to the point where he refuses to read whatever is printed as poetry at all. His illustrated edition will have given him an easy and pleasant experience which becomes an obstacle to the more laborious and unfamiliar effort involved in reading poetry straight, that is to say, as it was written and as it was meant to be read.

Perhaps it is not as important as I think it is that there should be a certain number of readers of poetry. But the fear that disturbs me can be exemplified by what occurred in a class of freshmen at one of the best universities in the world. The instructor, who was teaching English composition, asked the students to define blank verse. No student volunteered an answer. The instructor expressed his dismay and asked his class if they had not studied Shakespeare and other poets in high school. The students admitted that they had, and finally one student, perhaps feeling sympathy for the clearly distressed teacher, raised his hand and attempted a definition of blank verse: "Sir," he said, hesitantly, tentatively, and unsurely, "isn't blank verse something which looks like poetry, but is not poetry?" It turned out that the well-meaning student supposed that unless there were rhymes at the end of each line, he was not reading poetry. Now this class of students represented what was probably the most intensively and expensively educated young men in America. And as I have said, the incident and others like it occurred at one of the best schools in the world. If such a systematic misunderstanding of the nature of literature and poetry can exist among such young men what, after all, can be expected of a population which first comes upon great literature in the guise of cartoon editions? One can well imagine a student insisting to his instructor that *A Midsummer Night's Dream* cannot be a play in blank verse, since the student has seen with his own eyes that it was printed as prose. And it is certainly not fanciful to suppose that the day is swiftly approaching when one human being says to another: "Have you read *Hamlet?*" and is answered: "No, but I seen the comic book edition."

Yet certainly there is a good side to everything, however infamous. There always is. And the good side to Shakespeare's plays as cartoon strips might be that some juvenile readers who are oppressed and biased by the way in which Shakespeare is for the most part taught in high schools all over America will now come upon Shakespeare first of all as a cartoon and see that he is really a great deal of fun, he is not a painful assignment in homework and a difficult, outmoded, canonized ancient author who wrote strange plays which provide the teachers of English with inexhaustible and eminently respectable reasons for boring their students. But there must be other and less misleading ways of demonstrating the pleasures of poetry to juvenile readers.

It is true that to encounter a literary masterpiece in a dramatic or cinematic form sometimes gives the reader, juvenile or adult, a new view and a new interest in the work. The French films of Dostoevsky's *The Idiot* and *Crime and Punishment* not only gave me a new and clarified understanding of both novels, but it seemed to me that the changes that were made in the original text were often improvements. The same was true of the German film version of *The Brothers Karamazov*, even though the character of Alyosha and the fable of the Grand Inquisitor were omitted, probably for theatrical reasons. And it is even more true that when a Shakespearean film is made well, as *A Midsummer Night's Dream* and *Henry V* were, there is a great gain for the common reader of Shakespeare who is used to reading him in a book rather than grasping his plays as visual experiences.

The fundamental question, whether it is a matter of the filmed Shakespeare or the cartoon book Shakespeare, seems to me to be: will the juvenile reader ever arrive at the point where he wants to see the original as it was intended to be, in its full actuality as a work? And the answer which suggests itself is a depressing one. If you get used to getting literature with illustrations—"visualized" is the phrase, I think—then you are likely to feel deprived when there are no illustrations and you have to do all the work yourself, depending upon the book itself. Moreover, the vice of having your visualizing done for you is all too likely to make you unused if not unwilling to read books which have no pictures in them. The Chinese proverb, "A picture is worth a thousand words," is often quoted by American advertisers. But the Chinese meant something very different from what the advertisers are trying to say. The Chinese meant that the visual experience of an object was more likely to give the full concreteness of that object than many of the words about it, which are for the most part abstract, generalized, colorless, and the like. The advertisers mean that human beings are more interested in looking at things (and find it eas-ier) than in reading about them, so that the pictures in an ad are more efficacious in increasing sales than the words that accompany the pictures.

This fact is relevant to *Classics Illustrated* in the most direct way: the reader finds it easy and pleasant to look at words-with-pictures, he finds it more difficult and less pleasant to look at words which have no pictures to make them clear and visual. There is a tendency among some readers to read so much that their capac-ity to look at the visual world is spoiled. But far worse and far more prevalent is the tendency (of which masterpieces in cartoon form are an apt example) to read as lit-tle as possible and to prefer a thousand pictures to a single paragraph of intelligent reading matter. The over-all picture of the state of literacy was formulated two years ago by Gilbert Seldes in *The Great Audience*, a book which did not receive the atten-tion it deserved: "In fourteen million homes equipped with radios, *no* magazines are read; families with television sets read fewer magazines than those who do not have them; half the adults in America never buy books." It is simple to transpose this statement to the great juvenile audience and to their reading of comic books and of the classics in cartoon form.

When we turn to the cartoon book version of *Gulliver's Travels*, other aspects of juve-nile literacy (I was about to write, delinquency!) become clear. Of course *Gulliver's Travels* has been a children's classic for a long time as well as one of the greatest works of English literature for those who have reached the age of reason and con-sent. In the past, however; it is unquestionably true that the children's version of Swift's best work did not become a barrier to the interest of the same children in that work when they were old enough to want to enjoy the master-works of their native language. The cartoon book version, unlike the older children's editions of *Gulliver's Travels*, goes much further in mutilation. At the end of the cartoon version, there is no plea by the publisher, as there was in *Crime and Punishment*, and in *A Midsummer Night's Dream*, telling the reader that be ought to read this work in its original form. There is, however, as in all the *Classics Illustrated*, a biography of the author (these biographies vary in in-accuracy, but they are all inaccurate to some degree). Swift's cartoon biography contains a number of trivial errors—such as the statement that he began to write in 1704—but the important distortion is a truth which is stated in such a way that it is likely to mislead and deceive anyone who wants to find out the truth and is limited in the resources and skills necessary to finding out what the truth is (as, obviously, most juvenile readers are, whether they are quiz kids or not). The truth which is stated in such a way as to be entirely misleading is set forth in the cartoon biography of Swift as follows: "*Gulliver's Travels* was written by Swift as a savage commentary on the European world Swift knew, as a condemnation of the laws and customs of his own and other countries that led one of the characters in the story to describe the inhabitants of Europe as 'the most pernicious race of little odious vermin that nature ever suffered to crawl upon the surface of the earth.' In later years Swift's satire became more and more violently bitter, possibly the result of mental disease which, by 1736, caused him to become insane."

Whoever wrote the cartoon biography may not have a chance to read the cartoon version. For there is very little in the cartoon version to suggest that the original is a "savage commentary" in which human beings are condemned as "odious little vermin." Moreover, the cartoon biography suggests that Swift was commenting on the state of human nature in his own time, and not in all times and places which he knew about. There is also the suggestion that the bitterness and violence of his satire were probably due to the onset of mental disease. All of this apology is unnecessary, however, for the reader who only knows of Swift through the cartoon edition. And what the biography states is literally true and as true, deceptive. Swift did suffer from mental disease and the disappointment of his political ambition did inspire in part the savage indignation which makes *Gulliver's Travels* a masterpiece. But the juvenile reader has no need of reassurance as to the benign character of human nature and the one-sidedness of Swift's point of view. In the cartoon version Gulliver returns to England and we last see and hear him as he stands at the wheel of the ship which is coming into an English harbor. The captain of the ship, who is standing next to him, says: "There she is! Good old Brittania!" and Gulliver expresses his own pleasure in returning to civilized Europe and merry England by saying: "I certainly am happy to be back . . . but it will take me weeks to get used to moving among people my own size!" He has had strange and interesting adventures and now he is delighted to be home.

Surely no explanation that Swift was a disappointed man of genius who concluded in insanity is necessary if all the reader has read is the cartoon edition. If he reads the original, he is certainly bound to be disturbed. For the original concludes in a way which is very different from *Classics Illustrated*. Gulliver explains to the "Courteous Readers," on the next to the last page, that having lived among horses and among human beings, he still prefers horses to human beings. When he has just come back to his own house in England, his wife's kiss makes him faint: "My Wife took me in her Arms, and kissed me; at which, having not been used to the touch of that odious Animal for so many years, I fell in a Swoon for almost an Hour," and he feels disgusted with himself at the thought that he has become the father of human beings: the fact strikes him "with the utmost Shame, Confusion, and Horror." For the first year after his return to England "I could not endure my Wife or Children in my Presence, the Smell of them was intolerable." (I am quoting at length because anyone who has not read *Gulliver's Travels* recently will probably think any synopsis or paraphrase an exaggeration of Swift's satire.) As to the purpose of the work, Gulliver declares that "I write for the noblest End, to inform and instruct Mankind, over whom I may, without Breach of Modesty, pretend to some superiority, from the Advantages I received by conversing among the most accomplished Houyhnhnms. I write without any View toward Profit or Praise," which is to say that, having dwelt with horses, Gulliver feels Superior to mankind and capable of instructing human beings in how to improve. At the very end, having been back among civilized human beings for five years, Gulliver declares that he is now able to sit at the same dinner table with his wife, although since the smell of any civilized being is still offensive to him, he has to keep applying rue, lavender, or tobacco to his nose. And he adds that he would be able to accept human nature as it is in most of its follies and vices except for one unbearable trait, the vice of pride, which causes more viciousness than any other human trait. It is the viciousness of pride and vanity which make civilized existence insupportable.

Clearly, there is little likelihood that the juvenile reader of the cartoon version of *Gulliver's Travels* will be corrupted by Swift's cynicism and nihilism (which was inspired, we ought to remember, by an intense idealism and an intense purity as well as by the disappointment of ambition and the distortion of growing neurosis). But the important point here is not the juvenile reader himself or herself, but the adult publisher and editor who has exhibited a well-meaning solicitude for the juvenile reader's tender sensibility. For whoever is responsible for the cartoon version is very much aware of the true character of *Gulliver's Travels* and wishes to spare the feelings and the mind of the juvenile audience. But where does this solicitude stop?

I must turn to personal experience to show how far the solicitude and the censorship can go. When I taught English composition to freshmen and coeds ten years ago along with some twenty-five other instructors, a crisis occurred as a result of the modern novels which the students had been assigned to read. One of the coeds had been reading late at night at her English assignment, which was

John Dos Passos's *U.S.A.* Dos Passos's savage indignation, which resembles Swift's, and his explicit account of the sexual experiences of his characters, terrified the young lady to the point where she had to waken her father (not her mother!) and tell him that she had been scared and shocked by her reading assignment in English. The unhappy father conferred with the head of the English staff who in turn discussed the entire issue with the entire staff. The head of the staff was very much aware of both sides of the problem and he tried to be just to the interests and rights of his instructors as well as to the problems of adolescents who are in the first year of their undergraduate careers. But in such a situation, judiciousness and compromise can accomplish very little. Most of the instructors felt, whether rightly or wrongly, that they had been told not to assign Dos Passos, or Joyce, or Thomas Mann, or Proust, or Gide or Celine to their students. They felt that they probably would be fulfilling their duty as teachers of English composition and literature better if they went no further than such authors as Dickens, Thackeray, George Eliot, and George Meredith. Thomas Hardy was an ambiguous and questionable author, given the point of view which a shocked coed had brought to the fore, since *Jude the Obscure* and *Tess of the D'Urbervilles* were both books which might very well be shocking again as they had been when they first appeared (as a result of which scandal, the heartsick Hardy ceased to write novels).

The juvenile and adolescent reader certainly ought not to be scared and shocked. But he ought not to be cut off from the reality of great literature and of modern literature (the latter being, because of its contemporaneity, the best way of getting the ordinary adolescent reader interested in literature of any kind). And it is essential and necessary to remember that if a human being does not become interested in literature when he is an undergraduate, it is quite unlikely that he will become a devoted reader at any other time of life.

The teaching of English has a direct and continuous relationship to the kind of books which juvenile, adolescent, and adult readers are likely to desire to read. The cartoon version of *Gulliver's Travels* suggests still another incident in the teaching of English literature. The text in this instance was Swift's *A Modest Proposal*; in which Swift proposes among other things that the economic problem of Ireland might be solved if the Irish bred children and then butchered them for food. In the seven years during which, at some point during the year, I had to assign this little classic of satire to freshmen students, I naturally encountered a variety of impressions on their part. But the most frequent and representative comment was exemplified by a student of Armenian parents (he must have heard of the Turks) and a boy who was Irish (and who must have heard of the English in Ireland). Both students announced that Swift was "morbid." I was tempted to embark upon a self-indulgent excursion when I heard this comment and to say that I would not permit the greatest prose writer in English, except for Shakespeare, perhaps, to be called "morbid," and to recall to the students what they had heard about the Turks in Armenia, the English in Ireland, to say nothing of Buchenwald and Dachau. But I felt that the students would merely have concluded that I too was morbid. By questioning them with some degree of patience, I found out that after they had read comic books, listened to soap operas, and witnessed the sweetness and light of the motion pictures, they were inclined to regard anything which is serious satire as morbid sensationalism.

To return directly to the cartoon versions of the classics: it is customary and habitual, when one has expressed the point of view I have suggested here, to be asked, *What is to be done?* I do not suffer from the delusion that I know what is to be done. But I confess that I sometimes entertain certain modest guesses, the practicality of which I cannot determine. The reading of comic books, and cartoon versions of the classics (and listening to the radio, looking at the motion pictures and listening and looking at television programs) cannot be stopped. Mass culture is here to stay: it is a major industry and a very profitable one, and one can no more banish it than one can banish the use of automobiles because thirty-four thousand people are killed by cars every year. And even if the reading of cartoon books might be stopped, it is probable that prohibition and censorship would have the usual boomerang effect.

What can be done, I think (or rather, I guess), is to set a good example, or perhaps I should say an example which is the least of all the possible evil examples, namely: each adult and literate human being who feels that literature is one of the necessary conditions of civilized existence can set the example of reading *both* the original classics and the cartoon versions. By doing both, he is keeping his hold on literature at its best and at the same time he is remaining aware or the experience and thus the consciousness of any other reader: children, juveniles, adolescents, housewives, aged relatives, farmers, mechanics, taxi-drivers—in fact, everyone! For the products of mass culture preoccupy the minds of most human beings in America, whether they know it or not. And in setting the good or least evil example of maintaining his hold on great literature in the midst of forcing himself to be aware of the debased versions and mutilations and dilutions of it, he may make some other readers imitative enough to come or return to the classics in their full actuality. This proposal may seem very much like one of the labors of Hercules. But it is also a lot of fun, at least some of the time. Besides, Hercules was a hero, and as practically everyone knows, all human beings want to be heroic heroes and heroines, at least once in a while.

Robert Warshow

"Woofed with Dreams"

Partisan Review, vol. 13, November–December 1946. Reprinted by permission.

On the underside of our society, there are those who have no real stake at all in respectable culture. These are the open enemies of culture, despising indiscriminately a painting by Picasso and a painting by Maxfield Parrish, a novel by Kafka and a novel by A. J. Cronin, a poem by Yeats and a poem by Ella Wheeler Wilcox— these are readers of pulp magazines and comic books, potential book-burners, unhappy patrons of astrologers and communicants of lunatic sects, the hopelessly alienated and outclassed who can enjoy perhaps not even Andy Hardy but only Bela Lugosi, not even the *Reader's Digest* but only *True Detective.*

But their distance from the center gives them in the mass a degree of independence that the rest of us can approach only individually and by discipline. In the extremity of their alienation, they are ready to be assured and irresponsible; they are ready to say: Shoot the bankers, or Kill the Jews, or Let the Nazis come. They no longer care if the ship goes down, they go their own way. That is why an editorial in the *Daily News* is so much more interesting—and often so much nearer the truth—than an editorial in *PM. PM* has too many things to consider; only the *Daily News* can remain entirely reasonable and disinterested when it suggests that the human race is on the way to extinction.

When this *Lumpen* culture displays itself in mass art forms, it can occasionally take on a certain purity and freshness that would almost surely be smothered higher up on the cultural scale. The quality of a Marx Brothers movie, for example, comes from an uncompromising nihilism that is particularly characteristic of the submerged and dispossessed; the Marx Brothers are *Lumpen*, they spit on culture, and they are popular among middle-class intellectuals because they express a blind and destructive disgust with society that the responsible man is compelled to suppress in himself.

In *Krazy Kat*, a very sweet tempered fantasy, the gap between mass culture and respectable culture manifests itself not in an open rejection of society, but, more indirectly, in a complete disregard of the standards of respectable art.

Working for an audience completely out of touch with the concerns of the serious-minded, George Herriman had the advantage that Lewis Carroll got by writing for children: so long as the internal patterns of his work—the personal and physical relationships of the characters—remained simple, he was fairly sure to please. Where no art is important, *Krazy Kat* is as real and important a work of art as any other—it is only supposed to divert its reader for two minutes at a time. (While the intellectuals had to "discover" *Krazy Kat*, the comic-strip audience just read it.)

Thus Herriman's fantasy can be free and relaxed, it can go its own way. What came into his head went down on the paper. His language is built up of scraps of sound and meaning, all the echoes that his mind contained—Krazy talks an arbitrary dialect that has some connection with the speech of New York but is attributable in its finished form neither to foreignness nor to illiteracy but solely to the mind of its creator: "Et less my I'll korn butch yills a krop—now I will have korn bread, korn mill mutch, korn poems, korn plestas, korn kopias"; Offissa Pup tends to be high-flown: "I mean none other than Ignatz Mouse—who makes evil the day by tossing bricks at that dear Kat." While the characters stand still, a potted tree behind them becomes a distant plateau and then a house and then a tree again. The continual flux is never mentioned and has no meaning; it is just that Herriman felt no obligation either to keep the background still or to explain its mobility. This absolute fantasy sometimes becomes mechanical, but it is never heavy and it frequently achieves the fresh quality of pure play, freed from the necessity to be dignified or "significant" and not obviously concerned even with entertaining its audience.

This is the plot: Krazy, inoffensive creature of uncertain sex, loves Ignatz Mouse. Ignatz despises Krazy—for his inoffensiveness, for his impenetrable silliness, and for his unshakable affection—and Ignatz (therefore?) devotes all his intelligence and energy to the single end of hitting Krazy on the head with bricks. He buys bricks from a brickmaker especially for this purpose; he conceals the bricks in innocent-looking packages or disguises them in innocent-looking shapes, he makes appointments hours in advance so that Krazy will be in the right place at the right time to be hit by a brick. Somewhere in this single-minded effort there must be passion, but it is not apparent it is all channeled constructively into planning and action: Ignatz's métier is to hit Krazy on the head with a brick. The overt passion is all on Krazy's side; he can never get used to the routine, but waits every moment like a bride for the expected ecstasy, the blow always new and always the same and wonderful, the recurrent climax and reward of love. "L'il dahlink," Krazy murrnurs as the brick comes—ZIP through the air and POW when it hits—"l'il dahlink, is there anybody in this woil more constint than him?" Offissa Pup, the guardian of law, loves Krazy, with the gentle and protecting love of the practical man for the poet and dreamer—"Dear K," he says of Krazy, "his life is warped with fancy, woofed with dreams." Offissa Pup's occupation is to keep Ignatz from throwing the brick and to put him in jail when he has thrown it.

Offissa Pup is the sole authority in the universe and Ignatz the sole evildoer. Evil always triumphs—Ignatz always throws the brick; but authority always triumphs, too—Ignatz is always put in jail. Krazy lives happily between the two. It is a very nice universe for Krazy; if there is an issue, Krazy does not understand it; he loves to be hit by the brick, but he respects Offissa Pup's motives.

One is tempted to read into this the meanings that one finds in the serious world of respectable culture. E. E. Cummings talks in his introduction about the opposition between the individual and society. But if Ignatz and Krazy are very good examples of individuals, Offissa Pup is not much of a society: his jail is always empty the next day. we do best, I think, to leave *Krazy Kat* alone. Good fantasy never has an easy and explicit relation to the real world. Even *Through the Looking Glass* is weakest when Looking-Glass Land is *exactly* the opposite of the real world. The haphazard and irresponsible fancy of George Herriman was capable even of social comment, but it is not to be trusted with any systems. If Offissa Pup was society on Monday, that placed no restriction on his program for Tuesday. One thing remains the same: *Krazy Kat* is about a cat who gets hit on the head with bricks.

Krazy Kat is perhaps the best that the comic strip has produced. But it would be a mistake to think it a "higher" development of the comic strip. "Higher" development brings in the whole apparatus of respectable controls and produces *Joe Palooka* helping to sell the country on conscription, or the hygienic, progressive-school fantasy of *Barnaby*. "Higher" development makes *Krazy Kat* impossible. *Krazy Kat* is "pointless" and "silly," it comes from the peripheral world where the aims and pretensions of society are not regarded.

Something should be said also about the comic strip's dimension of time. *Krazy Kat* started before I was born, and it ended in 1944 only because Herriman died and the King Features Syndicate decided that there was no one who could continue his work. This was accidental; the usual practice is to appoint a successor to the dead artist—there is no internal reason why Orphan Annie, for instance, should not continue to face up to her troubles for ten million years. Thus the comic strip has no beginning and no end, only an eternal middle. It is an additional reality, running parallel with the *real* reality: for every day of one's own life, there is a day in the comic strip's life. This, too, is a characteristic of *Lumpen* culture: all gradations and distinctions are broken down, even the distinction between art and life. (The more realistic characters of the comic strips and the soap operas receive letters and gifts from their admirers.) A baseball game, an editorial, a comic strip, a kiss: all are experiences, varying in intensity but equally significant—none is significant, and none has any meaningful connection with another. Almost every day for more than thirty years, Ignatz hit Krazy with a brick.

Robert Warshow

"Paul, the Horror Comics, and Dr. Wertham"

Commentary, vol. 17 (1954), pp. 596–604. Reprinted in Robert Warshow, The Immediate Experience. (1962; expanded edition 2001). Reprinted from Commentary, June 1954 by permission; all rights reserved.

My son Paul, who is eleven years old, belongs to the E.C. Fan-Addict club, a synthetic organization set up as a promotional device by the Entertaining Comics Group, publishers of *Mad* ("Tales Calculated to Drive You MAD—Humor in a Jugular Vein"), *Panic* ("This is No Comic Book, This is a PANIC—Humor in a Varicose Vein"), *Tales from the Crypt, The Vault of Horror, Weird Science-Fantasy, Shock SuspenStories, Crime SuspenStories* ("Jolting Tales of Tension in the E.C. Tradition"), and, I imagine, various other such periodicals. For his twenty-five-cent membership fee (soon to be raised to fifty cents), the E.C. Fan-Addict receives a humorously phrased certificate of membership, a wallet-size "identification card," a pin and a shoulder-patch bearing the club emblem, and occasional mailings of the club bulletin, which publishes chitchat about the writers, artists, and editors, releases trial balloons on ideas for new comic books, lists members' requests for back numbers, and in general tries to foster in the membership a sense of identification with this particular publishing company and its staff. *E.C. Fan-Addict Club Bulletin* Number 2, March 1954, also suggests some practical activities for the members. "Everytime you pass your newsstand, fish out the E.C.'s from the bottom of the piles or racks and put 'em on top. . . . BUT PLEASE, YOU MONSTERS, DO IT NEATLY!"

Paul, I think, does not quite take this "club" with full seriousness, but it is clear that he does in some way value his membership in it, at least for the present. He has had the club shoulder-patch put on one of his jackets, and when his membership pin broke recently he took the trouble to send for a new one. He has recruited a few of his schoolmates into the organization. If left free to do so, he will buy any comic book which bears the E.C. trademark, and is usually quite satisfied with the purchase. This is not a matter of "loyalty," but seems to reflect some real standard of discrimination; he has occasionally sampled other comic books which imitate the E.C. group and finds them inferior.

67

It should be said that the E.C. comics do in fact display a certain imaginative flair. *Mad* and *Panic* are devoted to a wild, undisciplined machine-gun attack on American popular culture, creating an atmosphere of nagging hilarity something like the clowning of Jerry Lewis. They have come out with covers parodying the *Saturday Evening Post* and *Life*, and once with a vaguely "serious" cover in imitation of magazines like *Harper's* or the *Atlantic*. ("Do you want to look like an idiot reading comic books all your life? Buy *Mad*, then you can look like an idiot reading high-class literature.") The current issue of *Mad* (dated August) has Leonardo's Mona Lisa on the cover, smiling as enigmatically as ever and cradling a copy of *Mad* in her arms. The tendency of the humor, in its insistent violence, is to reduce all culture to indiscriminate anarchy. These comic books are in a line of descent from the Marx Brothers, from the Three Stooges whose funniest business is to poke their fingers in each other's eyes, and from that comic orchestra which starts out playing "serious" music and ends up with all the instruments smashed. A very funny parody of the comic strip *Little Orphan Annie*, in *Mad* or *Panic*, shows Annie cut into small pieces by a train because Daddy Warbucks's watch is slow and he has arrived just too late for the last minute; Annie's detached head complains: "It hurts when I laugh." The parody ends with the most obvious and most vulgar explanation of why Annie calls Daddy Warbucks "Daddy"; I had some difficulty in explaining that joke to Paul. One of the funnier stories in *Panic* tells of a man who finds himself on the television program "This IS Your Life"; as his old friends and neighbors appear one by one to fill in the story of his life, it becomes clear that nobody has seen his wife since 11:30 P.M. on the ninth of October 1943; shortly before that he had made some rather significant purchases: arsenic, a shovel, quicklime. Evidence piles up, including the actual bones of his wife (dug up by his old dog, Rover, who also appears on the program and will do nothing but growl at his former master). At the end of the program, of course, the man is arrested for murder; television's assault on privacy has reached its logical conclusion. I understand that *Mad* is rather popular among college students, and I have myself read it with a kind of irritated pleasure.

The straightforward crime and horror comics, such as *Shock SuspenStories*, *Crime SuspenStories*, or *The Vault of Horror*, exhibit the same undisciplined imaginativeness and violence without the leavening of humor. One of the more gruesome stories in *Crime SuspenStories* is simply a "serious" version of the story I have outlined from *Panic*: again a man murders his wife (this time with an ax) and buries her in the back yard, and again he is trapped on a television program. In another story, a girl some ten or eleven years old, unhappy in her home life, shoots her father, frames her mother and the mother's lover for the murder, and after their death in the electric to chair ("Mommy went first. Then Steve.") is shown living happily with Aunt Kate, who can give her the emotional security she has lacked. The child winks at us from the last panel in appreciation of her own cleverness. Some of the stories, if one takes them simply in terms of their plots, are not unlike the stories of Poe or other writers of horror tales; the publishers of such comic books have not failed to point this out. But of course the bareness of the comic-book form makes an enormous difference. Both the humor and the horror in their utter lack of modulation yield too readily to the child's desire to receive his satisfactions immediately, thus tending to subvert the chief elements in the process of growing up, which is to learn to wait; a child's developing appreciation of the complexity of good literature is surely one of the things that contribute to his eventual acceptance of the complexity of life.

I do not suppose that Paul's enthusiasm for the products of this particular publisher will necessarily last very long. At various times in the past he has been a devotee of the Dell Publishing Company (*Gene Autry, Red Ryder, Tarzan, The Lone Ranger,* etc.), National Comics (*Superman, Action Comics, Batman,* etc.), *Captain Marvel, The Marvel Family, Zoo Funnies* (very briefly), *Sergeant Preston of the Yukon,* and, on a higher level, *Pogo Possum.* He has around a hundred and fifty comic books in his room, though he plans to weed out some of those which no longer interest him. He keeps closely aware of dates of publication and watches the newsstands from day to day and from corner to corner if possible; when a comic book he is concerned with is late in appearing, he is likely to get in touch with the publishers to find out what has caused the delay. During the *Pogo* period, indeed, he seemed to be in almost constant communication with Walt Kelly and the Post-Hall Syndicate, asking for original drawings (he has two of them), investigating delays in publication of the comic books (there are quarterly 15 cents comic books, published by Dell, in addition to the daily newspaper strip and the frequent paperbound volumes published at one dollar by Simon and Schuster), or tracking down rumors that a Pogo shirt or some other object was to be put on the market (the rumors were false; Pogo is being kept free of "commercialization"). During the 1952 presidential campaign, Pogo was put forward as a "candidate," and there were buttons saying "I Go Pogo"; Paul managed to acquire about a dozen of these, although as he was told, they were intended primarily for distribution among college students. Even now he maintains a distant fondness for Pogo, but I am no longer required to buy the *New York Post* every day in order to save the strips for him. I think that Paul's desire to put himself directly in touch with the processes by which the comic books are produced may be the expression of a fundamental detachment which helps to protect him from them; the comic books are not a "universe" to him, but simply objects produced for his entertainment.

When Paul was home from school for his spring vacation this year, I took him and two of his classmates to visit the offices of the Entertaining Comics Group at 225 Lafayette Street. (I had been unable to find the company in the telephone book until I thought of looking it up as "Educational Comics"; I am told that this is one of five corporate names under which the firm operates.) As it turned out, there was nothing to be seen except a small anteroom containing a pretty receptionist and a rack of comic books; the editors were in conference and could not be disturbed. (Of course I knew there must be conferences, but this discovery that they actually occur at a particular time and place somehow struck me; I should have liked to know how the editors talked to each other.) In spite of our confinement to the anteroom, however, the children seemed to experience as great exaltation as if they had found themselves in the actual presence of, say, Gary Cooper.

One of Paul's two friends signed up there and then in the E.C. Fan-Addict Club (Paul had recruited the other one into the club earlier) and each boy bought seven or eight back numbers. When the receptionist obliging went into the inner offices to see if she could collect a few autographs, the boys by crowding around the door as she opened it managed to catch a glimpse of one of the artists, Johnny Craig, whom Paul recognized from a drawing of him that had appeared in one of the comic books. In response to the boys' excitement, the door was finally opened wide so that for a few seconds they could look at Mr. Craig; he waved at them pleasantly from behind his drawing board and then the door was closed. Before we left, the publisher himself, William Gaines, passed through the anteroom, presumably on his way to the men's room. He too was recognized, shook hands with the boys, and gave them his autograph.

I am sure the children's enthusiasm contained some element of self-parody, or at any rate an effort to live up to the situation—after all, a child is often very uncertain about what is exciting, and how much. It is quite likely that the little sheets of paper bearing the precious autographs have all been misplaced by now. But there is no doubt that the excursion was a great success.

A few weeks later Mr. Gaines testified before a Congressional committee that is investigating the effects of comic books on children and their relation to juvenile delinquency. Mr. Gaines, as one would expect, was opposed to any suggestion that comic books be censored. In his opinion, he said, the only restrictions on the editors of comic books should be the ordinary restrictions of good taste. Senator Kefauver presented for his examination the cover of an issue of *Crime Suspenstories* (drawn by Johnny Craig) which shows a man holding by its long blond hair the severed head of a woman. In the man's other hand is the dripping ax with which he has just carried out the decapitation, and the lower part of the woman's body, with the skirt well up on the plump thighs, appears in the background. It was an illustration for the story I have described in which the murderer is finally trapped on a television program. Did Mr. Gaines think this cover in good taste? Yes, he did—for a horror comic. If the head had been held a little higher, so as to show blood dripping from the severed neck, that would have been bad taste. Mr. Gaines went on to say that he considers himself to be the originator of horror comics and is proud of it. He mentioned also that he is a graduate of the New York University School of Education, qualified to teach in the high schools.

I did not fail to clip the report of Mr. Gaines's testimony from the *Times* and send it to Paul, together with a note in which I said that while I was in some confusion about the comic-book question, at least I was sure I did not see what Mr. Gaines had to be so proud about. But Paul has learned a few things in the course of the running argument about comic books that has gone on between us. He thanked me for sending the clipping and declined to be drawn into a discussion. Such discussions have not proved very fruitful for him in the past.

They have not been very fruitful for me either. I know that I don't like the comics myself and that it makes me uncomfortable to see Paul reading them. But it's hard to explain to Paul why I feel this way, and somewhere along the line it seems to have been established that Paul is always entitled to an explanation: he is a child of our time.

I said once that the gross and continual violence of the comic books was objectionable.

He said: "What's so terrible about things being exciting?"

Well, nothing really; but there are books that are much more exciting, the comics keep you from reading the books.

But I read books *too*. (He does, especially when there are no comics available.)

Why read the comics at all?

But you said yourself that *Mad* is pretty good. You gotta admit!

Yes, I know I did. But it's not that good. . . . Oh, the comics are just stupid, that's all, and I don't see why you should be wasting so much time with them.

Maybe they're stupid *sometimes*. But look at this one. This one is *really good*. Just read it! Why won't you just *read* it?

Usually I refuse to "just read it," but that puts me at once at a disadvantage. How can I condemn something without knowing what it is? And sometimes, when I do read it, I am forced to grant that maybe this particular story does have a certain minimal distinction, and then I'm lost. Didn't I say myself that *Mad* is pretty good?

I suppose this kind of discussion can be carried on better than I seem able to do, but it's a bad business getting into discussions anyway. If you're against comic books, then you say: no comic books. I understand there re parents who manage to do that. The best—or worst—that has happened to Paul was a limit on the number of comic books he was allowed to have in a week: I think it was three. But that was intolerable; there were special occasions, efforts to borrow against next week, negotiations for revision of the allotment; there was *always* a discussion.

The fundamental difficulty, in a way—the thing that leaves both Paul and me uncertain of our ground—is that the comics obviously do not constitute a serious problem in his life. He is in that Fan-Addict Club, all right, and he likes to make a big show of being interested in E.C. comics above all else that the world has to offer, but he and I both know that while he may be a fan, he is not an addict. His life at school is pretty busy (this has been his first year at school away from home) and comics are not encouraged, though they certainly do find their way in. Paul subscribes to *Mad* and, I think, *Pogo* (also to *Zoo Funnies* and *Atomic Mouse*, but he doesn't read those any more), and he is still inclined to haunt newsstands when he is in New York; indeed, the first thing he wants to do when he gets off the train is buy a comic. In spite of all obstacles, I suppose be manages to read a hundred in a year, at worst perhaps even a hundred and fifty—that would take maybe seventy-five to a hundred hours. On the other hand, he doesn't see much television or listen much to the radio, and he does read books, draw, paint, play with toads, look at things through a microscope, write stories and poems, imitate Jerry Lewis, and in general do everything that one could reasonably want him to do, plus a few extras like skiing and riding. He seems to me a more alert, skillful, and self-possessed child than I or any of my friends were at eleven, if that's any measure. Moreover, I can't see that his hundred or hundred and fifty comic books are having any very specific effects on him. The bloodiest of ax murders apparently does not disturb his sleep or increase the violence of his own impulses. *Mad* and *Panic* have helped to develop in him a style of humor which may occasionally be wearing but is in general pretty successful; and anyway, Jerry Lewis has had as much to do with this as the comics. Paul's writing is highly melodramatic, but that's only to be expected, and he is more likely to model himself on Erle Stanley Gardner or Wilkie Collins than on *Crime SuspenStories*. Sometimes the melodrama goes over the line into the gruesome, and in that the comic books no doubt play a role; but if there were no comic books, Paul would be reading things like "The Pit and the Pendulum" or *The Narrative of A. Gordon Pym*—which, to be sure, would be better. Now and then he has expressed a desire to be a comic book artist when he grows up, or a television comedian. So far as I can judge, he has no inclination to accept as real the comic-book conception of human nature which sees everyone as a potential criminal and every criminal as an absolute criminal.[1]

As you see, I really don't have much reason to complain; that's why Paul wins the arguments. But of course I complain anyway. I don't like the comic books—not even *Mad*, whatever I may have unguardedly allowed myself to say—and I would prefer it if Paul did not read them. Like most middle-class parents, I devote a good deal of over-anxious attention to his education, to the "influences" that play on him and the "problems" that arise for him. Almost anything in his life is likely to seem important to me, and I find it hard to accept the idea that there should be one area of his experience, apparently of considerable importance to him, which will have no important consequences. One comic book a week or ten, they must have an effect. How can I be expected to believe that it will be a good one?

Testifying in opposition to Mr. Gaines at the Congressional hearing was Dr. Fredric Wertham, a psychiatrist who has specialized in work with problem and delinquent

---

1. The assumption that human beings will always follow out the logic of their character to the limit is one of the worst elements in the comic books and is pretty widespread in them. If a man is a burglar, he will not hesitate to commit murder; and if he is going to commit murder, he is often as likely to think of boiling his victim in oil as of shooting him. In the radio serial "Mark Trial," a program no longer in existence which was based on the comic strip "Mark Trail," men engaged in such illegal activities as hunting beaver out of season would unhesitatingly shoot any game warden who came upon them. (The theme of the program was supposed to be conservation.) This kind of "logic" may seem very proper to children. When Paul was about four or five, a baby-sitter read him the story of Bluebeard. I was a little disturbed when he mentioned this to me the next morning and I tried to probe his reactions.

I said something like: "An exciting story, eh?"

"Oh, yes," said Paul.

"That Bluebeard was quite a nasty character, wasn't he?" I said.

"Oh, I don't know," said Paul.

"What do you mean you don't know? Didn't he try to murder his wife?"

"Well," said Paul, "he *told* her not to look in that closet."

children. Dr. Wertham has been studying and attacking the comic books for a number of years. His position on the question is now presented in full in his recently published book *Seduction of the Innocent*.

The most impressive part of the book is its illustrations: two dozen or so examples of comic-book art displaying the outer limits of that "good taste" which Mr. Gaines suggests might be a sufficient restraint upon the editors. There is a picture of a baseball game in which the ball is a man's head with one eye dangling from its socket, the bat is a severed leg, the catcher wears a dismembered human torso as chest protector, the baselines are marked with stretched-out intestines, the bases are marked with the lungs, liver, and heart, the resin-bag is the dead man's stomach, and the umpire dusts off home plate with the scalp. There is a close-up of a hanged man, tongue protruding, eyeballs turned back, the break in the neck clearly drawn. Another scene shows two men being dragged to death face down over a rocky road. "A couple more miles oughta do th' trick!" says the driver of the car. "It better," says his companion. "These * * * * !! GRAVEL ROADS are tough on tires!" "But you gotta admit," replies the driver, "there's nothing like 'em for ERASING FACES!" And so on. Dr. Wertham could surely have presented many more such examples if he had the space and could have obtained permission to reproduce them. From Paul's collection, I recall with special uneasiness a story in which a rotting corpse returns from the grave; in full color, the hues and contours of decay were something to see.

Among the recurrent motifs of the comic books, Dr. Wertham lists: hanging, flagellation, rape, torture of women, tying up of women, injury to the eye (one of the pictures he reproduces shows a horrifying close-up of a woman's eye about to be pierced by an ice-pick). If a child reads ten comics of this sort a week (a not unusual figure), he may absorb in the course of a year from fifteen hundred to two thousand stories emphasizing these themes (a comic book contains three or four stories). If he takes them with any seriousness at all—and it is difficult to believe that he will not—they surely cannot fail to affect his developing attitudes towards violence, sex, and social restraint.

What the effects will be, and how deep-seated, is not so easy to determine. And here Dr. Wertham is not very helpful. When he tells us of children who have been found hanging, with a comic-book nearby opened to a picture of a hanging, one can readily share his alarm. The fact that these children were probably seriously disturbed before they ever read a comic book, and the fact that fantasies of hanging are in any case common among children, does not relieve one of the feeling that comic books may have provided the immediate stimulus that led to these deaths.

Even if there were no children who actually hanged themselves, is it conceivable that comic books which play so directly and so graphically on their deepest anxieties should be without evil consequences? On the other hand, when Dr. Wertham tells us of children who have injured themselves trying to fly because they have read *Superman* or *Captain Marvel*, one becomes skeptical. Children always want to fly and are always likely to try it. The elimination of *Superman* will not eliminate this sort of incident. Like many other children, I made my own attempt to fly after seeing *Peter Pan*; as I recall, I didn't really expect it to work, but I thought: who knows?

In general, Dr. Wertham pursues his argument with a humorless dedication that tends to put all phenomena and all evidence on the same level. Discussing *Superman* he suggests that it wouldn't take much to change the "S" on that great chest to "S.S". With a straight face he tells us of a little boy who was asked what he wanted to be when he grew up and said, "I want to be a sex maniac!" He objects to advertisements for binoculars in comic books because a city child can have nothing to do with binoculars except to spy on the neighbors. He reports the case of a boy of twelve who had misbehaved with his sister and threatened to break her arm if she told anybody. "This is not the kind of thing that boys used to tell their little sisters," Dr. Wertham informs us. He quotes a sociologist who "analyzed" ten comic-book heroes of the *Superman* type and found that all of them "may well be designated as psychopathic deviates." As an indication that there are some children "who are influenced in the right direction by thoughtful parents," he tells us of the four-year-old son of one of his associates who was in the hospital with scarlet fever; when the nurses offered him some comic books, the worthy child refused them, "explaining that his father had said they are not good for children." Dr. Wertham take at face value anything a child tells him, either as evidence of the harmful effects of the comic books ("I think sex all boils down to anxiety," one boy told him; where could he have got such an idea except from the comics?) or as direct support for his own views: he quotes approvingly a letter by a thirteen-year-old boy taking solemn exception to the display of nudity in comic books, and a fourteen-year-old boy's analysis of the economic motives which lead psychiatrists to give their endorsements to comic books. I suspect it would be a dull child indeed who could go to Dr. Wertham's clinic and not discover very quickly that most of his problematical behavior can be explained in terms of the comic books.

The publishers complain with justice that Dr. Wertham makes no distinction between bad comic books and "good" ones. The Dell Pubishing Company, for instance, the largest of the publishers, claims to have no objectionable comics on its list, which runs to titles like *Donald Duck* and *The Lone Ranger*. National Comics Publications (*Superman*, etc.), which runs second to Dell, likewise claims to avoid objectionable material and has an "editorial code" which specifically forbids the grosser forms of violence or any undue emphasis on sex. (If anything, this "code" is too puritanical but mechanically fabricated culture can only be held in check by mechanical restrictions.) Dr. Wertham is largely able to ignore the distinction between "bad" and "good" because most of us find it hard to conceive of what a "good" comic book might be.[2]

Yet in terms of their effect on children, there must be a significant difference between *The Lone Ranger* or *Superman* or *Sergeant Preston of the Yukon* on the one hand and, say, the comic book from which Dr. Wertham took that picture of a baseball game played with the disconnected of a human body. If *The Lone Ranger* and *Superman* are bad, they are bad in a different way and on a different level. They are crude, unimaginative, banal, vulgar, ultimately corrupting. They are also, as Dr. Wertham claims violent—but always within certain limits. Perhaps the worst thing they do is to meet the juvenile imagination on its crudest level and offer it an immediate and stereotyped satisfaction. That may be bad enough, but much the same things could be said of much of our radio and television entertainment and many of our mass-circulation magazines. The objection to the more unrestrained horror and crime comics must be a different one. It is even possible that these outrageous productions may be in one sense "better" than *The Lone Ranger* or *Sergeant Preston*, for in their absolute lack of restraint they tend to be somewhat livelier and more imaginative; certainly they are often less boring. But that does not make them any less objectionable as reading matter for children. Quite the contrary, in fact: *Superman* and *Donald Duck* and *The Lone Ranger* are stultifying; *Crime SuspenStories* and *The Vault of Horror* are stimulating.

A few years ago I heard Dr. Wertham debate with Al Capp on the radio. Mr. Capp at that time had introduced into *Li'l Abner* the story of the shmoos, agreeable little animals of 100 per cent utility who would fall down dead in an ecstasy of joy if one merely looked at them hungrily. All the parts of a shmoo's body, except the eyes, were edible, tasting variously like porterhouse steak, butter, turkey, probably even chocolate cake; and the eyes were useful as suspender buttons. Mr. Capp's fantasy was in this—as, I think, in most of his work—mechanical and rather tasteless.

---

2. I leave out of consideration a few comics like *Pogo Possum* and *Dennis the Menace* which I think could be called good without quotation marks, though it is possible Dr. Wertham might find grounds for objection to these also.

But Dr. Wertham was not content to say anything like that. For him, the story of the shmoos was an incitement to sadistic violence comparable to anything else he had discovered in his reading of comics. He was especially disturbed by the use of the shmoo's eyes as suspender buttons, something he took to be merely another repetition of that motif of injury to the eye which is exemplified in his present book by the picture of a woman about to be blinded with an ice-pick. In the violence of Dr. Wertham's discourse on this subject one got a glimpse of his limitations as an investigator of social phenomena.

For the fact is that Dr. Wertham's picture of society and human nature is one that a reader of comic book—at any rate, let us say, a reader of the "good" comic books—might not find entirely unfamiliar. Dr. Wertham's world, like the world of the comic books, is one where the logic of personal interest is inexorable, and *Seduction of the Innocent* is a kind of crime comic book for parents, as its lurid title alone would lead one to expect. There is the same simple conception of motives, the same sense of over-hanging doom, the same melodramatic emphasis on pathology, the same direct and immediate relation between cause and effect. If a juvenile criminal is found in possession of comic books, the comic books produced the crime. If a publisher of comic books, alarmed by attacks on the industry, retains a psychiatrist to advise him on suitable content for his publications, it follows *necessarily* that the arrangement is a dishonest one. If a psychiatrist accepts a fee of perhaps $150 a month for carrying out such an assignment (to judge by what Dr. Wertham himself tells us, the fees are not particularly high), that psychiatrist has been "bought"; it is of no consequence to point out how easily a psychiatrist can make $150. It is therefore all right to appeal to the authority of sociologist who has "analyzed" Superman "according to criteria worked out by the psychologist Gordon W. Allport" and has found him a "psychopathic deviate," but no authority can be attached to the "bought" psychiatrist who has been professionally engaged in the problem of comic books. If no comic-book publisher has been prosecuted under the laws against contributing to the delinquency of minors, it cannot be because those laws may not be applicable; it must be because "no district attorney, no judge, no complainant, has ever had the courage to make a complaint."

Dr. Wertham also exhibits a moral confusion which, even if it does not correspond exacdy to anything in the comic books, one can still hope will not gain a footing among children. Comic-book writers and artists working for the more irresponsible publishers have told Dr. Wertham of receiving instructions to put more violence, more blood, and more sex into their work, and of how reluctantly they have carried out these instructions. Dr. Wertham writes: "Crime-comic-book writers should not be blamed for comic books. They are not free men. They are told what to do and they do it or else. They often are, I have found, very critical of comics. . . . But of course . . . they have to be afraid of the ruthless economic power of the comic-book industry. In every letter I have received from a writer, stress is laid on requests to keep his identity secret." What can Dr. Wertham mean by that ominous "or else" which explains everything and pardons everything? Will the recalcitrant writer be dragged face down over a rocky road? Surely not. What Dr. Wertham means is simply that the man might lose his job and be forced to find less lucrative employment. This economic motive is a sufficient excuse for the man who thought up that gruesome baseball game—I suppose because he is a "worker." But it is no excuse for a psychiatrist who advises the publishers of *Superman* and sees to it that no dismembered bodies are played with in that comic book. And of course it is no excuse for a publisher—he is "the industry." This monolithic concept of "the industry" is what makes it pointless to discover whether there is any difference between one publisher and another; it was not men who produced that baseball game—it was "the industry." Would Dr. Wertham suggest to the children who come to his clinic that they cannot be held responsible for anything they do so long as they are doing it to make a living? I am sure he would not. But he does quote with the greatest respect the words of that intelligent fourteen-year-old who was able to see so clearly that if a psychiatrist receives a fee, one can obviously not expect that he will continue to act honestly. And it is not too hard to surmise where this young student of society got the idea.

Apparently also, when you are fighting a "ruthless industry" you are under no obligation to be invariably careful about what you say. Dr. Wertham very properly makes fun of the psychiatric defenders of comic books who consider it a sufficient justification of anything to say that it satisfies a "deep" need of a child. But on his side of the argument he is willing to put forward some equally questionable "deep" analysis of his own, most notably in his discussion of the supposedly equivocal relation between Batman and the young boy Robin; this particular analysis seems to me a piece of utter frivolity. He is also willing to create the impression that all comic books are on the level of the worst of them, and that psychiatrists have endorsed even such horrors as the piercing of woman's eyes and the whimsical dismemberment of bodies. (In fact, the function performed by the reputable psychiatrists who have acted as advisers to the publishers has been to suggest what kind of comic books would be "healthy" reading for children. One can disagree with their idea of what is "healthy," as Dr. Wertham does, or one can be troubled, as I am, at the addition of this new element of fabrication to cultural objects already so mechanical; but there is no justification for implying that these psychiatrists have been acting dishonestly or irresponsibly.)

None of this, however, can entirely destroy Dr. Wertham's case. It remains true that there is something questionable in the tendency of psychiatrists to place such stress on the supposed psychological needs of children as to encourage the spread of material which is at best subversive of the same children's literacy, sensitivity, and general cultivation. *Superman* and *The Three Musketeers* may serve the same psychological needs, but it still matters whether a child reads one or the other. We are left also with the underworld of publishing which produced that baseball game, which I don't suppose I shall easily forget, and with Mr. Gaines's notions of good taste, with the children who have hanged themselves, and with the advertisements for switch-blade knives, pellet guns, and breast developers which accompany the sadistic and erotic stimulations of the worst comic books.[3] We are left above all with the fact that for many thousands of children comic books, whether "bad" or "good," represent virtually their only contact with culture. There are children in the schools of our large cities who carry knives and sometimes guns. There are children who reach the last year of high school without ever reading a single book. Even leaving aside the increase in juvenile crime, there seem to be larger numbers of children than ever before who, without going over the line into criminality, live almost entirely in a juvenile underground largely out of touch with the demands of social responsibility, culture, and personal refinement, and who grow up into an unhappy isolation where they are sustained by little else but the routine of the working day, the unceasing clamor of television and the juke boxes, and still, in their adult years, the comic books. This is a very fundamental problem; to blame the comic books, as Dr. Wertham does, is simpleminded. But to say that the comics do not contribute to the situation would be like

---

3. An advertisement on the back cover of a recent issue of *Panic* and *Weird Science* strikes a loftier note:

BOYS, GIRLS, MEN, WOMEN!
The World is on FIRE
Serve the LORD
And You Can Have These PRIZES!

We will send you the wonderful prizes pictured on this page . . . all WITHOUT ONE PENNY OF COST. *Crime, sin, graft, wars are the greatest they have ever been. Our leaders say a reawakening of Christianity is needed to save us. You can do your share by spreading the gospel into every house in your community. Merely show your friends and neighbors inspiring, beautiful Religious Wall Motto plaques. Many buy six or more . . . only 35cents . . . sell on sight. . . . Serve the* LORD *and earn prizes you want.*

denying the importance of the children's classics and the great English and European novels in the development of an educated man.

The problem of regulation or even suppression of the comic books, however, is a great deal more difficult than Dr. Wertham imagines. If the publication of comic books were forbidden, surely something on an equally low level would appear to take their place. Children do need some "sinful" world of their own to which they can retreat from the demands of the adult world; as we sweep away one juvenile dung heap, they will move on to another. The point is to see that the dung heap does not swallow them up, and to hope it may be one that will bring forth blossoms. But our power is limited; it is the children who have the initiative: they will choose what they want. In any case, it is not likely that the level of literacy and culture would be significantly raised if the children simply turned their attention more exclusively to television and the love, crime, and movie magazines. Dr. Wertham, to be sure, seems quite ready to carry his fight into these areas as well; ultimately, one suspects, he would like to see our culture entirely hygienic. I cannot agree with this tendency. I myself would not like to live surrounded by the kind of culture Dr. Wertham could thoroughly approve of, and what I would not like for myself I would hardly desire for Paul. The children must take their chances like the rest of us. But when Dr. Wertham is dealing with the worst of the comic books he is on strong ground; some kind of regulation seems necessary—indeed, the more respectable publishers of comic books might reasonably welcome it—and I think one must accept Dr. Wertham's contention that no real problem of "freedom of expression" is involved, except that it may be difficult to frame a law that would not open the way to a wider censorship.

All this has taken me a long way from Paul, who doesn't carry a switch-blade knife and has so far been dissuaded even from subscribing to Charles Atlas's body-building course. Paul only clutches at his chest now and then, says something like "arrgh," and drops dead; and he no longer does that very often. Perhaps even Dr. Wertham would not be greatly alarmed about Paul. But I would not say that Paul is not involved in the problem at all. Even if he "needs" *Superman*, I would prefer that he didn't read it. And what he does read is not even *Superman*, which is too juvenile for him; be reads some of the liveliest, bloodiest, and worst material that the "ruthless" comic-book industry has to offer—he is an E.C. Fan-Addict.

I think my position is that I would be happy if Senator Kefauver and Dr. Wertham could find some way to make it impossible for Paul to get *any* comic books. But I'd rather Paul didn't get the idea that I had anything I to do with it.

Harold Rosenberg

"The Labyrinth of Saul Steinberg"

From *The Anxious Object: Art Today and Its Audience* (New York: Horizon Press, 1966), pp. 163–66; reprinted in 1990 by University of Chicago Press. © 1990 by the Estate of Harold Rosenberg, administered by the University of Chicago Press.

Steinberg's line is the line of a master penman and artist; it is also a "line"—that is, a kind of organized talk. The pen of this artist-monologist brings into being pictures that are also words, e.g. the odd *birds* at a cocktail party. Or they are visualizations of things said, as in the drawings in his book, *The Labyrinth*, where people utter flowers, strings of beads, heraldic decorations.

Both because of his superb penmanship and the complex intellectual nature of his assertions, I think of Steinberg as a kind of writer, though there is only one of his kind. He has worked out an exchange between the verbal and the visual that makes possible all kinds of revelations. For instance, there is a drawing in which a triangle on one end of a scale weighs down an old patched-up, decrepit question mark on the other. Axiom: A NEAT FORMULA OUTWEIGHS A BANGED-UP PROBLEM.

To build his labyrinth, Steinberg had only to draw a line from A to B on the principle that the truth is the longest distance between two points: the result is an enormous scrawl within which the original two dots appear as the eyes of the Minotaur.

As if the relations between words and objects were not complicated enough, Steinberg has thrust between them the illusions of the drawing paper. "There is perhaps no artist alive," testifies E.H. Gombrich in *Art And Illusion*, "who knows more about the philosophy of representation." A long straight line keeps changing its pictorial functions—first it represents a table edge, then a railroad trestle, then a laundry line, until it ends up in an abstract flourish. Steinberg is the Houdini, of multiple meanings: the line with which he creates his labyrinth and entangles himself in it is also the string that leads him out of it.

Logician of stereotypes and repetitive social situations, Steinberg brings to life dramas of abstract entities masquerading as people, animals, landscapes. All his formulas, comical mainly through their magical terseness, have deep contemporary reference. A sequence of drawings shows a serpentine line penetrating, or being swallowed by (Is it the same thing?), a cube and coming out on the other side organized into a geometrical pattern—a spoof about Cubism, yet also a reminder of the forced straightening out of our ideas (our "lines"). Steinberg's dialectic, however, also recognizes that we desire this straightening: on the facing page, a roughly sketched cube dreams of one drawn with a ruler and with its corners lettered in ABC order. Then comes a sketch in which an artist's line leaves the canvas and fills up the room around him—the labyrinth again; while on the following page, the line organizes itself into a road map of success labeled with the motto inside the crest of the Pall Mall cigarette package: *per aspera ad astra* . . . I know of no American novelist or poet today who is saying these things more astringently.

In Steinberg's conceptual reality, words have the substantiality of things. Elaborating on the speech balloons of the comic strips, the series of word-visualizations mentioned above shows ephemeral persons enunciating huge constructions, solid grills, architectural designs; a dog barks a zigzag; while on a mountain of gibberish he is in the process of emitting gesticulates an orator who is a scribble.

Counterpointing this theme of the materiality of speech is that of words behaving as "characters," as in the incomparable group where SICK lies flattened out on a cot, HELP topples off a cliff, TANTRUM explodes into a rocket display.

Irresistible as a juggling act, Steinberg never satisfied himself with the merely entertaining—the reason, I should say, why his vein has shown no sign of running out. His translations of words into pictures and pictures into writing continuously scoop meaning out of platitudinous situations and set phrases. This is a labor of philosophy. Specifically, Steinberg is a philosopher of identity, a subject he dreams about all day and reasons about in his dreams. His illusionist double language is, in the most complete sense, an autobiographical record, notations of a prolonged research into the artist's self within surroundings at times menacing and always full of strangeness. And Steinberg reveals that meditating on who one is cannot be carried on by mere remembering and analyzing but involves a game with devices of the imagination that are not unlike those let loose by mental disorder. Foremost among these risky toys indispensable to poetic investigation is the device of the projected self—the device of the mask, ancient device of comedy and tragedy and symptom of the split personality. On the jacket of *The Labyrinth* is a profile of the author as a square-jawed Solid Citizen whose head is a cage out of which a white rabbit peers fearfully through the eye socket. On the inside flap, Steinberg turns up in a full length photograph wearing a mask of Steinberg drawn on a paper bag. Behind the solid citizen, the rabbit, the caricature on the bag, is the unknown

Steinberg who watches the others—and who in the collaboration with them is the creator of his drawings. Steinberg's fictions make him visible to himself by exaggerating him: a living face can be deadpan, but not as dead a pan, nor capable of challenging the world with so fierce a stare, as the same face drawn on a bag.

Steinberg is present under disguise in most of his drawings; in all, if one accepts the view that everything Steinberg draws is Steinberg in contour (the exceptions are some beautiful pen-and-wash drawings done for their own sake as well as from a perverse desire to mislead). In the past, in addition to being the little man at cocktail parties and art galleries, Steinberg used to be a cat. Lately, he has become a fish. As a cat he was engaged in domesticating himself (an early book was called *The Passport*). As a fish he's out to catch himself (another meaning for the "line"). The axiom of one drawing might be: THE FISH IS A SPHINX TO THE CAT.

Steinberg lives in a world of Steinberg (e.g., drawing of the Trojan Steinberg into which all the little men climb), of quasi-Steinberg (e.g., this author, through the formula, a Stein is a Rose is a berg), of anti-Steinberg (scenes in Florida, Russia, the Far West). Anti-Steinberg is the mask of the unfamiliar, including the crowd and public applause: a harpy queen is determined to clamp laurels on the brow of a fleeing little man. Drawings of monuments and glories end with one of the hero with his foot on his own head. In another, the laurel-lavishing harpy repeats her bid to Steinberg-laureate standing on a base adorned with Steinberg *couchant*, the whole ensemble hanging over an abyss. Such is fame, declares the artist-student of self, listening for the crash.

Since his drawings are themselves "words," their meanings flowing, as in Baudelaire's *Correspondences*, from sense to sense and from thought into materiality, captions would be superfluous and Steinberg never supplies any. His images retain their silence, and this is a source of their pathos, even when the joke is strongest.

PART THREE

The Postwar Mavericks

As Irving Howe noted, by the 1960s the criticism of mass culture offered by the New York Intellectuals was itself being attacked as "heavy and humorless" by advocates of a new sensibility, most notably Susan Sontag. Howe quoted a younger writer, Seymour Krim, who objected to "the overcerebral, Europeanish, sterilely citified, pretentiously alienated" style of the New York writers. Yet, the seeds of this 1960s critique had already been planted by a motley crew of postwar maverick thinkers, who as a group were aware of the *Partisan Review* crowd but dissatisfied with their approach to cultural criticism.

We've labeled the writers in this section "post-war mavericks" in part because they don't share a common approach and argue about comics from a host of perspectives. McLuhan and Ong wrote as Catholics interested in the liturgical possibilities of popular culture. Phelps and Farber were visually-sensitive essayists, trying to cobble together a vocabulary to describe the new surfaces they saw on the movie screen and in the newspaper. Writing with prophetic rage, Gershon Legman was a cranky lay psychologist who wanted to overturn his culture's combination of violence-obsession and sexual repression. A castaway of the Trotskyist Left Opposition, C. L. R. James looked for glimmers of an emerging socialist culture in the everyday art of modern life. Unlike the New York intellectuals with whom he shared a common political past, James still had hope for a vibrant working class culture. Leslie Fiedler was a relentlessly iconoclastic myth critic who looked for larger mythic patterns that defined the American mind. Just as Fiedler set the stage for cultural studies, Umberto Eco was a pioneer of semiotics. Eco's cool, analytical approach nicely contrasts with Fiedler's snappy, agitated prose.

Despite these differences a few common themes can be seen in most of these essays: whereas the New York writers relied on categories of economic class, these writers are much more likely to speak in the language of psychology. Words like repression (with its Freudian overtones) and myth (legitimized by the 1950s craze for Jung) start becoming commonplace critical terms. (Aside from its Jungian coloration, the language of myth also drew on the works of Robert Graves and James George Fraser, both of whom had a postwar vogue). This psychological language bespeaks not only of a greater respect for therapeutic values, but also a cultural turn towards the internal and personal.

Gershon Legman emerges as a surprisingly central figure in this era. His *Love and Death: A Study in Censorship* (1949) not only anticipated Wertham's more famous critique, it was considerable agitated and influenced other critics on the subject. Marshall McLuhan wrote for Legman's journal *Neurotica* and admired Legman's ability to uncover the underside of mass culture. Legman read and adopted Ong's critique of superhero comics as a fascist genre. Fiedler and Farber both polemicized against Legman (as did Warshow in a review not reprinted here). Yet these critics were also shaped by Legman: Fiedler's *Love and Death in the American Novel* (1960) took not only its title but also some of its conceptual apparatus from Legman's *Love and Death*. Perhaps because his writing was frequently overblown and bombastic, Legman was often dismissed out of hand by critics. Certainly intellectual historians have yet to come to terms with his legacy. Fortunately Donald Phelps wrote a typically penetrating essay which nicely adjudicates between Legman and his many critics.

Among the postwar mavericks, Walter Ong and Marshall McLuhan stand out because of their religious interest. In 1938, while pursuing a master's degree in English at Saint Louis University as a budding Jesuit scholar, Ong met Marhall McLuhan, a young professor from Canada who had converted to Catholicism the previous year.

McLuhan would later become famous, of course, as a media guru—widely celebrated and reviled in the 1960s a prophet of the death of books and the rise of television. Yet this image of as a pop intellectual does a great disservice to McLuhan, a complex thinker who fruitfully linked the study of technology with the humanist concerns of literary criticism and broad spiritual questions.

In his early years as a teacher, long before his rise to fame, Mcluhan was supremely gifted as a mentor. He excited the imagination of bright young students like Ong by confidently linking together disparate phenomena, ranging from modernist art to neo-Thomist theology, into a single worldview. Around himself in these years McLuhan gathered a circle of fledgling scholars, largely but not exclusively Roman Catholics, who were eager to join in his quest to make sense of the modern techno-communication landscape (what we now, thanks in part to McLuhan, call "the media").

In their early work, the members of the McLuhan circle tended to be harshly critical of mass culture—hence Ong's attack on Mickey Mouse ("Mr. Disney's West-Coast rodent") and McLuhan's imputation of a totalitarian philosophy to Superman.

Yet very quickly, the members of the McLuhan circle began to become more appreciative of their subject, finding possibilities for creativity and even liturgical beauty in a mass culture aimed at a broad audience. A decade after lambasting Mickey Mouse Ong celebrated Walt Kelley's *Pogo*, noting that the linguistic playfulness of the strip represented a popularization of the high modernism of James Joyce and Gertrude Stein.

In their shifting attitudes towards popular culture, the McLuhan circle were harbingers of changes within Catholicism. The middle decades of the twentieth century were an exciting time to be a Catholic intellectual—Vatican II was gestating, but there was great uncertainty as to how the church should deal with the modern world. Thoughtful Catholics felt the competing tug of tradition and change.

In a larger sense, even outside the ranks of Catholic thinkers, the "postwar mavericks" of the 1950s were also trying to find a balance between tradition and change. They were deeply aware of the critique of mass culture that had been developed by their predecessors (indeed Legman would take that critique to a new level of intensity), but wanted to move beyond the ad-hoc approach of earlier writers. The best of the "post-war mavericks" were more systematic and deep-ranging than previous writers. Instead of looking at just individual comic strips, writers like Fiedler, Eco, and McLuhan tried to examine genres and think of the aesthetic of the medium as whole. By pushing the argument of comics to a new level of sophistication, the post-war mavericks set the state for the rise of cultural studies and the proliferation of comics scholarship we are now seeing.

Manny Farber

"Comic Strips"

From *The New Republic*, September 4, 1944, p. 279. Reprinted with permission.

Comic strips are not what they used to be. Those in the *New York Post*, which are the ones I read, are getting increasingly genteel, naturalistic and like the movies, moving away from the broad comedy of their beginnings and into the pulp field. The old style in comic strips was to trip everything—drawing, dialogue, place, action—for laughs. The new style is almost never concerned with being funny; rather it tries to be as much like a soap opera as possible. The stories are either very gentle affairs full of cliches, corn and cozy morals (Mary Worth says: "I always thought old age was a genial companion"), or they are full of adventures starring a child named Dickie Dare, a woman in a slinky evening gown which is being endlessly ripped off named Miss Fury—easily one of the most difficult comics to follow—and the man in the union suit named Superman, easily the least romantic figure of all time.

The technique and behavior in comic strips have been increasingly refined. Nowadays they show all kinds of people how to act, look, and what to expect from life, with a craftsmanship that is as flashy, high-powered and canny as the best advertising art in Vogue. Their drawing has become as realistic as it formerly was comically distorted and imaginative. A living example of this development goes on daily in the *Post* comic, *Debbie Dean*, which started looking as if its artist were drawing with wooden slats rather than pen and ink; since then everything in it has been dramatically and slowly turning more realistic and less wooden. The other comic which started recently in the *Post*, *The Goldbergs*, indicates how well meaning and well mannered they have become. In the early days of the comics, some national group was ragged by almost every cartoon in a crudely comic or merely vulgar way: the Swedes caught it daily in *Yens Yenson*, the French in *Alphonse and Gaston*, the Germans in the *Katzenjammers*, the Irish in three or four strips, and the Jews in *Abie the Agent*; in that strip, Abie Kabibble was ridiculed for his Jewishness in dialect, dress, profession, look and every action. *The Goldbergs*—taking up the old custom and particularly the Jews—is thoroughly civilized, dedicated to good works like encouraging nurseries, and is an awfully weak sort of pleasantness: the loss in

89

intent since *Abie* died and *The Goldbergs* was born has been far more than one of ridiculing nationalities.

The *Post* runs three daily comics, called *Nancy*, *The Bungle Family* and *Silly Milly*, and two ancients on Saturday, *The Captain and the Kids* and *Mutt and Jeff*, which seem to deserve the name of comic and are holding out against the movies. It is probable that *Nancy* is the best comic today, principally because it combines a very strong, independent imagination with a simplification of best tradition of comic drawing. *Nancy* is daily concerned with making a pictorial gag either about or on the affairs of a group bright, unsentimental children who have identical fire-plug shapes, two-foot heights, inch-long names (Sluggo, Winky, Tilly, Nancy) and genial self-powered temperaments. This comic has a remarkable, brave, vital energy that its artist, Ernie Bushmiller, gets partly from seeing landscape in large clear forms and then walking his kids, whom he sees in the same way, with great strength and well being, through them. Bushmiller's kids have wonderfully integrated personalities combining smart sociability with tough independence. They also have wonderful heads of hair—Sluggo hasn't any and calls his a "baldy bean," Nancy's is a round black cap with prickles, Tilly has an upsweep tied around the middle like a shock of wheat. *Nancy* is one of the few dominantly pantomimic strips left (*Cicero*, the baggy cat, being another).

Stan MacGovern's *Silly Milly* very insolently and precociously kids news items in three or four daily take-off, starring the heroine. Silly Milly is drawn in typical MacGovern style, as though by a wind current, and has a prehistoric animal for a hair-do, a very expressive, giant-sized eye, and a perfectly oval profile. It is one of those comics with animated decor, like *Smoky Stover*, with adjoining family portraits shaking hands, and one that tries for laughs in every part of the box. It has its pet vocabulary—all names are Frammis, laughter is Yuk Yuk, and the language of animals is Coo. It is the most sophisticated of comics, smart-alecky, corny, sloppy and half unlikable, but produces its eyedropper of humor each day without fail.

The Bungles is an ageless, peculiarly static, talkative comic in which the most mild-looking creatures carry on lives that are subtly rebellious and fantastic. Harry Tuthill confines their visual idiosyncracies almost totally to noses, so that the people seem to be suspended by their noses and look very proud-spirited on that account, and when they talk they inevitably join noses, and fight by grabbing noses. Tuthill has a talent for whimsy, being the inventor of The Dookus, Stilletta, Mrs. Dardanella, Uncle Willie the Honest Plumber, and of remarkable dialogue like Josie Bungle's comment when George rushes out, "What! Going out at midnight to that phony

Inspector's? How dippy." But *The Bungles* unfortunately share the chronic disease in modern comics of running a story for months and losing it in midpassage.

The major influence on the new strips seems to be the movies, and anything that influences movies. It probably started on the day someone discovered that a strip could be drawn as realistically as camera images; since then the comics have been picking the Hollywood process of everything but its talking machines. They are now as full of Hollywood's kind of sunshine as the old ones like *Krazy Kat* were full of sadism. Their heroes, in the manner of Humphrey Bogart and Gary Cooper, hardly draw a newspaper breath that they don't save someone good and destroy someone evil, while in the old days a hero like Krazy Kat or Jiggs was inevitably an anarchist and doomed to be laid out by a brickbat. The comics have also taken over the movie trick of sparking up a story with cheesecake and of touching superficially and pleasantly on enough different sides of existence to attract a variety of reader interest: for instance a typical day in the mewling *Abbie an' Slats* is devoted to one box of patriotism, one of cheesecake and one of plot, and cartoons like *Mary Worth's Family*, *Scorchy* and *Terry and the Pirates* add a cute, flashy dialogue for people who are attracted by such dialogue: "What's the score, brief me." Technically, the cartoons have taken over the close-up, the angle shot and dramatic lighting, and have learned the advantage of variegated views of a subject and scenes packed with décor, people and shadows to simulate liveliness.

Manny Farber

"Comic Strips"

The Nation, June 16, 1951; reprinted in Brushes With History: Writing on Art from The Nation: 1865–2001, (edited by Peter G. Meyer), page 233–35. Reprinted with permission.

Top comic-strip artists like Al Capp, Chet Gould, and Milt Caniff are the last in the great tradition of linear composers that started with Giotto and continued unbroken through Ingres. Until the Impressionists blurred the outlines of objects and diffused the near, middle, and far distance into a smog of light and dark, design had been realized in terms of outline and the weight of the enclosed shape. Today the only linear surgeons carrying on the practice—except for some rearguard opportunists like Shahn—are the pow-bam-sock cartoonists, whose masterful use of a dashing pen line goes virtually unnoticed in the art world. (Once in a lifetime a curator takes time off from Klee, Disney, and Dadaism to throw up a slipshod retrospective like the recent show "American Cartooning," at the Metropolitan.) The rococo, squiggling composition of the average comic strip is too intricate, difficult, and unorthodox for cultured eyes grown lazy on the flaccid drawing-with-color technique and the pillow-like form of modern painting.

The comic stripper—a funereal-faced craftsman who draws with his hat on and usually looks like an ex-saxophone-playing Republican—has good reason to wear a Ned Sparks expression. To start with, he has to meet over four hundred deadlines a year—one daily plus two on Sundays—while serving up his uniquely personal Karakters in a format squeezed to a fraction of its original size because his colleagues multiply like rabbits. He is bedeviled by aesthetic arid moral do-gooders for contributing to a "debauch in flamboyant color and violent drawing," for his "fishing about in the murky depths of mass reactions." His earliest slapstick creations were rebuked for glamourizing "the cheeky, disrespectful child"; then the girlie-girlie strips were hounded by cheesecake censors; some of the religious newspapers run his stuff but jerk out pipes, cigarettes, and clouds of smoke; the newer strong-arm brigade catches monthly blasts from psychiatrists like Wertham and psyched-up little magazines like

Neurotica. Worst of all, he is continually criticized for not being "funny" when from the beginning, from the first *Yellow Kid* strip in the 1890s, his humor has been of a jaundiced, whiplashing, Goyaesque type, too sour for articulate laughs.

The key to the success of cartoons is not the vulgar, violent subject matter but the dinky, cocky pen stroke, which unfortunately gets less virile every day. Gilbert Seldes' complaint about the weak conception and execution of the *Katzenjammers* was an apt damnation of Knerr's designs but completely unjust to the small, beautifully well-fed details: readers drool over Knerr's just-baked pies drawn rather sloppily but with bloated, seductive lines that stream taste and texture out of the page; his plump and sassy roadster tires, his stylish oval rumble seats have more aesthetic kick than the effects of his most industrious competitor—Peter Paul Rubens. Despite their latter day shortcomings, the strippers still have a full grasp of the objects in our world and throw them up with a quick spendthrift exhibitionism delightful to Americans who have been raised on the idea that drawing skill is hard won.

At that, the comic creators start with stolidly traditional tactics ("First learn how to draw—then go to a good art school and get a firm foundation in the arts"—Billy DeBeck, Barney Google's accoucheur.) Bisect almost any box from *L'il Abner* with two diagonals and you will find the lines crossing all important details: bosoms, hag's face, fleeing bachelors, six-shooter barrel peeled back like a banana. Capp, a veteran of four art schools, also spots his ducks in a circular path with a firm anchorage in one corner or another—a typical student maneuver. Another old-master orthodoxy is his serpentine pattern of figures across the page, each slob aimed this way or that so as to contrast and link with his neighbor. Yet every panel is distorted into life because Capp plays enough rage and gloom into each Dogpatch person and thing to bury his conventional moves under a forest of weird lettering and decisively stylized curiosities.

Unfortunately, Capp and his contemporaries have softened cartoonism by overdrawing figure and overworking the intellectual-literary vein. The old standbys were arrogant show-offs who confounded their fans with ambiguously brilliant-bitter touches. George McManus stuck a hideously aggressive face on Maggie and then gave her a beautiful body and legs; this insidious combination was drawn with the clean sharp elegance of a Botticelli nude. Another unforgettable resolution of contradictions was DeBeck's sagging, ponderous Spark Plug, who always found graceful fluid motion in the home stretch.

There have been three major "periods" in American cartooning, and each step has been a change for the worse. The founding fathers—Swinnerton, Outcault,

Dirks—were strictly caricaturists, hardly bothering about backgrounds: their stock in trade was exposing the smashable character of ordinary people with a style based on doodles. When adults started reading the funnies, style changed to suit their timid suburban outlook. Domesticity and illustration crept in for the benefit of the henpecked and the lovelorn; rooms were drawn in perspective, lamps were with a ruler, potbellies shrank, and everything suggested a solid hunk of marital doom. The most dispiriting change was ushered in by *Tarzan* in 1929. With this, funnies turned into pseudo-movies—taking over close-ups, tricky lighting, and the rest. There have been some miraculous cinematic inkers like Caniff (*Terry, Canyon*), who draws incredibly sharp and delicate faces with a crowquill pen and exciting clothing with a shadownicking brush; yet even Caniff fondles his troubled adventurers like a cosmetic man making up a glamour girl.

Good or bad, uphill or down, comic strips are read by sixty or seventy million daily devotees. They satisfy a demand for inventiveness, energetic drawing, and a roughneck enthusiasm for life that other plastic arts cannot meet.

Walter J. Ong

"Mickey Mouse and Americanism"

America, October 4, 1941, pp. 719–20. Reprinted by permission.

It is no easy task to find any common denominator in the various mixtures of ideologies existing in the minds of American men and women. But from our Victorian ancestors we nearly all seem to have inherited one first principle in common—an abiding faith in youth when it is accompanied by vigorous animal activity and a healthy grin. For confirmation of this fact, we need only look at the puppies and children in the advertisements.

Hence it is ticklish business to undertake a critique of Mickey Mouse. For if all normal human beings are supposed to like young creatures engaged in physical activity and grinning, they do not all put the same value on this sort of thing. But suppose we examine what Mickey Mouse is, not in himself, but in his relation to our national culture, and see if, thereby, we can arrive at something that is very difficult to attain to—an evaluation of our own culture. Today, when whole civilizations are being revised, peaceably as well as forcibly, close inspection of all aspects of our national life is of pressing importance.

This is especially true of those aspects which we have taken for granted. Thus, if a product of an age is entirely free from criticism, it is something of great interest. Its immunity from critical examination is the guarantee that such a product has risen out of those principles which are considered so basic as never to be questioned. If we can, then, bring our critical attention to focus upon such an adventitious being universally taken for granted, we will be in a position to see our age somewhat in the way it will appear to succeeding generations.

Now, Mickey Mouse is singularly free from criticism. He is taken for granted because if he does not represent the entire scheme of values that Americans live by, at least his scheme of values is fitted into theirs without demanding for itself any readjustment in the process. The artists who have brought Mickey into being have always worked with some of their fingers on the pulse of the American public. And, since Hollywood, at least in this one instance, is functioning frankly and freely to produce movies and not canned stage plays, little has stood in the way of their realizing the artistic effects desired. The result is the creation of a world which offends almost no one and meets with uncritical and enthusiastic acclaim.

There can be no doubt that the quality and extent of Mickey's popularity has some kind of deep significance. There is, of course, nothing wrong with liking juvenile activity and juvenile grinning, but there is something distinctive about an age which makes a fetish of this sort of thing.

Mickey's popularity is a popularity that has come with the living of a mechanically busy life in an intellectual and moral vacuum. In most of the "stories" we watch Mickey's quaint smile and queer poses. We watch the characters making faces or pirouetting at the vortices of multi-colored whirlwinds or rocketing along with blasts of vapor in their wakes. We watch Pluto's flexible muzzle as it crawls across the screen. And that is all.

Though Mickey's animal ancestry is very old, none of his animal forebears were quite like Mickey. Animal stories reach far back toward the beginnings of the human race, and yet the Mickey Mouse stories differ vastly from all the traditional varieties. As for the earliest animal stories with which everyone is familiar, a very brief recollection of Aesop will make it plain that Mickey has swung wide of this tradition.

It is true that Aesop's characters are more conscious of being animals than Disney's figures are: Mickey does not diet on cheese, nor even refer to himself as a mouse, nor to Dippy as a dog, and actually keeps a real dog named Pluto. But differences of this sort are found even among the traditional animal stories and are not to be much made much of. The more important difference lies in the depths of being to which the roots of the stories strike. Aesop's stories all have deep moral connections. The morals themselves may be simple and easily gathered. But they are serious, and the story, entertaining as it may be, is inextricably involved with the ordinary moral issues which confront human beings.

This connection between beast fable and the serious things of existence is the usual thing. It is found in the Sanscrit *Panchatantra*, in the medieval beast fables and epics such as Reynard the Fox, and down to La Fontaine, and Hans Christian Andersen's *Ugly Duckling*.

Yet these stories, like the Disney stories, are entertaining. It has not always been necessary to sidestep every serious issue in order to amuse. Perhaps a more entertaining animal story will never be told than the popular medieval account of the fox who fell into the well and talked his old enemy, the wolf, into riding the other windlass bucket down into the depths (where he had given the wolf to understand a veritable paradise was to be found), thus enabling himself to ride back up in the other bucket. But for all its sheerly amusing qualities, the tale quite obviously involves itself in the question of flattery and of the man who lives off society by his wits.

Similarly, opening my Chaucer at *The Nun's Priest's Tale*, I find some pretty serious connections established. On the first page that strikes my eye, the name of God appears seven times in the very speeches of Chaunticleer the Cock and his wife, Dame Pertelote. On the next page comes Chaunticleer's prayer, which begins:

O blissful God, that art so just and trewe,
Lo, how that thou bewrayest mordre alway!

Now I wish to avoid the religious suicide which identifies all that was medieval with all that is Catholic. The medieval authors, like their contemporaries in other fields than literature, had their faults in plenty, and they often lapsed into or failed to emerge from paganism. But even then they were religious, and in the height of their fun and merrymaking, as in everything else, they were incapable of the studied secularism which Mr. Disney's characters, in accord with our public school tradition, so carefully affect. The references to God in *The Nun's Priest's Tale* do not occur simply because a cleric tells the story.

An artificial secularism puts Mickey Mouse outside this tradition, delimiting the field in which he operates and effectively blocking off connections with basic and serious truths which have characterized his animal forerunners. Thus, the Disney picture-stories whether movies or newspaper strips, gravitate toward the shallowly spectacular. Mickey in his own way is merely following out the segregative processes of a secularism which has eaten the marrow out of our national culture by isolating religious and moral considerations from everything except the most private departments of each individual's life. And our being so taken with Mickey's vacuous existence is a tacit acknowledgment of our own weakness.

It is entirely true that we can find in other ages certain forms of art with which Mickey Mouse has as close affinities as he has with the animal stories. There is the dumb show, the Punch-and-Judy show, or the jig, in all of which antics might be antics and nothing more. But apart from the fact that in these forms of entertainment there is not quite the studied isolation from all serious meaning that we find in Mickey, no age has opened its arms to such things in the way we have to Mr. Disney's world. Further, although every age has its slapstick and a certain measure of entertainment built around mere moving and smiling, in no other age have these phenomena achieved the complete divorce from everything of importance that we find in Mickey Mouse. And in no other age have the individual and national ideals of a people found such satisfactory expression on this level. Certainly no other age has a similar figure been apotheosized and reproduced in so many forms of idols as Mr. Disney's West-Coast rodent has today.

Not only is Mickey one of the best known and most loved fictional creations of our age, but it is become prudish and snobbish to question his place it in the world. To love a character of another type may indeed be conceded to an individual as a kind of personal crotchet. But one who is incapable of the usual to-do over Mickey Mouse is hardly recognizable as a normal "red-blooded" American. For Mickey Mouse has succeeded in living the good life, as this life is taught by the school of Mr. Dewey and by the loudest advocates of a devitalized Americanism— the life which involves a maximum of fuss and activity with the blinking at all truly fundamental questions.

As an instance of how far matters have gone, we are now given the information by the press that the Disney studios have recently received a new assignment— this time from Uncle Sam. It has been decided that the insignia for our men in the service should be designed in the true Mickey Mouse tradition. Photographs of the designs recently published disclose a Laughing Jackass, Butch the Falcon, Dusty (a cuddlesome winged calf sprawled on a cloud and wearing an airman's helmet and a moonish smile), and a genuine Disney eagle with boxing gloves which evidently supersedes the traditional American eagle that appears rather diffidently in the background of the design.

Here, it seems, we have a kind of plenary treatment of Mickey Mousism. When a nation prepares for war, it is in a serious mood. Even in peace time its emblems and insignia, such as the flag or the American eagle, give expression to the highest national aspirations, and in a time that threatens war we may reasonably assume that there is an all-out on inspirational devices. Presumably at such a time the most inspirational must be seized upon. And thus is betrayed where Mickey's scheme of values fits into our national life. For, although all these new insignia are not recognizable Mickey Mouses, they are most unmistakably in the Mickey Mouse tradition and stand for what it stands for and for no more.

But are not these insignia performing merely the function of mascots? Yes. And a mascot is the proper attribute of an athletic team. Of course, a mascot may serve a function even in an army—a recreational function. Recreation and a spirit of jovial comaraderie are certainly in order. But it is not in order to substitute a mascot appeal for a serious appeal.

Mickey Mouse motivation is sure to crumple before one of the serious major ideologies. It is late now to start to rehabilitate the deliberately secularized and emasculated set of values which we have allowed to spring up and flourish in our nation and especially in our public schools. But we had better begin. We cannot erect a defense of democracy on a set of national ideals where the things for which Mickey Mouse stands find place so near the top.

Walter J. Ong

"Bogey Sticks for Pogo Men"

America, January 11, 1951, pp. 434–35. Reprinted by permission.

Those who have set their faces against what they like to style "modern" art and literature are given something to think about in a current comic strip. For, strangely enough, a pa'cel of characters fished out of a swamp in the Deep South have been making fame for themselves and money for their creator by exploiting, at the most popular of popular levels, a linguistic which we had been assured was a private horror dripped from the brains of the most decadent of *avant-garde* intellectuals—meaning people like James Joyce, Gertrude Stein, or E. E. Cummings—and quite unthinkable to any save persons such as these.

But here we are: "Oh, pick a pock of peach pits, pockets full of pie, foreign twenty blackboards baked until they cry." The lines might well have been lifted from Joyce. As a matter of fact, they are a little song from the comic strip in question, *Pogo*, whose characters not only sing like this but talk like this frequently and with abandon. And everybody loves it. The strip is in seventh place among all comic strips in the United States today.

When we are told that *avant-garde* experimentation is inhuman and unreal and totally unrelated to the levels of popular awareness or the "real" issues of life, there are other things besides *Pogo*'s linguistic which come to mind. There is the stylization in posters and even in store-window displays so thoroughly reminiscent of the cubism which many decades ago was supposed to be an effete phenomenon illustrating the complete divorce between the "modern" artistic sensibility and the man in the street. Or there are the faces, half front and half side, which since Virgil Partch have become a commonplace in humorous cartoons, but which exploit the same sort of multi-angle viewing and stylization found in the Picasso of thirty or forty years ago. Or there are the montage and collage effects associated with the period of dadaism or with even earlier periods but nowadays repeated week after week on the thoroughly effective covers of *Time* magazine. *Time*'s bourgeois readers love them and write letters to the editor telling him how fine they are, although it is hard to imagine their grandparents sixty years ago, or even Mr. Lewis's Babbitt, doing the same thing about art such as this.

It seems that the "effeteness" which the man in the street opposes is really something like upsetting strangeness, and that the man in the street is quite willing to accept anything, provided that it has been on the market long enough for his responses to be grooved to its measure. Perhaps the "effete" or "decadent" *avant-garde* is really not so dissociated from the sensibility of the man in the street as some persons have pretended. It may be that it is often genuinely *avant-garde*—representing (with understandable inaccuracy and exaggeration) the sensibilities everybody is on the way to developing, only well ahead of the mass of people.

This is not to say, of course, that Pogo and his pals are exactly the same as the characters in *Four Saints in Three Acts*. They are not. But there are definite affinities. Moreover, Pogo and his friends provide a commentary on Miss Stein's work as much as it provides a commentary on them. Notably, Pogo specializes in infantile effects—it is in a way the most infantile of comic strips if we by-pass the infantilism of toughness in such a strip as *Dick Tracy* or the infantilism of made-to-order sophistication in something like *Terry and the Pirates*. In *Pogo* a high percentage of the chuckles are the kind you get from the helpless linguistic errors of a child, who, however unfortunate, could never blunder so frequently and accurately and delightfully as Pogo and his friends, "nature's screetures."

The strip capitalizes not on real baby talk but on the part of baby talk which attracts particular adult attention, subsisting in the kind of world parents like to create around their children (not the kind children really experience). The characters are named like toys: Pogo himself, who is a winsome little possum, or Porky Pine. Or for names they are given mispronunciations of semi-sophisticated terms sure to be distorted if a child should use them, e.g. Churchy LaFemme. The characters, moreover, one and all, are made to seem diminutive, toy-like. As in a world of toys, insects here become more or less commensurate with alligators and get a respectful hearing from them. This is the habitat in which emerges something like automatic writing for the common man.

The fact that the disintegrated and reassembled language which linguistic experimentalists have been tinkering with emerges at the popular level within an adult's vision of a child's universe is perhaps of some importance in assessing its significance. So, too, is the fact that the world which the experimenters take in a variety of attitudes, including that of dead seriousness, enters the popular consciousness only in terms of gentle Southern sentimentality and laughter. One recalls the Victorian sentimentality of Lewis Carroll's and Edward Lear's nonsense verse. Facts such as these are certainly of more importance than observations which brush aside the later experimenters with the observation that they are all effete.

And such facts do not lend countenance to this observation. Indeed, they upset the obscurantist applecart completely. For back of the hostility which, in many semi-educated circles, still cripples an intelligent approach to the problems of the modern artist, lies the supposition (in part an heritage from Rousseau, who may be followed in fact where he is disowned in principle) that the common man is always right in his attitudes and instincts and that it is high time effete "modern" artists or writers returned to him and his point of view, whatever that is. But here there seem to be signs that the common man, in his own instinctive way, has perhaps vague symptoms of the disease supposed to be the prerogative of the decadent intellectual. Popular art—and, if there was ever popular art, it is the comic ships—is like the thing most opposed to it. What do you do then?

Two things at least can be recognized. First, the mere fact that the common man likes a thing carries no assurance that his reasons for liking it are simple and easy to account for, and thus that they afford an easily managed touchstone for assaying pure artistic or literary metal. The reasons of the common man are hard to catch sight of, for they retreat deep into the difficult territory of cultural heritage and learned attitudes. Secondly, a tendency to damn indiscriminately an assortment of things vaguely apprehended as "modern" art or literature in favor of the "common man's" likes or dislikes, with the implication that these mustn't be inspected too closely either, may well indicate that we are quite unprepared to account for any art or literature, popular or private, ancient or new—that we are happy only with a high degree of unawareness, that we don't want to face honestly the implications of any art or literature until these cam be blurred into the background of our emotional life by at least several decades of time.

From this state of mind, *avant-garde* productions may conceivably waken us to something in ourselves that is worth while and usable in terms of what we really are now. This is not to recommend the indiscriminate use of dangerous material, for some *avant-garde* work, like a tremendous amount of the Latin and Greek classics and much medieval literature, is dangerous material. Nor is it to intimate that all *avant-garde* work is worth while. But it is to recommend an attitude, happily growing but needing encouragement, which will help us, Catholics, too—indeed, Catholics especially—to know what it is that today we live by. There is no virtue in accumulating a collection of bogey men. Let those who do so be beaten with Pogo sticks.

Marshall McLuhan

From *The Mechanical Bride: Folklore of Industrial Man*

(New York: The Vanguard Press, 1951): Orphan Annie," pp. 64–66 and "Superman," pp. 102–3. *The Mechanical Bride: Folklore of Industrial Man*, by Marshall McLuhan, is published by Gingko Press. Copyright © The Estate of Herbert Marshall McLuhan. Used by permission.

Orphan Annie

Harold Gray's strip finds a natural setting and sponsor in the Patterson-McCormick enterprise. From this strip alone it is possible to document the central thesis of Margaret Mead's excellent book, *And Keep Your Powder Dry*. As an anthropologist, Margaret Mead works on the postulate of the organic unity or "cultural regularity" of societies. Her own example of this postulate is that of the sudden fame of a movie star which must be explained to the public as the result not of luck but of know-how. Before being successful, the star had to have her teeth capped, her nose rebuilt, her dresses designed to hide a big tummy, and special music written to distract attention from her clumsy, shambling walk. Her publicity must suggest that any well-fed youngster would have *deserved* the same success.

Working on this postulate of "cultural regularity," the very strangeness of this version of the Cinderella story suggests to the anthropologist that the pressures behind the movie-star publicity are the same as those producing the normal patterns of the same society. And so Margaret Mead concludes that it is our Puritan view that work must be rewarded and that failure is the mark of moral deficiency which is behind the need to make luck appear to be the reward of virtue. For this Puritan view of work versus luck is socially constitutive. It confers cultural regularity. Seeming exceptions will therefore prove to be variations on this theme rather than contradictions of it.

Obviously speaking from her teaching experience, Dr. Mead says: "American girls of college age can be thrown into a near panic by the description of cultures in which parents do not love their children." In our Puritan culture, she insists, where even parental love is unconsciously awarded to the child who is meritorious in eating, in toilet habits, in dress, and in school grades, the majority of children feel insecure because they know they do not merit this parental love. So they fall back on the *instinct* of maternal love, which they feel will insure some small increment of affection even to their unworthiness. When they hear an anthropologist undermine this residual conviction, they become very upset. For, as a famous American educator has remarked, "No one can love unconditionally a child with an I.Q. over ninety." The moron may gather in a bit of unearned love, but not the normal child. The ordinary child must be on its toes, brimful of "promise" and precocity in order to assure himself of human affection.

In addition to an anxiety engendered by a parental love awarded on a basis of competitive merit, Dr. Mead points out, the American child is typically limited to the affection of two parents. The very housing conditions nowadays forbid the regular presence of numerous relatives and the generalized presence of the whole community in the form of adopted "uncles" and "aunts":

> *So the young American starts life with a tremendous impetus towards success. His family, his little slender family, just a couple of parents alone in the world, are the narrow platform on which he stands.*

The plot begins to get exciting at this point in the success story, according to Dr. Mead. For success consists not only in winning the approval of parents but in surpassing them. On that premise rests the American way of life, she says. We must, in the most signal way, show our superiority to our parents in every department, or we have failed to give meaning to their efforts and to our own selves.

In a social and economic sense, success, it would appear, means the virtual rejection of the parents, so that in a symbolic way the child bitten with the success spirit is already an orphan. A Lincoln could stimulate himself with the belief that he was the illegitimate child of an aristocrat, but the child of today, says Dr. Mead, nurses the feeling of being only "adopted."

At this level Tom Sawyer and Huck Finn have a basic position among our folk myths. They are contrasted symbols that focus complex feelings and ideas. Huck is the shiftless, unambitious son of a disreputable father. Impossible for him to earn marks for progressive behavior. He cannot sink, he cannot rise. He simply exists, however gloriously, a horror to the parents but the envy of the boys: snoozing in an old hogshead; publicly and openly smoking his corn-cob pipe; indifferent to truant officers; hunting, fishing, drifting on a raft. But Tom is a craft on other lines. He is marked out for success. And *he has no parents*. He is the *adopted* child of his Aunt

Sally. That means he recognizes that he must make his way by his own wits and energy in an unfriendly world.

And such is the position of Orphan Annie today, in a strip and in a press dedicated to individual enterprise and success. Annie finds affection and security mainly in her dog Sandy, as she circumvents and triumphs over weasel-like crooks and chiselers. Always on the move, brimful of Eden-innocence and goodness, she embodies that self-image of a knight in shining armor nursed in the bosom of every tycoon as the picture of his true self. Girded only with her own goodness, but menaced on every hand by human malice and stupidity, she wins through by shrewdness, luck, and elusiveness.

Apart from Daddy Warbucks (a war profiteer of transcendant virtue), her allies are the little people, who, like Annie, have to contend with the frustrations brought about by bureaucratic bungling and interference. In a recent episode she discovered a fortune of many millions in an old cave, and at once formed a scheme to found orphanages and hospitals. But Washington locked up the cave pending the imposition of taxes, and then, in a forceful move to get at the treasure, blew up the mountain. Result, no orphanages or hospitals.

Daddy Warblucks, the benevolent war profiteer, is less a piece of folklore than of special pleading. His operations are on a world scale, and he maintains private "police" and an information bureau in every country in the world. His great enemy is "the Count," type and pattern of European ruthlessness and corruption. All of which is obvious enough as Republican journalism. But not so Orphan Annie herself. In her isolation and feminine "helplessness" Harold Gray has portrayed for millions of readers the central success drama of America—that of the young, committed to the rejection of parents, that they may justify both the parents and themselves.

Curiously, it is not a theme that "serious" writers have chosen to exploit since Mark Twain. We have here just one instance of popular entertainment keeping in play a major psychological tension in America to which the sophisticated writers are often blind.

Superman

Superman was dreamed up by two high school boys in about 1935. That in itself is indicative of the "science fiction" mentality to which the strip appeals. But this strip works at two levels. It provides fantasies of the usual *Super Science Stories* variety, in which the reader plays hopscotch and leapfrog with the centuries and with solar systems alike, in such stories as "The Voyage that Lasted 600 Years." But *Superman* is not only a narrative of the conquests, actual or imagined, of a technological age; it is also a drama of the psychological defeat of technological man. In ordinary life Superman is Clark Kent, a nobody. As a third-rate reporter whose incompetence wins him the pity and contempt of the virile Lois Lane, his hidden superself is an adolescent dream of imaginary triumphs. While Clark Kent can't win even the admiration of Lois Lane, Superman is besieged by clamorous viragos. Superman accepts a self-imposed celibacy with the resignation of a stamping forge, while Kent is merely resigned.

It was this character and situation which Danny Kaye portrayed in the movie version of *The Secret Life of Walter Mitty*. The Thurber fans protested that the movie was a travesty of Thurber's original Walter Mitty. And it is true that Thurber denies any fantasy triumphs to his character. Thurber prefers to keep Mitty in a state of bitter humiliation, permitting him an occasional frantic revenge.

The attitudes of Superman to current social problems likewise reflect the strong-arm totalitarian methods of the immature and barbaric mind. Like Daddy Warbucks in *Orphan Annie*, Superman is ruthlessly efficient in carrying on a one-man crusade against crooks and anti-social forces. In neither case is there any appeal to process of law. Justice is represented as an affair of personal strength alone. Any appraisal of the political tendencies of *Superman* (and also its many relatives in the comic-book world of violent adventure known as the "Squinky" division of entertainment) would have to include an admission that today the dreams of youths and adults alike seem to embody a mounting impatience with the laborious processes of civilized life and a restless eagerness to embrace violent solutions. For the reading public of this type of entertainment cuts across all boundaries of age and experience quite as much as the pressures of the technological world are felt alike by child and adult, by sad sack and sage. Unconsciously, it must be assumed, the anonymous oppression by our impersonal and mechanized ways has piled up a bitterness that seeks fantasy outlets in the flood of fictional violence which is now being gulped in such a variety of forms.

Some readers may be interested in the way in which Superman corresponds to the medieval speculations about the nature of angels. The economist Werner Sombart argued that modern abstract finance and mathematical science was a realization at the material level of the elaborate speculations of medieval philosophy. In the same way it could be argued that Superman is the comic-strip brother of the medieval angels. For the angels, as explained by Thomas Aquinas, are quite superior to time or space, yet can exert a local and material energy of superhuman kind. Like Superman, they require neither education nor experience, but they possess, without effort, flawless intelligence about all things. Men have dreamed of becoming like these beings for quite a while. However, fallen angels are known as devils. And imperfect men, possessing superhuman material power, are not a reassuring prospect.

Marshall McLuhan

"Comics: *Mad* Vestibule to TV"

From *Understanding Media* (New York: McGraw-Hill, 1964), pp. 164–69. *Understanding Media*, by Marshall McLuhan, is published by Gingko Press. Copyright © The Estate of Herbert Marshall McLuhan. Used by permission.

It was thanks to the print that Dickens became a comic writer. He began as a provider of copy for a popular cartoonist. To consider the comics here, after "The Print," is to fix attention upon the persistent print-like, and even crude woodcut, characteristics of our twentieth-century comics. It is by no means easy to perceive how the same qualities of print and woodcut could reappear in the mosaic mesh of the TV image. TV is so difficult a subject for literary people that it has to be approached obliquely. From the three million dots per second on TV, the viewer is able to accept, in an iconic grasp, only a few dozen, seventy or so, from which to shape an image. The image thus made is as crude as that of the comics. It is for this reason that the print and the comics provide a useful approach to understanding the TV image, for they offer very little visual information or connected detail. Painters and sculptors however, can easily understand TV, because they sense how very much tactile involvement is needed for the appreciation of plastic art.

The structural qualities of the print and woodcut obtain, also, in the cartoon, all of which share a participational and do-it-yourself character that pervades a wide variety of media experiences today. The print is clue to the comic cartoon, just as the cartoon is clue to understanding the TV image.

Many a wrinkled teenager recalls his fascination with that pride of the comics, the *Yellow Kid* of Richard F. Outcault. On first appearance, it was called *Hogan's Alley* in the *New York Sunday World*. It featured a variety of scenes of kids from the tenements, Maggie and Jiggs as children, as it were. This feature sold many papers in 1898 and thereafter. Hearst soon bought it, and began large-scale comic supplements. Comics (as already explained in the chapter on The Print), being low in definition, are a highly participational form of expression, perfectly adapted to the mosaic form of the newspaper. They provide, also, a sense of continuity from one day to the next. The individual news item is very low in information and requires completion or fill-in by the reader, exactly as does the TV image, or the wirephoto. That is the reason why TV hit the comic-book world so hard. It was a real rival, rather than a complement. But TV hit the pictorial ad world even harder, dislodging the sharp and glossy, in favor of the shaggy, the sculptural, and the tactual. Hence the sudden eminence of *Mad* magazine which offers, merely, a ludicrous and cool replay of the forms of the hot media of photo, radio, and film. *Mad* is the old print and woodcut image that recurs in various media today. Its type of configuration will come to shape all of the acceptable TV offerings.

The biggest casualty of the TV impact was Al Capp's *Li'l Abner*. For eighteen years Al Capp had kept Li'l Abner on the verge of matrimony. The sophisticated formula used with his characters was the reverse of that employed by the French novelist Stendhal, who said, "I simply involve my people in the consequences of their own stupidity and then give them brains so they can suffer." Al Capp, in effect, said, "I simply involve my people in the consequences of their own stupidity and then *take away* their brains so that they can do nothing about it." Their inability to help themselves created a sort of parody of all the other suspense comics. Al Capp pushed suspense into absurdity. But readers have long enjoyed the fact that the Dogpatch predicament of helpless ineptitude was a paradigm of the human situation, in general.

With the arrival of TV and its iconic mosaic image, the everyday life situations began to seem very square indeed. Al Capp suddenly found that his kind of distortion no longer worked. He felt that Americans had lost their power to laugh at themselves. He was wrong. TV simply involved everybody in everybody more deeply than before. This cool medium, with its mandate of participation in depth, required Capp to refocus the Li'l Abner image. His confusion and dismay were a perfect match for the feelings of those in every major American enterprise. From *Life* to General Motors, and from the classroom to the Executive Suite, a refocusing of aims and images to permit ever more audience involvement and participation has been inevitable. Capp said: "But now America has changed. The humorist feels the change more, perhaps, than anyone. Now there are things about America we can't kid."

Depth involvement encourages everyone to take himself much more seriously than before. As TV cooled off the American audience, giving it new preferences and new orientation of sight and sound and touch and taste, Al Capp's wonderful brew also had to be toned down. There was no more need to kid Dick Tracy or the suspense routines. As *Mad* magazine discovered, the new audience found the scenes and themes of ordinary life as funny as anything in remote Dogpatch. *Mad* magazine simply transferred the world of ads into the world of the comic book, and it did this just when the TV image was beginning to eliminate the comic book by direct rivalry. At the same time, the TV image rendered the sharp and clear photographic images blur and blear. TV cooled off the ad audience until the continuing vehemence of the ads and entertainment suited the program of the *Mad* magazine world very well. TV, in fact, turned the previous hot media of photo, film, and radio into a comic-strip world by simply featuring them as overheated packages. Today the ten-year-old clutches his or her *Mad* ("Build up your Ego with *Mad*") in the same way that the Russian beatnik treasures an old Presley tape obtained from a G.I. broadcast. If the "Voice of America" suddenly switched to jazz, the Kremlin would have reason to crumble. It would be almost as effective as if the Russian citizens had copies of Sears Roebuck catalogues to goggle at, instead of our dreary propaganda for the American way of life.

Picasso has long been a fan of American comics. The high-brow, from Joyce to Picasso, has long been devoted to American popular art because he finds in it an authentic imaginative reaction to official action. Genteel art, on the other hand, tends merely to evade and disapprove of the blatant modes of action in a powerful high definition, or "square," society. Genteel art is a kind of repeat of the specialized acrobatic feats of an industrialized world. Popular art is the clown reminding us of all the life and faculty that we have omitted from our daily routines. He ventures to perform the specialized routines of the society, acting as integral man. But integral man is quite inept in a specialist situation. This, at least, is one way to get at the art of the comics, and the art of the clown.

Today our ten-year-olds, in voting for *Mad*, are telling us in their own way that the TV image has ended the consumer phase of American culture. They are now telling us what the eighteen-year-old beatniks were first trying to say ten years ago. The pictorial consumer age is dead. The iconic age is upon us. We now toss to the Europeans the package that concerned us from 1922 to 1952. They, in turn, enter their first consumer age of standardized goods. We move into our first depth-age of art-and-producer orientation. America is Europeanizing on as extensive a pattern as Europe is Americanizing.

Where does this leave the older popular comics? What about *Blondie* and *Bringing Up Father?* Theirs was a pastoral world of primal innocence from which young America has clearly graduated. There was still adolescence in those days, and there were still remote ideals and private dreams, and visualizable goals, rather than vigorous and ever-present corporate postures for group participation.

The chapter on The Print indicated how the cartoon is a do-it-yourself form of experience that has developed an ever more vigorous life as the electric age advanced. Thus, all electric appliances far from being labor-saving devices, are new forms of work, decentralized and made available to everybody. Such is, also, the world of the telephone and the TV image that demands so much more of its users than does radio or movie. As a simple consequence of this participational and do-it-yourself aspect of the electric technology, every kind of entertainment in the TV age favors the same kind of personal involvement. Hence the paradox that, in the TV age, Johnny can't read because reading, as customarily taught, is too superficial and consumerlike an activity. Therefore the highbrow paperback because of its depth character, may appeal to youngsters who spurn ordinary narrative offerings. Teachers today frequently find that students who can't read a page of history are becoming experts in code and linguistic analysis. The problem, therefore, is not that Johnny can't read, but that, in an age of depth involvement, Johnny can't visualize distant goals.

The first comic books appeared in 1935. Not having anything connected or liter-ary about them, and being as difficult to decipher as the Book Of Kells, they caught on with the young. The elders of the tribe, who had never noticed that the ordinary newspaper was as frantic as a surrealist art exhibition, could hardly be expected to notice that the comic books were as exotic as eighth-century illuminations. So, hav-ing noticed nothing about the form, they could discern nothing of the contents, either. The mayhem and violence were all they noted. Therefore, with naïve literary logic, they waited for violence to flood the world. Or, alternatively, they attributed existing crime to the comics. The dimmest-witted convict learned to moan, "It wuz comic books done this to me."

Meantime, the violence of an industrial and mechanical environment had to be lived and given meaning and motive in the nerves and viscera of the young. To live and experience anything is to translate its direct impact into many indirect forms of awareness. We provided the young with a shrill and raucous asphalt jungle, beside which any tropical animal jungle was as quiet and tame as a rabbit hutch. We called this normal. We paid people to keep it at the highest pitch of intensity because it paid well. When the entertainment industries tried to provide a reasonable facsimile of the ordinary city vehemence, eyebrows were raised.

It was Al Capp who discovered that until TV, at least, any degree of Scragg may-hem or Phogbound morality was accepted as funny. He didn't think it was funny. He put in his strip just exactly what he saw around him. But our trained incapacity to relate one situation to another enabled his sardonic realism to be mistaken for humor. The more he showed the capacity of people to involve themselves in hideous difficulties, along with their entire inability to turn a hand to help themselves, the more they giggled. "Satire," said Swift, "is a glass in which we see every countenance but our own."

The comic strip and the ad, then, both belong to the world of games, to the world of models and extensions of situations elsewhere. *Mad* magazine, world of the woodcut, the print, and the cartoon, brought them together with other games and models from the world of entertainment. *Mad* is a kind of newspaper mosaic of the ad as entertainment, and entertainment as a form of madness. Above all, it is a print- and woodcut-form of expression and experience whose sudden appeal is a sure index of deep changes in our culture. Our need now is to understand the formal character of print, comic and cartoon, both as challenging and changing the consumer-culture of film, photo, and press. There is no single approach to this task, and no single observation or idea that can solve so complex a problem in changing human perception.

Gershon Legman

From *Love and Death: A Study in Censorship*

New York: Breaking Point, 1949, pp. 33–43

Disguises are still necessary. The public can hardly be told what is being done to it. And so, super-imposed on the pattern violence of its children's comics, there is a variety of titles, a variety of formulas suited to the age-groups and sexes the industry proposes to exploit: under six, six to ten, ten to fourteen, fourteen to sixteen, and up. The principal formulas, in the chronology of the age-groups they appeal to, are: the floppity-rabbit or kid comics, representing a tenth or less; the crime comics, one tenth last year, this year—having been legalized—a third or more; classical and educational, a tenth between them; Superman and his imitators, the most popular formula until the advent of crime, with about one third last year, this year a fifth; the squinkie or sex-horror group, another fifth; and the teen-age or sex-hate group, a final fifth specifically for adolescent girls.

At the lowest age-level the necessary violence is presented as between little anthropomorphic animals—gouging, twisting, tearing, and mutilating one another (as will be seen) to a running accompaniment of all the loud noises and broad swift motions enjoyed by, and forbidden to, small children. The Katzenjammer pattern is abandoned. Menaces are created, because, against a menace, no extreme of brutality is forbidden, where, against Der Captain or Foxy Grandpa, or 'Uncle' Donald Duck, nothing rougher than a pea-shooter and ridicule may be used. Also, and very importantly, where even the slightest overt hostility against these real parent-surrogates will inevitably be followed by punishment; no punishment at all, but rather rewards, will follow the total brutalization of a "menace."

In our culture the perversion of children has become an industry. When Mr. Walt Disney, the dean of that industry, sits down with his artists to put a nursery story into animated pictures, color, and sound, what do they do to it, to insure their investment of time & money? What did they do to *The Three Little Pigs*, their greatest triumph? They changed a story of diligence rewarded and laziness punished into a Grand Guignol of wolf-tortured-by-pigs, complete with house-sized "Wolf Pacifier" beating the wolf over the head with six rolling-pins, kicking him in the rump with as many automatic boots, and reserving bombs and TNT beneath, and a potty-chair overhead, to finish him off with. Pictures of this mechanism may be examined in Alfred H. Barr's *Fantastic Art* (1937) item 536.

The explanation—if anyone ever notices that an explanation is called for—is never, frankly, that the wolf is papa, tricked out in animal falseface so he can be righteously beaten to death. At most, one is privately given to understand that without this continual drug of violence, parents could not be protected from their children. The horse-dosage of sadism supplied for this purpose to nursery and crib, gives pause even to murder-movie director, John Houseman. Says Mr. Houseman—observing, naturally the mote in his neighbor's eye to the exclusion of the beam in his own—

I remember the time when Disney and his less successful imitators concerned themselves with the frolicsome habits of bees, birds, and the minor furry animals. Joie-de-vivre was the keynote. Sex and parenthood played an important and constructive role, illustrated by such cheerful fertility-symbols as storks, Easter eggs, bunnies, et cetera. Now all this is changed. The fantasies which our children greet with howls of joy run red with horrible savagery. Today the animated cartoon has become a bloody battlefield through which savage and remorseless creatures, with single-track minds, pursue one another, then rend, gouge, twist, tear, and mutilate each other with sadistic ferocity. ("What makes American movies tough?" Vogue Jan. 15, 1947 pages 88, 120.)

One thing is certain: in our violent popular arts—and comic-books and Disney cartoons and Punch & Judy shows are only a few of them—children do not generally identify themselves with the victims of the violence. These are daydreams not nightmares. It is the child who is gloriously violent in these fantasies, as he dare not be in fact. And his victim is everyone else.

It was for lack of discernment on this point that critical surprise was expressed during the war—as by "George Orwell" (Eric Blair) and the rest of the shabby-genteel school—when murder-mysteries consumption outsold all other pocket reprints into the hundred millions, while comic-books were the favorite, and practically the only, reading of the American soldier, outselling at PX's, by ten to one, *Life, Liberty, Reader's Digest* and the *Saturday Evening Post* combined. It seemed odd that, after being exposed to violence and the fear of violence all day soldiers and civilians should want to read about it all night. But the significant difference is again that in the violent fantasies of murder-mysteries and comic-books the reader is not being shot at—he does the shooting. He is no helpless victim, as he is in life. While he reads, he is the hero. While he reads, he is no well-bullied cog in the wheel—he is bigger than the wheel: he protects the wheel, and breaks it if he likes.

The glorification of crime is, by common consensus, unfit for children. That one third of all fiction printed, and two thirds of all comic-books, are nevertheless devoted to crime—specifically to the crime of murder—has been made possible by the Poe-esque shifting of the accent, and the reader's identification-image, from the criminal to the avenger. The crime-content remains the same, even increases, since the reader no longer need have any sense of guilt in reading.

Until recently, fiction and comics simple-mindedly glorifying criminals instead of Supersleuths, or cowboy outlaws instead of G-men, had fallen upon lean days. Their formula was so closely watched, so loaded down with apologies and pious protestations of educational and didactic intent, that no one cared to read them. Hardly a tenth of all comic-books openly glorified crime, and even these to take it all back in fatuous exhortations to law & order at the top of every page. It was also necessary, after every seven pages of glorious cop-killing and lawbreaking, to show the outlaw or gangster, at the bottom of page eight, full of bullet-holes and covered with blood. In other words, the Katzenjammer formula, but with killing instead of spanking as the punishment, since killing and not "naughtiness" was the crime. This teaches the reader that CRIME—in big letters—and then in little letters underneath: *does not pay*. That's the title of the most successful crime-comic.

From 1937, when comic-books got under way, until the spring of 1948, when the United States Supreme Court struck down, in the Winters decision, all state laws against printed "bloodshed, lust or crime" under which crime- and similar comics might have been suppressed (but never were), twenty crime comics were being published. By the end of the year, one hundred new crime comics opened shop—first gangster, then cowboy when the publishers' nerve failed—with no similar increase in any other type. GANGSTERS—*can't win*. LAWBREAKERS—*always lose*. CRIME-*and punishment*. CRIMINALS—*on the run* (formerly *Young King Cole*), GUNS—*of fact and fiction* (formerly *A-1*). Or the apologetics can come first, in the usual small type, and the selling plug last: *Justice traps the* GUILTY, *Crime must pay the* PENALTY, *There is no escape for* PUBLIC ENEMIES, or, as the final bathetic convolution of a publisher's bad conscience (the distributors have none), *Hard-hitting agents of the law strike at the* ... UNDERWORLD, with a cover-illustration showing a criminal slapping a woman in the face. And ninety-odd more.

The manufacturers are not as proud of their new abundance as they might be, disguising the first issue of their two new crime-kicks a week as #3 (*Saddle Justice*), #33 (*Crime must pay the* PENALTY), and #103 (*All-American Western*) but the total is not hard to cast. In ten years, twenty. In one year, a hundred. When the highest court in the land protects it, crime pays.

Like the toy gun and cowboy suit that are its concomitants, the crime-comic is for the younger child. When children get to be nine or ten, and parents begin to realize that thumbing through little pictures of talking animals massacring one another can hardly called literate, while similar massacres as between cops & robbers can hardly be called constructive, the necessary violence gets a quick coat of literary paint by the industry, and re-appears under the respectable camouflage of being "classic." What is meant by "classic" is that all the most violent children's books of the last two centuries are condensed into forty-eight-page picture-sequences, omitting every literary element but the rougher dialogue, and stringing and squeezing together into four dozen pages every violent scene that can be found anywhere in the three hundred or more text-pages of the original "classic." Dickens becomes a library of terror. Dumas, Cooper, Stevenson, and Scott—massacres complete. And if the chosen "classic" should happen to run short on violence, extra violence can always be added, as in the *Three Little Pigs*.

After being processed in this way, no classic, no matter who wrote it, is in any way distinguishable from the floppity-rabbit and crime comics it is supposed to replace, except that it has a sort of seal of approval: it's been printed in "hard-cover" books—as they're called by people who do not read them—and so it must be all right. As the final meretricious touch to the disguise, one sequence in every "classic" comic must always be some tender little sob-story like *Laddie* or *Black Beauty*, teaching that we should all be kind to dumb animals, This not only adds an elevating flavor of humanitarianism to the whole enterprise, but also helps the reader to graduate, at the age of ten, from animal victims to human.

Parent-Teacher associations assemble. They are worried—not by the violence in comic-books: they approve of that. They are worried by the exclusive absorption with which the children lap it up. Their education is being neglected, the very education that this mad-dog biscuit of violence was supposed to protect. And the manufacturers are spurred to action. They hire child-psychologists, educators, clergy-men, quiz-kids, criminologists, public-opinion pollsters; and under their supervision the comics become "educational," meaning that instead of fictional violence, factual violence will be substituted.

History and biography are ransacked. Science is turned upside down. Every war since Cain & Abel's is retold in the usual fifty little pictures as one continuous jamboree of corpses. The Indians are killed off twice a week, and, when they are gone, outlaws and sheriffs battle it out with six-guns for the American dirt the Indians no longer need. Alfred Nobel is made educational in eight pages of dynamite explosions, Florence Nightingale in eight pages of Crimean war horror. Teddy Roosevelt, eight pages of buffalo-killing and boxing gloves. Louis Pasteur—this was a hard one—eight pages of corpuscles killing germs. This is "educational." There are even Bible comics: eight pages of Jesus Christ flagellated, on the cross, dripping blood. Why not? It's not only classic, it's sacred; it can be enjoyed on the walls of any Catholic church. And for the cover-illustration: David cutting off Goliath's head with a bloody sword. The more famous part of that particular story is that David hit him with a slingshot, but a sword and blood and a severed head are more "educational."

It is hard to believe that the child-psychologists and educators who accept fees for signing their names to the mast-heads of "classic" and "educational" comics are really so naive as not to realize that the products they are fronting for are immeasurably more harmful than the crime comics they intend to replace (when they do not turn into them, as in *Parents' Magazine*'s FBI and *Fighting Frontier Sheriff* comics, formerly *True* and *Calling All Boys*). Hypocritically or not, the crime-comic does tell the child that murder is the act of a criminal, and will be punished. The educational comic tells him the opposite. It gives murder prestige. It *sells* children on murder the way tooth-paste is sold. Movie stars do it, duchesses do it, men of distinction do it—why don't you? The educational comic glorifies murder, as the crime comic cannot, with all the prestige of science, classics, the Bible, patriotism. *Geheimpolizei* and every other possible incentive to emulation. Captain Eddie Rickenbacker killed so many and so many men. Go thou and do thou likewise. Not only murder is no longer a crime, and need not be punished; in the educational comic, murder is rewarded. Murder is heroic.

It is this same ability to transcend all human law, and be honored for it instead of punished, that makes the Superman formula so successful, Crime comics are generally frowned upon because of the obvious insincerity of their last-page exhortations to law and order. And so, Superman reverses the formula. He takes the crime for granted, and then spends thirty pages violently avenging it. He can fly, he can see through brick walls, he can stop the sun in its orbit like a second Joshua; and all this godlike power he focuses on some two-bit criminal or crackpot, who hasn't even pulled a trigger yet but is only threatening to. Giant the Jack-killer. And of course, all of Superman's violence being on the side of right, there is no necessity for any Katzenjammer-Kid punishment on the last page. If Superman is punished at all, his punishment is something like Blondie's: implicit in his status, in the fact that he is really only an unvirile clerk who wears glasses and can't get the girl—like the reader. And this obvious flimflam suffices to blind parents & teachers to the glaring fact that not only Superman, and his even more violent Imitators, invest violence with righteousness and prestige—something that the crime comics can never do, and that the "educationals" can only hope to, since children will not read them—but that the Superman formula is essentially lynching.

In the hands of the Supermen, private justice takes over. Legal process is completely discounted and contemptuously by-passed. No trial is necessary, no stupid policemen hog all the fun. Fists crashing into faces become the court of highest appeal. And if Superman himself does not shed blood, few of his imitators are quite so careful. The question is not whether Superman flies because children object to the law of gravity, or because the flying dream is a disguised and therefore allowable eroticism. (Sigmund Freud: *Die Traumdeutung*, 1900, chapter 5) The question is: what has become of the law & order that all the Supermen are supposedly upholding?

After six thousand pictures (per child) super-flying, -swimming, -bouncing, -jumping, and otherwise contra-gravitationally progressing gazeebos taking the law into their own hands for its own good—the black mask constant among all their copyrightable peculiarities—of what, precisely, has the reader been convinced by Aquaman, Batman, Blackhawk, Black Hood, Black Knight, Blackstone, Black Terror (his insignia a skull & crossbones), Black X, Blue Beetle (a policeman in his spare time), Boy Commandos, Captain America, Captains Marvel and Marvel Jr., Captain Midnight, Captain Triumph, Catman & Kitten (a girl-helper for a change), Doc Strange, Doll Man, Dr. Mid-nite, Dynamic Man, Fighting Yank, Funnyman (Superman's second-string imbecility), Golden Archer, Golden Arrow, Golden Lad, Green Hornet, Green Lantern & Doiby, Green Mantle, Human Torch & Toro, Ibis the Invisible, The Jester (another policeman), Kid Eternity, Mad Hatter, Magno & Davey, Manhunter & his faithful dog Thor (still another policeman. but "police are limited"), Marvel Man & Vana, Master Key, Minute Man, Mr. Scarlet & Pinky (goak), Phantasmo, Phantom Eagle & Commando Yank, Plastic Man, Professor Supermind & Son—not getting bored, are you? the kids eating this up by the thousand ton—Pyroman, The Reckoner & Chipper, Red, White & Blue, Rocket Man, The Scarab, Silver Streak, Skyman, Spirit of '76 & Tubby, Star Pirate, Sub-mariner, Superboy ("Crime-fighting Poet"), Superman, Super Rabbit, Supersnipe, Target & the Targeteers Yankee Boy, Yankee Doodle Jones & Dandy (who gets his strength from a hypodermic needle), and Wonderman. An abbreviated list, of course.

The truth is that the Superman formula is, in every particular, the exact opposite of what it pretends to be. Instead of teaching obedience to law, Superman glorifies the "right" of the individual to take that law into his own hands. Instead of preaching the 100 percent Americanism that he and his cruder imitators express in hangmen's suits of red-white-&-blue, Superman—as Sterling North long ago pointed out (*Chicago Daily News*, May 8th, 1940)—is really peddling a philosophy of "hooded justice" in no way distinguishable from that of Hitler and the Ku Klux Klan. Instead of being a gallant hangover from the feudal knighthood of *combat seul*—the sort of thing aviators like to play at—Superman is actually not above accompanying his endless rights to the jaw with snide wisecracks like "I do wish you fellows would listen to reason," or "Ho hum, here we go again."

Most significant of all, instead of being brave and fearless, Superman lives really in a continuous guilty terror, projecting outward in every direction his readers' paranoid hostility. Every city in America is in the grip of fiends. Every mayor, governor, senator, president—even a district attorney or two—is totally corrupt and/or in cahoots with spies. Every country in the world is about to attack us—with our own bombs. Mars is almost ready to blow us out of the cosmos—with our own rockets. And of course the army, the navy, the police and the FBI, and all the resources of civilization are powerless. Only the Nazi-Nietzschean *Ubermensch*, in his provincial apotheosis as Superman, can save us.

> The constant traffic with the world of crime [says Walter J Ong], provides a suitable culture for the paranoic patriotism . . . found festering at the roots of recent Germany . . . "Clark Kent," Superman is told, "you're a pessimist! To listen to you, anyone would think this town was full of crooks!" The guardian of American ideals glances casually over his shoulder. Crooks everywhere. It is not far to go from this world of total crime to the persecution complex of the neurotic. (Arizona Quarterly, Autumn 1945, page 41.)

Americans are the only modern people (except the Boers) who, within living memory, have killed off the original population of the country in which they live. Only in America, therefore, has a national bad conscience had to be stilled by inventing the type-myth of the "bad Injun" to replace the plain historical fact of an honorable Redskin unsuccessfully defending his land from gun- and Bible-bearing invaders. Our merited punishment can be averted only by denying that evil has been done, by throwing the blame upon the victim, by proving—to our own satisfaction at least—that in striking the first and only blow we were acting simply in self-defense . . . as against the Indians, who owned this country before we got here, and are now nowhere to be seen.

Stunned by our own guilt—as now again with the atom-bomb—we find ourselves desperate either to fasten this guilt upon someone else, or to confuse our fear of punishment with the disproportionate aggression against which we struck. The daily conviction that we are menaced in our innocence, and not by our guilt, must at all costs be maintained. Our mental "preparedness" must be kept at the exploding point, looking always outward and never in. When bad Injuns run short, the ubiquitous rustler is raised up to replace them. When both disappear, and the gangster along with them, it becomes necessary to go shopping for victims. Whole literatures produce fantasy scapegoats for us to murder by the bookful—flogging-blocks, daily to pummel and destroy—all leering horribly, as per contract, in synthetic menace.

It was in conformity with this pattern that Americans leapt into the street with shotguns and brickbats when, on Hallowe'en 1938, on the eve of war, the radio assured them that octopedal Martians had landed in Sleepyville, New Jersey. It would have been inconceivable—as much to Ringmasters H. G. and Orson Welles as to the public—that the Martians might come with the outstretched tentacle of friendship, eager to exchange folk-dances and encyclopedias. No. If we went to Mars—yes, and if we *do* go to Mars—it will be with the naked sword, the cocked gun, the long-nosed bomber (with the motor behind), or with whatever the current camouflage-symbol for aggressive virility with the prepuce retracted may be. To excuse ourselves in advance, we have merely to project our intended aggression upon our intended victim.

Into this well-manured soil of national guilt, fear, and renewed aggression—in ascending spirals—the Superman virus was sown. Not, of course, by the two nice Jewish boys who take the credit, Messrs. Shuster and Siegel, but by Hitler. With only this difference that, in the ten-year effort to keep supplying sinister victims for the Supermen to destroy, comic-books have succeeded in giving every American child a complete course in paranoid megalomania such as no German child ever had, a total conviction of the morality of force such as no Nazi could even aspire to

Nor are the comic-books lacking in any of the trappings of their Naziism. It may even be that they are not unconscious of their function as pilot-plants for the fascist state. There is the same appeal to pagan gods for totally unearned powers—Wodin, Thoth, Oom, Ug, and the rest of that pantheon. There is the same exploitation of magical insignia: Superman's big "S" without which he is powerless, The Flash's thunderbolt, also Captain Marvel's—a swastika is two thunderbolts crossing, one on the sleeve as the *Turnverein* symbol the other in the pocket waiting for *der Tag*—the Lone Ranger's even clearer monogram, lacking only one leg of being a swastika complete.

There is the same needful creation of a super-menace to excuse the creation of the super-avenger. There is the same anti-intellectuality, not only in the worship of "coat-hanger shoulders and nutcracker jaws" (Marya Mannes, in *Town Meeting of the Air*, March 2, 1948, page 9), and in the stock character of the "mad" scientist, but in actual propaganda strips showing whole hordes of scientists in white coats setting out to enslave and destroy the world. When the comic-book reader hears the word "culture," he too reaches for the safety-catch of his revolver. There is of course the same anti-Semitism: *all* the more sinister villains have "Jewish" noses. In some cases the hook-nose is the only way to tell the equally bloodthirsty villain and (snub-nosed) hero apart. There is the same glorification of uniforms, riding boots, and crushed caps: Blackhawk, for instance, and his international lynch mob, are dressed from tip to toe in the Gestapo uniform, but in state-trooper blue instead of black. And there is the same undercurrent of homosexuality and sado-masochism.

The exploitation of brutality and terror is blatantly apparent. The homosexual element lies somewhat deeper. It is not—at least, not importantly—in the obvious faggotry of men kissing one another and saying "I love you," and then flying off through space against orgasm backgrounds of red and purple, not in the transvestist scenes in every kind of comic-book from floppity-rabbits to horror-squinkies, not in the long-haired western killers with tight pants (for choice). Neither is it in the explicit Samarai subservience of the inevitable little-boy helpers—theoretically identification shoe-horns for children not quite bold enough to identify themselves with Superprig himself—nor in the fainting adulation of thick necks, ham fists, and well-filled jock-straps; the draggy capes and costumes, the shamanistic talismans and superstitions that turn a sissified clerk into a one-man flying lynch-mob with biceps bigger than his brain. It is not even in the two comic-book companies staffed entirely by homosexuals and operating out of our most phalliform skyscraper.

The really important homosexuality of the Superman theme—as deep in the hub of the formula as the clothes and kisses are at the periphery—is in the lynching pattern itself, in the weak and fearful righteousness with which it achieves its wrong. No matter how bad criminals (or even crime-comics) may be, in identifying himself with them the child does consummate his Oedipean dream of strength: the criminal does break through his environment. The Supermen, the Supersleuths, the Super-cops do not. They align themselves always on the side of law, authority, the father; and accept their power passively from a bearded above. They are not competing—not for the forbidden mother, not for any other reward. Like Wild Bill Hickok, our own homosexual hero out thar where men were men—with his long silk stockings and his Lesbian side-kick, Calamity Jane—they are too unvirile to throw off fear, and kill as criminals. Instead, unseen and unsuspected in some corner, they put on a black mask, a sheriff's badge and a Superman suit, and do all their killing on the side of the law.

Leslie Fiedler

"The Middle Against Both Ends"

Encounter, August 1955, pp. 16–23. Reprinted in *The Collected Essays of Leslie Fiedler*, Volume II (Stein and Day, 1971). Reprinted by permission.

I am surely one of the few people pretending to intellectual respectability who can boast that he has read more comic books than attacks on comic books. I do not mean that I have consulted or studied the comics—I have read them, often with some pleasure. Nephews and nieces, my own children, and the children of neighbors have brought them to me to share their enjoyment. An old lady on a ferry boat in Puget sound once dropped two in my lap in wordless sympathy: I was wearing, at the time, a sailor's uniform.

I have somewhat more difficulty in getting through the books that attack them. I am put off, to begin with, by inaccuracies of fact. When Mr. Geoffrey Wagner in his *Parade of Pleasure* calls Superboy "Superman's brother" (he is, of course, Superman himself as a child), I am made suspicious. Actually, Mr. Wagner's book is one of the least painful on the subject; confused, to be sure, but quite lively and not in the least smug; though it propounds the preposterous theory that the whole of "popular literature" is a conspiracy on the part of the "plutos" to corrupt an innocent American people. Such easy melodrama can only satisfy someone prepared to believe, as Mr. Wagner apparently does, that the young girls of Harlem are being led astray by the *double entendres* of blues records!

Mr. Wagner's notions are at least more varied and subtle than Mr. Gershon Legman's, who cries out in his *Love and Death* that it is simply our sexual frustrations which breed a popular literature dedicated to violence. But Mr. Legman's theory explains too much: not only comic books but Hemingway, war, Luce, Faulkner, the status of women—and, I should suppose, Mr. Legman's own shrill hyperboles. At that, Mr. Legman seems more to the point in his search for some deeply underlying cause than Fredric Wertham, in *Seduction of the Innocent*, with his contention that the pulps and comics in themselves are schools for murder. That the undefined aggressiveness of disturbed children can be given a shape by comic books, I do not doubt; and one could make a good case for the contention that such literature standardizes crime woefully or inhibits imagination in violence, but I find it hard to consider so obvious a symptom a prime cause of anything. Perhaps I am a little sensitive on this score, having heard the charge this week that the recent suicide of one of our college freshmen was caused by his having read (in a course of which I am in charge) Goethe, Dostoevsky, and *Death of a Salesman*. Damn it, he *had* read them, and he *did* kill himself!

In none of the books on comics[1] I have looked into, and in none of the reports of ladies' clubs, protests of legislators, or statements of moral indignation by pastors, have I come on any real attempt to understand comic books: to define the form, midway between icon and story; to distinguish the subtypes: animal, adolescent, crime, Western, etc.; or even to separate out, from the dead-pan varieties, tongue-in-cheek sports like *Pogo*, frank satire like *Mad*, or semisurrealist variations like *Plastic Man*. It would not take someone with the talents of an Aristotle, but merely with his method, to ask the rewarding questions about this kind of literature that he asked once about an equally popular and bloody genre: what are its causes and its natural form?

A cursory examination would show that the superhero comic (*Superman*. *Captain Marvel, Wonder Woman*, etc.) is the final form; it is statistically the most popular with the most avid readers, and it provides the only new legendary material invented along with the form rather than adapted to it.

Next, one would have to abstract the most general pattern of the myth of the superhero and deduce its significance: the urban setting, the threatened universal catastrophe, the hero who never uses arms, who returns to weakness and obscurity, who must keep his identity secret, who is impotent, etc. Not until then could one ask with any hope of an answer: what end do the comics serve? Why have they gained an immense body of readers precisely in the past fifteen or twenty years? Why must they be disguised as children's literature though read by men and women of all ages? And having answered these, one could pose the most dangerous question of all: why the constant, virulent attacks on the comics, and, indeed, on the whole of popular culture of which they are especially flagrant examples?

Strategically, if not logically, the last question should be asked first. Why the attacks? Such assaults by scientists and laymen are as characteristic of our age as puritanical

---

1. Oddly enough in the few years since 1955, this became a historic essay. The comic book is dead, killed, perhaps, by the tit-magazines, *Playboy*, etc.—or by TV, on which violence has retreated to the myth from which it began, the Western.

diatribes against the stage of the Elizabethan Era, and pious protests against novel reading in the later eighteenth century. I suspect that a study of such conventional reactions reveals at least as much about the nature of a period as an examination of the forms to which they respond. The most fascinating and suspicious aspect of the opposition to popular narrative is its unanimity; everyone from the members of the Montana State Legislature to the ladies of the Parent Teachers Association of Boston, Massachusetts, from British M.P.s to the wilder Post-Freudians of two continents agree on this, though they may agree on nothing else. What they have in common is, I am afraid, the sense that they are all, according to their lights, righteous. And their protests represent only one more example (though an unlikely one) of the notorious failure of righteousness in matters involving art.

Just what is it with which vulgar literature is charged by various guardians of morality or sanity? With everything: encouraging crime, destroying literacy, expressing sexual frustration, unleashing sadism, spreading antidemocratic ideas, and, of course, corrupting youth. To understand the grounds of such charges, their justification and their bias, we must understand something of the nature of the subart with which we are dealing.

Perhaps it is most illuminating to begin by saying that it is a peculiarly American phenomenon, an unexpected by-product of an attempt, not only to extend literacy universally, but to delegate taste to majority suffrage. I do not mean, of course, that it is found only in the United States, but that wherever it is found, it comes first from us, and is still to be discovered in fully developed form only among us. Our experience along these lines is, in this sense, a preview for the rest of the world of what must follow the inevitable dissolution of the older aristocratic cultures.

One has only to examine certain Continental imitations of picture magazines like *Look* or *Life* or Disney-inspired cartoon books to be aware at once of the debt to American examples and of the failure of the imitations. For a true "popular literature" demands a more than ordinary slickness, the sort of high finish possible only to a machine-produced commodity in an economy of maximum prosperity. Contemporary popular culture, which is a function of an industrialized society, is distinguished from older folk art by its refusal to be shabby or second-rate in appearance, by a refusal to know its place. It is a product of the same impulse which has made available the sort of ready-made clothing which aims at destroying the possibility of knowing a lady by her dress.

Yet the articles of popular culture are made, not to be treasured, but to be thrown away; a paperback book is like a disposable diaper or a paper milk container. For all

its competent finish, it cannot be preserved on dusty shelves like the calf-bound volumes of another day; indeed, its very mode of existence challenges the concept of a
library, private or public. The sort of conspicuous waste once reserved for an elite is
now available to anyone; and this is inconceivable without an absurdly high standard of living, just as it is unimaginable without a degree of mechanical efficiency
that permits industry to replace nature and invents—among other disposable
synthetics—one for literature.

Just as the production of popular narrative demands industrial conditions most
favorably developed in the United States, its distribution requires the peculiar conditions of our market places: the mass or democratized market. Subbooks and sub-
arts are not distributed primarily through the traditional institutions: museums,
libraries, and schools, which remain firmly in the hands of those who deplore mass
culture. It is in drugstores and supermarkets and airline terminals that this kind of
literature mingles without condescension with chocolate bars and soap flakes. We
have reached the end of a long process, begun, let us say, with Samuel Richardson,
which the work of art has approached closer and closer to the status of a commodity. Even the comic book is a last descendant of *Pamela*, the final consequence of
letting the tastes (or more precisely, the buying power) of a class unpledged to maintaining the traditional genres determine literary success or failure.

Those who cry out now that the work of a Mickey Spillane or *The Adventures of
Superman* travesty the novel forget that the novel was long accused of travestying
literature. What seems to offend us most is not the further downgrading of literary
standards so much as the fact that the medium, the very notion and shape of a
book, is being parodied by the comics. Jazz or the movies, which are also popular
urban arts, depending for their distribution and acceptance on developments in
technology (for jazz the gramophone), really upset us much less.

It is the final, though camouflaged, rejection of literacy implicit in these new
forms which is the most legitimate source of distress; but all arts so universally consumed have been for illiterates, even stained glass windows and the plays of
Shakespeare. What is new in our present situation, and hence especially upsetting,
is that this is the first art for *post*-literates, i.e., for those who have refused the benefit for which they were presumed to have sighed in their long exclusion. Besides,
modern popular narrative is disconcertingly not oral; it will not surrender the bene-
fits of the printing press as a machine, however indifferent it may be to that press as
the perpetrator of techniques devised first for pen or quill. Everything that the press
can provide—except matter to be really read—is demanded: picture, typography,

even in many cases the illusion of reading along with the relaxed pleasure of illiteracy. Yet the new popular forms remain somehow prose narrative or pictographic substitutes for the novel; even the cognate form of the movies is notoriously more like a novel than a play in its handling of time, space and narrative progression.

From the folk literature of the past, which ever since the triumph of the machine we have been trying sentimentally to recapture, popular literature differs in its rejection of the picturesque. Rooted in prose rather than in verse, secular rather than religious in origin, defining itself against the city rather than the world of outdoor nature, a by-product of the factory rather than agriculture, present-day popular literature defeats romantic expectations of peasants in their embroidered blouses chanting or plucking balalaikas for the approval of their betters. The haters of our own popular art love to condescend to the folk; and on records or in fashionable night clubs in recent years, we have had entertainers who have earned enviable livings producing commercial imitations of folk songs. But contemporary vulgar culture is brutal and disturbing: the quasi-spontaneous expression of the uprooted and culturally dispossessed inhabitants of anonymous cities, contriving mythologies which reduce to manageable form the threat of science, the horror of unlimited war, the general spread of corruption in a world where the social bases of old loyalties and heroisms have long been destroyed. That such an art is exploited for profit in a commercial society, mass produced by nameless collaborators, standardized and debased, is of secondary importance. It is the patented nightmare of us all, a packaged way of coming to terms with one's environment sold for a dime to all those who have rejected the unasked-for gift of literacy.

Thought of in this light, the comic books with their legends of the eternally threatened metropolis eternally protected by immaculate and modest heroes (who shrink back after each exploit into the image of the crippled newsboy, the impotent and cowardly reporter) are seen as inheritors, for all their superficial differences, of the *inner* impulses of traditional folk art. Their gross drawing, their poverty of language, cannot disguise the heritage of aboriginal violence, their exploitation of the ancient conflict of black magic and white. Beneath their journalistic commentary on A-bomb and communism, they touch archetypal material: those shared figures of our lower minds more like the patterns of dream than fact. In a world where men threaten to dissolve into their most superficial and mechanical techniques, to become their borrowed newspaper platitudes, they remain close to the impulsive, subliminal life. They are our not quite machine-subdued Grimm, though the Black Forest has become, as it must, the City; the wizard, the Scientist; and Simple Hans, Captain Marvel. In a society which thinks of itself as "scientific"—and of the Marvelous as childish—such a literature must seem primarily children's literature, though, of course, it is read by people of all ages.

We are now in a position to begin to answer the question. What do the righteous really have against comic books? In some parts of the world, simply the fact that they are American is sufficient, and certain homegrown self-contemners follow this line even in the United States. But it is really a minor argument, lent a certain temporary importance by passing political exigencies. To declare oneself against "the Americanization of culture" is meaningless unless one is set resolutely against industrialization and mass education.

More to the point is the attack on mass culture for its betrayal of literacy itself. In a very few cases, this charge is made seriously and with full realization of its import; but most often it amounts to nothing but an accusation of "bad grammar" or "slang" on the part of some schoolmarm to whom the spread of "different than" seems to threaten the future of civilized discourse. What should set us on guard in this case is that it is not the fully literate, the intellectuals and serious writers, who lead the attack, but the insecure semiliterate. In America, there is something a little absurd about the indignant delegation from the Parent Teachers Association (themselves clutching the latest issue of *Life*) crying out in defense of literature. Asked for suggestions, such critics are likely to propose the *Reader's Digest* as required reading in high school or to urge more comic book versions of the "classics": emasculated Melville, expurgated Hawthorne, or a child's version of something "uplifting" like "The Fall of the House of Usher." In other countries, corresponding counterparts are not hard to find.

As a matter of fact, this charge is scarcely ever urged with much conviction. It is really the portrayal of crime and horror (and less usually sex) that the enlightened censors deplore. It has been charged against vulgar art that it is sadistic, fetishistic, brutal, full of terror; that it pictures women with exaggeratedly full breasts and rumps, portrays death on the printed page, is often covertly homosexual, etc., etc. About these charges, there are two obvious things to say. First, by and large, they are true. Second, they are also true about much of the most serious art of our time, especially that produced in America.

There is no count of sadism and brutality which could not be equally proved against Hemingway or Faulkner or Paul Bowles—or, for that matter, Edgar Allan Poe. There are certain more literate critics who are victims of their own confusion in this regard; and who will condemn a Class B movie for its images of flagellation or blood-shed only to praise in the next breath such an orgy of high-minded sadism as *Le Salaire de la Peur*. The politics of the French picture may be preferable, or its photography; but this cannot redeem the scene in which a mud-and-oil-soaked truck driver crawls from a pit of sludge to reveal the protruding white bones of the multiple fracture of the thigh. This is as much horror-pornography as *Scarface* or *Little Caesar*. You cannot condemn *Superman* for the exploitation of violence, and praise the existentialist-homosexual-sadist shockers of Paul Bowles. It is possible to murmur by way of explanation something vague about art or catharsis; but no one is ready to advocate the suppression of anything merely because it is aesthetically bad. In this age of conflicting standards, we would all soon suppress each other.

An occasional Savonarola is, of course, ready to make the total rejection; and secretly or openly, the run-of-the-mill condemner of mass culture does condemn, on precisely the same grounds, most contemporary literature of distinction. Historically, one can make quite a convincing case to prove that our highest and lowest arts come from a common antibourgeois source. Edgar Allan Poe, who lived the image of the Dandy that has been haunting high art ever since, also, one remembers, invented the popular detective story; and there is a direct line from Hemingway to O'Hara to Dashiell Hammett to Raymond Chandler to Mickey Spillane to Richard S. Prather.

Of both lines of descent from Poe, one can say that they tell a black and distress-ing truth (we are creatures of dark impulse in a threatened and guilty world), and that they challenge the more genteel versions of "good taste." Behind the opposi-tion to vulgar literature, there is at work the same fear of the archetypal and the unconscious itself that motivated similar attacks on Elizabethan drama and on the eighteenth-century novel. We always judge Gosson a fool in terms of Shakespeare; but this is not the point—he was just as wrong in his attack on the worst written, the most outrageously bloody and bawdy plays of his time. I should hate my argument to be understood as a defense of what is banal and mechanical and dull (there is, of course, a great deal!) in mass culture; it is merely a counterattack against those who are aiming through that banality and dullness at what moves all literature of worth. Anyone at all sensitive to the life of the imagination would surely prefer his kids to read the coarsest fables of Black and White contending for the City of Man, rather than have them spell out, "Oh, see, Jane. Funny, funny Jane," or read to themselves hygienic accounts of the operation of supermarkets or manureless farms. Yet most school-board members are on the side of mental hygiene; and it is they who lead the charge against mass culture.

Anyone old enough to have seen, say, *Rain* is on guard against those who in the guise of wanting to destroy savagery and ignorance wage war on spontaneity and richness. But we are likely to think of such possibilities purely in sexual terms; the new righteous themselves have been touched lightly by Freud and are firm believers in frankness and "sex education." But in the midst of their self-congratulation at their emancipation, they have become victims of a new and ferocious prudery. One who would be ashamed to lecture his masturbating son on the dangers of insanity, is quite prepared (especially if he has been reading Wertham) to predict the electric chair for the young scoundrel with a bootlegged comic. Superman is our Sadie Thompson. We live In an age when the child who is exposed to the "facts of life" is protected from "the facts of death." In the United States, for instance, a certain Doctor Spock has produced an enlightened guide to child care for modern mothers—a paperback book which sold, I would guess, millions of copies. Tell the child all about sex, the good doctor advises, but on the subject of death—hush!

By more "advanced" consultants, the taboo is advanced further toward absurdity: no blood-soaked Grimm, no terrifying Andersen, no childhood verses about cradles that fail—for fear breeds insecurity; insecurity, aggression; aggression, war. There is even a "happy," that is to say, expurgated, Mother Goose in which the three blind mice have become "kind mice"—and the farmer's wife no longer hacks off their tails, but "cuts them some cheese with a carving knife." Everywhere the fear of fear is endemic, the fear of the very names of fear; those who have most ardently desired to end warfare and personal cruelty in the world around them, and are therefore most frustrated by their persistence, conspire to stamp out violence on the nursery bookshelf. This much they can do anyhow. If they can't hold up the weather, at least they can break the bloody glass.

This same fear of the instinctual and the dark, this denial of death and guilt by the enlightened genteel, motivates their distrust of serious literature, too. Faulkner is snubbed and the comic books are banned, not in the interests of the classics or even of Robert Louis Stevenson, as the attackers claim, but in the name of a literature of the middle ground which finds its fictitious vision of a kindly and congenial world attacked from above and below. I speak now not of the few intellectual converts to the cause of censorship, but of the main body of genteel book-banners, whose idol is Lloyd Douglas or even A. J. Cronin. When a critic like Mr. Wagner is led to applaud what he sees as a "trend" toward making doctors, lawyers, etc. the heroes of certain magazine stories, he has fallen into the trap of regarding middling fiction as a transmission belt from the vulgar to the high. There is no question, however, of a slow climb from the level of literature which celebrates newspaper reporters, newsboys, radio commentators (who are also superheroes in tight-fitting uniforms with insignia), through one which centers around prosperous professionals, to the heights of serious literature, whose protagonists are suicides full of incestuous longings, lady lushes with clipped hair, bootleggers, gangsters, and broken-down pugs. To try to state the progression is to reveal its absurdity.

The conception of such a "trend" is nothing more than the standard attitude of a standard kind of literature, the literature of slick-paper ladies' magazines, which prefers the stereotype to the archetype, loves poetic justice, sentimentality, and gentility, and is peopled by characters who bathe frequently, live in the suburbs, and are professionals. Such literature circles mindlessly inside the trap of its two themes: unconsummated adultery and the consummated pure romance. There can be little doubt about which kind of persons and which sort of fables best typify our plight, which tell the truth—or better: a truth in the language of those to whom they speak.

In the last phrase, there is a rub. The notion that there is more than one language of art, or rather, that there is something not quite art, which performs art's function for most men in our society, is disquieting enough for anyone, and completely unacceptable to the sentimental egalitarian, who had dreamed of universal literacy leading directly to a universal culture. It is here that we begin to see that there is a politics as well as a pathology involved in the bourgeois hostility to popular culture. I do not refer only to the explicit political ideas embodied in the comics or in the literature of the cultural elite; but certainly each of these arts has a characteristic attitude: populist-authoritarian on the one hand, and aristocratic-authoritarian on the other.

It is notorious how few of the eminent novelists or poets of our time have shared the political ideals we (most readers of this magazine and I) would agree are the most noble available to us. The flirtations of Yeats and Lawrence with fascism, Pound's weird amalgam of Confucianism, Jeffersonianism, and Social Credit, the modified Dixiecrat principles of Faulkner—all make the point with terrible reiteration. Between the best art and poetry of our age and the critical liberal reader there can be no bond of shared belief; at best we have the ironic confrontation of the skeptical mind and the believing imagination. It is this division which has, I suppose, led us to define more and more narrowly the "aesthetic experience," to attempt to isolate a quality of seeing and saying that has a moral value quite independent of *what* is seen or heard.

> *Time that with this strange excuse*
> *Pardoned Kipling and his views,*
> *And will pardon Paul Claudel,*
> *Pardons him for writing well.*

But the genteel middling mind which turns to art for entertainment and uplift, finds this point of view reprehensible, and cries out in rage against those who give Ezra Pound a prize and who claim that "to permit other considerations than that of poetic achievement to sway the decision world . . . deny the validity of that objective perception of value on which any civilized society must rest." We live in the midst of a strange two-front class war: the readers of the slicks battling the subscribers to the "little reviews" and the consumers of pulps; the sentimental-egalitarian conscience against the ironical-aristocratic sensibility on the one hand and the brutal-populist mentality on the other. The joke, of course, is that it is the "democratic" center which calls here and now for suppression of its rivals; while the elite advocate a condescending tolerance, and the vulgar ask only to be let alone.

It is disconcerting to find cultural repression flourishing at the point where middling culture meets a kindly, if not vigorously thought-out, liberalism. The sort of right-thinking citizen who subsidizes trips to America for Japanese girls scarred by the Hiroshima bombing and deplores McCarthy in the public press also deplores, and would censor, the comics. In one sense, this is fair enough; for beneath the veneer of slogans that "crime doesn't pay" and the superficial praise of law and order, the comics do reflect that dark populist faith which Senator McCarthy has exploited. There is a kind of "black socialism" of the American masses which underlies formal allegiances to one party or another: the sense that there is always a conspiracy at the centers of political and financial power; the notion that the official defenders of the commonwealth are "bought" more often than not; an impatience with moral scruples and a distrust of intelligence, especially in the expert and scientist; a willingness to identify the enemy, the dark projection of everything most feared in the self, with some journalistically-defined political opponent of the moment.

This is not quite the "fascism" it is sometimes called. There is, for instance, no European anti-Semitism involved, despite the conventional hooked nose of the scientist-villain. (The inventors and chief producers of comic books have been, as it happens, Jews.) There is also no adulation of a dictator figure on the model of Hitler or Stalin; though one of the archetypes of the Deliverer in the comics is called Superman, be is quite unlike the Nietzschean figure—it is the image of Cincinnatus which persists in him, an archetypical that has possessed the American imagination since the time of Washington: the leader who enlists for the duration and retires unrewarded to obscurity.

It would be absurd to ask the consumer of such art to admire in the place of images that project his own impotence and longing for civil peace some hero of middling culture—say the good boy of Arthur Miller's *Death of a Salesman*, who, because he has studied hard in school, has become a lawyer who argues cases before the Supreme Court and has friends who own their own tennis courts. As absurd as to ask the general populace to worship Stephen Dedalus or Captain Ahab! But the high-minded petty-bourgeois cannot understand or forgive the rejection of his own dream, which he considers as nothing less than the final dream of humanity. The very existence of a kind of art based on allegiances and values other than his challenges an article of his political faith; and when such an art is "popular," that is, more read, more liked, more bought than his own, he feels his *raison d'être*, his basic life defense, imperiled. The failure of the petty bourgeoisie to achieve cultural hegemony threatens their dream of a truly classless society; for they believe, with some justification, that such a society can afford only a single culture. And they see, in the persistence of a high art and a low art on either side of their average own, symptoms of the re-emergence of classes in a quarter where no one had troubled to stand guard.

The problem posed by popular culture is finally, then, a problem of class distinction in a democratic society. What is at stake is the refusal of cultural equality by a large part of the population. It is misleading to think of popular culture as the product of a conspiracy of profiteers against the rest of us. This venerable notion of an eternally oppressed and deprived but innocent people is precisely what the rise of mass culture challenges. Much of what upper-class egalitarians dreamed for him, the ordinary man does not want—especially literacy. The situation is bewildering and complex, for the people have not rejected completely the notion of cultural equality; rather, they desire its symbol but not its fact. At the very moment when half of the population of the United States reads no *hard-cover* book in a year, more than half of all high school graduates are entering universities and colleges; in twenty-five years almost all Americans will at least begin a higher education. It is clear that what is demanded is a B.A. for everyone, with the stipulation that no one be forced to read to get it. And this the colleges, with "objective tests" and "visual aids," are doing their reluctant best to satisfy.

One of the more exasperating aspects of the cultural defeat of the egalitarians is that it followed a seeming victory. For a while (in the Anglo-Saxon world at least) it appeared as if the spread of literacy, the rise of the bourgeoisie, and the emergence of the novel as a reigning form would succeed in destroying both traditional folk art and an aristocratic literature still pledged to epic, ode, and verse tragedy. But the novel itself (in the hands of Lawrence, Proust, Kafka, etc.) soon passed beyond the comprehension of those for whom it was originally contrived; and the retrograde derivations from it—various steps in a retreat toward wordless narrative: digests, pulp fiction, movies, picture magazines—revealed that middling literature was not in fact the legitimate heir of either folk art or high art, much less the successor of both, but a *tertium quid* of uncertain status and value.

The middlebrow reacts with equal fury to an art that baffles his understanding and to one which refuses to aspire to his level. The first reminds him that he has not yet, after all, *arrived* (and, indeed, may never make it); the second suggests to him a condition to which he might easily relapse, one perhaps that might have made him happier with less effort (and here exacerbated puritanism is joined to baffled egalitarianism)—even suggests what his state may appear like to those a notch above. Since he cannot on his own terms explain to himself why anyone should choose any level but the highest (that is, his own), the failure of the vulgar seems to him the product of mere ignorance and laziness—a crime! And the rejection by the advanced artist of his canons strikes him as a finicking excess, a pointless and unforgivable snobbism. Both, that is, suggest the intolerable notion of a hierarchy of taste, a hierarchy of values, the possibility of cultural classes in a democratic state; and before this, puzzled and enraged, he can only call a cop. The fear of the vulgar is the obverse of the fear of excellence, and both are aspects of the fear of difference: symptoms of a drive for conformity on the level of the timid, sentimental, mindless-bodiless genteel.

Donald Phelps

"Over the Cliff"

From *Covering Ground: Essays for Now* (New York: Croton Press Books, 1969), pp. 128–33. Reprinted by permission.

In the decade since I wrote "Cliffhanger Comic", about Al Capp's *Li'l Abner*, the most crucial event by far in the Yokum saga has been Abner's marriage to Daisy Mae. This occurred in 1951, as the result, I take it, of those "public pressures" which are so often misread, as they were in this case. For Abner's implacable virginity was—next to Downwind Jaxon's permanently averted face in *Smilin' Jack*—the arch tease of the comic-strip world. Too, it was central to that secrecy which gave *Li'l Abner* its tone, its unity and—beyond the rather specious satire and fantasy—its fascination.

The trouble was that obviously, for Al Capp, this permanent virginity conditioned Abner's world: a world permanently suspended, a cliffhanger world, equally imperiled by the prospect over the cliff, or that of level ground. Capp, after considerable wobbling, settled for over-the cliff. I can only assume that he thus decided to take seriously the doowah long circulated about the "self-contained world" of Abner; than which a world less self-contained would be hard to find off the stage of the old Palace. *Li'l Abner* was all missing walls, open ends and breakaway chairs. Its glory was its two-dimensionality, not the cheesy fantastic-realism accorded it by academicians and other sentimentalists. Capp's very imagination—I'm not talking about ingenuity—lacked one wall. Billy DeBeck, who divorced Barney Google with such brusque and jovial aplomb, might have met the challenges of marrying off Abner, assuming he'd have considered Abner worth his time. Capp, who built a career on making shift with his stunted and fractured inventive power, found his strength in mockery of his characters' humanity. To make Abner's marriage (a) funny, (b) humanly persuasive, would have entailed an imaginative coup of which he had never shown himself capable; not to mention a total refutation of his strip's basic premise. His reaction was very nearly as interesting: he wrenched the typical parody of his strip into something more openly acrid and rancidly grotesque than had ever appeared theretofore. Those strips following Daisy Mae's wedding with Abner are probably the strangest, most distasteful and most idiosyncratic comic strips to appear in America at that time. Immediately, on the honeymoon, Abner was entrusted by Mammy Yokum with an enormous phallus-shaped ham—the Family Ham—which, like the family pig, Salomey, was inviolate (one of Capp's typically askew introductions of his Jewish background; another being that the Yokum family subsists on pork chops). Li'l Abner's solicitude for this monstrous, vaguely animate ("I kin hear its heart beatin'!" he reassures himself, when the ham has been struck by the railroad engine) talisman, comes between and his bride in every respect including, of course, the most agonizing. The eerie, travestied sexuality of these episodes caused several panels to be banned by local papers.

Like so many primitive societies, Dogpatch in upheaval was attended by all manner of prodigies and portents. Foremost among these: Mammy Yokum "gave birth" to a younger brother for Abner—a blonde, even more-lumpish near duplicate named Tiny. Mammy had produced Tiny while visiting a neighbor—then had absent-mindedly left him, deeming the experience an attack of indigestion. Obviously, Capp, his *jeune premier* deposed, felt pressed to rush in a surrogate Li'l Abner. But the most striking feature of his ploy was the naked ugliness of its grotesquerie, and the bilious contempt implied in it. Mammy Yokum's standard role, of course, had been emblem and (Capp's usual jugglery) caricature of motherhood—as institution, not as biological process. But beyond that, the grotesquerie and scorn of the episode—neither element unfamiliar to Capp's readers—took their heavy, mordant tone from the rawness of Capp's importunity: he had to do this; and, for the first time, his desperation seemed remote from sport, from daredevil enterprise. The pressure which he had acknowledged by marrying off Abner was simply too hectoring, too obvious. And it was the pressure not of commercial expediency alone, but of biological reality: that reality which he had flouted so long. His sole retaliation against this triumphant reality was a snarling disconsolate mockery of marriage and birth. But that act of retaliation was many-sided. For Daisy Mae, for instance, honeymoon frustration was the lightest affliction. During successive months she became monstrously fat (through compulsively eating mad mushrooms); lost all her hair; broke her nose and was forced to wear a sack over her head. What made these—well, yes, assaults—so singularly shocking, beyond the hyperbolic dilemmas of other episodes, was, first, their common physical basis—heavily outlined by the contorted naturalism of Capp's drawing style—and the common implication, which seemed only then to have dawned on Capp, that, as marriageable, reproducible creatures, his characters were also perishable: they could die. Marriage predicated death; therefore, let her, the one most responsible, bear the ugly brunt of physical liability.

Once again: Abner's marriage rent the veil of teasing ambiguity, which had sustained it, bodying forth its originality. Except for *Little Orphan Annie*, no comic strip—probably—was so distinguished by what it did *not* say, did *not* show, *Li'l Abner's* power came from its underground rivers of hostility and repressed sexual energy and irony, which thanks to the shagginess of Capp's narrative, the gnarliness of his drawing—were *felt* more than they were specifically perceived. If the content skittered away from sexuality, the drawing—the winding black line, the use of silhouettes—squirmed with sexual implications, straight and kinky. When the drawing soft-pedaled violence, the dialogue played it *fortissimo*.

Throughout, Capp's tactic was giving with one hand what he took away with the other. As a mama-figure, Mammy Yokum was both benign and haggish, often simultaneously. Capp derided the situation of an urban Jew exploiting hillbilly primitives, not only in the use of "in" Yiddishisms, but by oblique references—sardonically reversed—to Jewish culture. Thus pigs—or the pig Salomey—is taboo for dietary purposes in the Dogpatch canon; although the Yokums subsist on pork chops, the source of which is never identified. Domestic virtues are fondled and chaffed in the Yokums' sweetly troglodyte household. This repertoire of ambiguities and withheld secrets, all refers to the anality of Li'l Abner; which, I think, has flourished its sexual hangup as blatantly and as indefatigably as any family-oriented strip. Buttocks in every guise and situation (no office scene is complete without a curvy secretary stooping to that bottom file-drawer); excrement (Senator Phogbound, the manure expert; outhouse jokes in quantity sufficient to wrinkle Chic Sale's brow); corporal punishment whenever indicated, even tentatively. Recently Capp's tastes have obtruded themselves so as to cloy even the connoisseur: one episode, a couple of months ago, had Salomey pursued by a foreign delegate named Rumpelmayer, who yearned for roast rump; was referred to on an average of once an episode as "our greatest asset"; with a cataract of puns, calculated to beggar the combined memories of the above mentioned Chic Sale, Pat Henning, and any team of Minsky's writers.

Anality means the separation of experiences, each safely packeted, so as to have the best of each: as in *Li'l Abner*, squalor and dirt and ugliness (but also, the Noble Savage in his shaggy purity) alternating with luxury, glamour, svelte beauty (also, selfishness and megalomania). Anality means the harboring of secrets, the inviolate cache. All such symptoms are rooted in anxiety about the body, and about its vulnerability to the dirt and pain of reality. When Capp married off Abner, he imperiled the separation of experiences: Abner's insulation from sex, and its piquant side products. He sacrificed his cache—the mystery of Abner's continuous virginity, and how far it could be placed in jeopardy. And he included in the package a sacrifice graver and less reparable: the sacrifice of his emotional commitment to the strip, the creatively anxious involvement, which one felt as a transmitter-wave day after day: that gambler's enthusiasm and mock cynicism, *Li'l Abner*'s real warranty of youth. When Abner married, it was like a departure from Shangri-La; he and Daisy Mae did not grow up, but they grew very old.

The ultimate result of this impasse was that Capp should turn "conservative"—a conservatism as meretricious as his liberalism of a decade ago. For conservatism in its valid forms, entails giving—giving, with full acknowledgment of the giver's boundaries, personal and proprietary. Capp's reaction against his past liberalism was entirely self-protective—a scrambling makeshift of identity, to replace the identity which has been jeopardized by his vast concession.

That is half the trouble—his conservatism now has no more integrity than his liberalism then. Then, too, he opposed big business and establishment meddling—remember General Bullmoose, and Bet-A-Million Bashby? Senator Jack S. Phogbound was lanced against quaint provincials as much (at least) as political reactionaries. Only a Swift could sustain the change—or what has remained unchanged.

And Al Capp is no Swift—the other part of the reason mentioned before. The strongest instincts of *Li'l Abner*—discernable by the most casual or lowbrow reader—were duplicity and self-insulation. And their justifying force was a devil-may-care excitement and abandon. Now, Capp is still playing to popular response—but with all his cards face up. I agree and sympathize with many of his present-day sentiments, and still turn up some amusing episodes—Pappy Yokum's experiences with today's judicial labyrinths—but good conservative satire—and most good satire is fundamentally conservative—requires a more solvent more enterprising bile. Conservatives must be more concerned with principles than the liberals and Capp never showed concern with any principle between self-preservation and genital preservation. Joan Baez as Joanie Phonie, just isn't enough.

Reading it mainly in sorrow and embarrassment, I recall the awful bleak dignity of *Little Orphan Annie* in its last episodes, when its author, Harold Gray, was dying of cancer. Would such dignity ever be imaginable for *Li'l Abner*? Is it ever imaginable for the old who frantically pretend to youth?

Donald Phelps

"Reprise: 'Love and Death' "

From *Covering Ground: Essays for Now* (New York: Croton Press Books, 1969), pp. 255–59. Reprinted by permission.

George Alexander (Gershon) Legman's *Love and Death* is a thunderous, overloaded, angry juggernaut, surmounted by a loudspeaker system which continuously blares Legman's message: American censorship thwarts the imagery of normal sex, and encourages images of brutality, perverted violence and blood-letting. Legman published the book himself, late in 1949, after submitting it with methodical pessimism, to an alphabet of publishers, from A for Aberdeen Press, through X, for Xavier Publishers for the Blind. The critics were hardly more receptive: Malcolm Cowley, in the *New Republic*, contributed a mildly sympathetic review, bristling with reservations; Robert Warshow, in the *Partisan Review*, was angrily contemptuous.

The edgy reception given *Love and Death* can probably be partly explained by Legman's affiliation with Jay Landesmann's now-defunct magazine, *Neurotica*, in which sections of *Love and Death* had appeared during the writing. Despite its hospitality toward vigorous or even brilliant writers, like Legman and Jack Jones, *Neurotica* was inflected with the same defiant comedy which permeated *Love and Death*, and which defines a great deal of beatnik writing today. This reckless self-parody, so often close to self-contempt, could hardly invite party manners from Warshow or Cowley.

Beyond this, however, the aversion to *Love and Death*—Warshow's, especially— reflects the difference of two critical worlds. Warshow's partiality, as critic and editor, was toward hermetically solid essay-writing, in which every idea and attitude was buttressed by an opposition-proof wall of logic, illustration, paradox and, occasionally, sophistry. At its worst, this approach tended to neutralize the original idea, and the emotion it contained, into near-emptiness, and to reduce all argument to the issue of plausibility. On the other hand, it disabled Warshow entirely for dealing with the virtues of Legman's book: whose crude moral urgency and angry excitement propelled it beyond any question of technique or self-justification.

But time is the polemicist's chief witness, and time has certified *Love and Death*. The extent of violence within the mass entertainment industry—both as substitute for emotion and insulation against emotion—has almost corroborated Legman's jocular, ruthless hyperbole, and makes us forget, momentarily, the absence of discrimination, of critical finesse or of deep-reaching sensitivity in *Love and Death*. For this, undoubtedly, Legman must share credit with Time, which has its obliging way of confirming rhetoric.

His favorite technique, like that of the 19th-century French authors, Balzac or Mirabeau (*Love and Death* suggests occasionally the declamatory passages of Mirabeau's *Torture Garden*), starts with a large, free-floating generalization which he then bombards, like a scientist assaulting a raincloud with sand, with a volley of concrete examples. He exploits his basic irony—the togetherness of sexual repression and untethered violence—as a furnace-heated metaphor, rather than an occasion for fine-spun critical analysis. His material consists primarily of comic-strips, movies, and paperback novels; although—in one of the most effective chapters of this book—he has not neglected to anatomize at least one hard-covered bestseller, and, later on—more regrettably—turns his rather frantic attention to Hemingway. Legman's impatient questing and hoarse-throated rhetoric make you, every so often, miss the number of ripe and exact insights he can achieve when he slows down a little. In the rather sketchy and secondary section on detective stories, he gets precisely the spinsterishness of Raymond Chandler's private eye heroes, the covert woman-baiting of Richard Powell's Mr. and Mrs. mysteries, and the way in which Hammett, in *The Maltese Falcon* and *The Thin Man*, presents sex as an atmospheric vapor, as indefinite and nearly as phoney as the opium in Chinese melodramas of the twenties.

The theme that Mr. Legman extracts from such material is a growing hostility toward women which is both reflected in, and exploited by, popular art. He might as easily have discovered that the hostility is toward all pliability, tenderness and generosity of emotion. The virtue of good polemic like *Love and Death* is the way it occasionally, by its perception and vehemence, extends itself to allegory and symbolism. The theme which nudges us throughout Legman's essay, is the threat to our culture of a violence which underlies even the violence of bludgeonings, murders and mutilations which Legman itemizes. This primary violence is the violence of bad art; the violence of unremitting contempt. This contempt is evident in the later movies of Elia Kazan, with their wracking, mechanical abuse of the emotions, no less than in TV shows like *Rifleman*, or *Surfside 6*. And this contempt is a hundred times more potent today than twenty years ago, because it is bolstered with the apparatus of pseudointelligence, which offers the toys of complexity without the responsibilities. Such violence is no less virulent, because it is dedicated to self-preservation: see Harold Rosenberg's comments on the middlebrow in *The Noble Savage* #1.

The most important disclosure Legman makes is that our popular literature at present is deficient in an imagery, a vocabulary, of normal heterosexual love. Even the "four letter words," which cop most of the blame for sexual excitement, are not the descriptive images which one finds in the Oriental languages, or in the Song of Songs. They are grunts and gutturals, the pure extract of aversion and contempt. They suggest the warning sound you might hear from a lookout "laying chickie" at the doorway of a poolroom or cathouse. The real attraction of beatings, bindings and kidnappings in the movies, is that these events offer *specific images* of sex, which give the frustrated viewer a sense of palpable rapport with what he is looking at.

I wish that Legman had taken a bit of time to make these points more explicit; for *Love and Death* shares with so much other polemic a basic conventionality of moral and artistic attitudes. The function of the polemicist, of course, is to tell the public what it is supposed to know. The forcefulness of his argument always depends heavily on the impress of personality which he gives it, far more than on the cogency or originality of his reasoning, Mr. Legman sees the contrast between "normal love" and sadistic violence; but he chooses not to see the extent to which normal love and violence, in life as in art, may fortify each other. Instead—like the sadists whom he seems to be attacking—he tries to *isolate* sexual pleasure and pain. His attitude toward any psychology much beyond a Psych I course occasionally suggests a man embarrassedly paying off his poor relation. His points about anti-feminism, and the exaltation of the cutie-bitch, Dotty Dripple type in popular art, seem to be shrewdly taken; but he doesn't make sufficiently clear whether he is offering these observations as explanation of the violence kick, or merely as corroboration of it.

Legman's most serious weakness, though, is a deficiency of taste: what should have been his heaviest gun. By "taste," I mean the ability to notice the identity of a creative work, and to relate that identity to the world outside. Legrnan, I feel, has deliberately withheld this sort of taste from his investigations; and the result is, occasionally, to reduce the decent outrage of his writing to the self-satisfied peeping of a village gossip. A humorous remark by Stephen Leacock about his passion for murder mysteries is "worthy of any compleat lyncher's consideration"; and, so we'll know he isn't kidding, Legman, a little later, snaps that: "Make no mistake about it: the murder mystery reader is a lyncher." His comment on Hemingway resounds like a pennywhistle in Lewisohn Stadium, besides which he misses the most interesting characteristic of Hemingway's writing: the essential *feminism* of the esthetic taste, graceful reticence, reliance on forms and modes of behavior.

Despite its occasionally faulty brakes and erratic steering, however, the Legman cannonball heads a forceful and often exhilarating course. The deficiency of clean, abandoned anger in our recent criticism should make *Love and Death* a preferred item today.

C. L. R. James

"C. L. R. James on Comic Strips"

From *American Civilization* [1950]. Oxford: Blackwell, 1993, pp. 118–99.

To state it crudely, where formerly we had to look at the economic relations of society, the political and social movements and the great artistic expressions to get a whole, complete and dynamic view of the society, while as far as the great mass was concerned, we had to guess; today it is not so. The modern popular film, the modern newspaper (the *Daily News*, not the *Times*), the comic strip, the evolution of jazz, a popular periodical like *Life*, these mirror from year to year the deep social responses and evolution of the American people in relation to the fate which has overtaken the original concepts of freedom, free individuality, free association, etc. To put it more harshly still, it is in the serious study of, above all, Charles Chaplin, *Dick Tracy*, *Gasoline Alley*, James Cagney, Edward G. Robinson, Rita Hayworth, Humphrey Bogart genuinely popular novels like those of Frank Yerby (*Foxes of Harrow, The Golden Hawk, The Vixen, Pride's Castle*), men like David Selznick, Cecil deMille, and Henry Luce, that you find the clearest ideological expression of the sentiments and deepest feelings of the American people and a great window into the future of America and the modern world. This insight is not to be found in the works of T. S. Eliot, of Hemingway, of Joyce, of famous directors like John Ford and Rene Clair.

[. . .]

We have to first consider the conditions (unique for over two thousand years) in which these films, strips, etc. are produced. The producer of the film or the newspaper publisher of a strip aims at millions of people, practically the whole population, and must satisfy them. *Dick Tracy* appears today in newspapers with a circulation of 43 millions. Of every four books that appear today one is a detective story.

If even for the sake of argument, it is agreed that the publishers, the movie magnates, the newspaper proprietors and the banks which directly or indirectly control them, are interested in distracting the masses of the people from serious problems or elevated art, then the question still remains, why, at this particular time, this particular method of distraction should have arisen and met with such continuous success. To believe that the great masses of the people are merely passive recipients of what the purveyors of popular art give to them is in reality to see people as dumb slaves.

C. L. R. James

"Letter to Daniel Bell"

June 1953. Taken from *The C. L. R. James Reader.* Anna Grimshaw, ed. Oxford: Blackwell, 1992, pp. 223–24.

Future historians will write that in the twentieth century a new art began, and that the great masterpieces of the age, both in form and in impact upon the generations that they served, were the films of Chaplin and Griffith.

These movies in their day were no doubt treated with the same lack of interest by critical intellectuals as comic strips are being treated today. The movies were new in that they were conditioned by the suffrage of the whole nation. The same quality of newness distinguishes the soap opera, the comic strip and jazz music because of the peculiar conditions of the twentieth century—the impact of the mass audience on the one hand and the fact that some artists set out to fill the needs of this vast population.

I have picked up here and there some information about comic strips. Al Capp states that the comic strip was at first what its name declared it to be. It was a strip designed to make people laugh. But somewhere about 1931, one of those sharp-eyed newspapermen, sensing something in the population, told Chester Gould that he was now ready for what finally became the *Dick Tracy* comic; and it is something to read how Gould was told to draw the bullets entering into people, all the paraphernalia of cruelty and sadism that we know so well today. Why did it come just then? I believe that, as a result of the depression, rage, anger and bitterness were surging through the people of the United States; and the savage comic strip of Chester Gould supplied some sort of artistic expression of this. Since that time, as Capp said, the comic strip has changed completely and now it has joined the great band of representations of shooting, plotting, murdering, police-chasing thieves and gangsterism which is one of the most significant features of artistic production today.

At the same time there is expressed in strips not only gangster and police activities of people like Tracy and others, but also the lives of the great masses of the people, the things they would like to do. Joe Palooka must be the aim and aspiration of God knows how many millions of young American boys, who would like to be champion of the world and live a pleasant and interesting life.

The people need these things. Is this all the people need? I do not say that for one minute. Given more freedom, would the people need more, would they attempt to penetrate more deeply into the life among them, would the things that they look at have to be of a different quality? I haven't the slightest doubt of it. But I cannot believe that it is accidental or something passing that there is this response in the early 1930s to a profound change in the attitude of the population and a corresponding change in the things at which they look.

Umberto Eco

"The Myth of Superman"

Originally published as "Il mito di Superman e la dissolozione del tempo," in *Demitizzazione e immagine*, ed. E. Castelli (Padua: Cedam, 1962); translated by Natalie Chilton for *Diacritics* 2.1 (1972), 14–22. © The Johns Hopkins University Press. Reprinted with permission of The Johns Hopkins University Press.

The hero equipped with powers superior to those of the common man has been a constant of the popular imagination—from Hercules to Siegfried, from Roland to Pantagruel, all the way to Peter Pan. Often the hero's virtue is humanized, and his powers, rather than being supernatural, are the extreme realization of natural endowments such as astuteness, swiftness, fighting ability, or even the logical faculties and the pure spirit of observation found in Sherlock Holmes. In an industrial society, however, where man becomes a number in the realm of the organization which has usurped his decision-making role, he has no means of production and is thus deprived of his power to decide. Individual strength, if not exerted in sports activities, is left abased when confronted with the strength of machines which determine man's very movements. In such a society the positive hero must embody to an unthinkable degree the power demands that the average citizen nurtures but cannot satisfy.

Superman is not from Earth; he arrived here as a youth from the planet Krypton. Growing up on Earth, Superman finds he is gifted with super-human powers. His strength is practically unlimited. He can fly through space at the speed of light, and, when he surpasses that speed, he breaks through the time barrier and can transfer himself to other epochs. With no more than the pressure of his hands, he can subject coal to the temperature required to change it into diamond; in a matter of seconds, at supersonic speed, he can fell an entire forest, make lumber from trees; and construct a ship or a town; he can bore through mountains, lift ocean liners, destroy or construct dams; his X-ray vision allows him to see through any object to almost unlimited distances and to melt metal objects at a glance; his superhearing puts him in extremely advantageous situations permitting him to tune in on conversations however far away. He is kind, handsome, modest, and helpful; his life is dedicated to the battle against the forces of evil; and the police find him an untiring collaborator.

Nevertheless, the image of Superman is not entirely beyond the reach of the reader's self-identification. In fact, Superman lives among men disguised as the journalist Clark Kent; as such, he appears fearful, timid, not overintelligent, awkward, nearsighted, and submissive to his matriarchal colleague, Lois Lane, who, in turn, despises him, since she is madly in love with Superman. In terms of narrative, Superman's double identity has a function, since it permits the suspense characteristic of a detective story and great variation in the mode of narrating our hero's adventures, his ambiguities, his histrionics. But, from a mythopoeic point of view, the device is even subtle: in fact, Clark Kent personifies fairly typically the average reader who is harassed by complexes and despised by his fellow men; though an obvious process of self-identification, any accountant in any American city secretly feeds the hope that one day, from the slough of his actual personality, there can spring forth a superman who is capable of redeeming years of mediocre existence.

I: The structure of myth and the "civilization" of the novel

With the undeniable mythological connotation of our hero established, it is necessary to specify the narrative structure through which the myth is offered daily or weekly to the public. There is, in fact, a fundamental difference between the figure of Superman and the traditional heroic figures of classical and nordic mythology or the figures of Messianic religions.

The traditional figure of religion was a character of human or divine origin, whose image had immutable characteristics and an irreversible destiny. It was possible that a story, as well as a number of traits, backed up the character; but the story followed a line of development already established, and it filled in the character's features in a gradual, but definitive, manner.

In other words, a Greek statue could represent Hercules or a scene of Hercules' labors; in both cases, but more so in the latter, Hercules would be seen as someone who has a story, and this story would characterize his divine features. The story has taken place and can no longer be denied. Hercules has been made real through a development of temporal events. But once the development ended his image symbolized, along with the definitive character, the story of his development, and it became the substance of record and judgments about him. Even the account greatly favored by antiquity was almost always the story of something which had already happened and of which the public was aware.

One could recount for the nth time the story of Roland the Paladin, but the public already knew what happened to the hero. New additions and romantic embellishments were not lacking, but neither would they have impaired the substance of the myth being narrated. A similar situation existed in the plastic arts and the paintings of Gothic cathedrals or of Counter-Reformation and Renaissance churches. What had already happened was often narrated in moving and dramatic ways.

The "civilization" of the modern novel offers a story in which the reader's main interest is transferred to the unpredictable nature of *what will happen* and, therefore, to the plot invention which now holds our attention. The event has not happened *before* the story; it happens *while* it is being told, and usually even the author does not know what will take place.

At the time of its origin, the *coup de théâtre* where Oedipus finds himself guilty as a result of Tiresias' revelation "worked" for the public, not because it caught them unaware of the myth, but because the mechanism of the "plot," in accordance with Aristotelian rules, succeeded in making them once more co-participants through pity and terror. The reader is brought to identify both with the situation and with the character. In contrast, there is Julien Sorel shooting Madame de Rênal, or Poe's detective discovering the party guilty of the double crime in Rue de la Morgue, or Javert paying his debt of gratitude to Jean Valjean, where we are spectators to a *coup de théâtre* whose unpredictable nature is part of the invention and, as such, takes on aesthetic value. This phenomenon becomes important in direct proportion to the popularity of the novel, and the *feuilleton*, for the masses—the adventures of Rocambole and of Arsene Lupin—have, as craft, no other value than the ingenious invention of unexpected events.

This new dimension of the story sacrifices for the most part the mythic potential of the character. The mythic character embodies a law, or a universal demand, and therefore must be in part *predictable* and cannot hold surprises for us; the character of a novel wants, rather, to be a man like anyone else, and what could befall him is as unforeseeable as what may happen to us. Such a character will take on what we will call an "aesthetic universality," a capacity to serve as a reference point for behavior and feelings which belong to us all. He does not contain the universality of myth, nor does he become an archetype, the emblem of a supernatural reality. He is the result of a universal rendering of a particular and eternal event. The character of a novel is a "historic type." Therefore, to accommodate this character, the aesthetics of the novel must revive an old category particularly necessary when art abandons the territory of myth; this we may term the "typical."

The mythological character of comic strips finds himself in this singular situation: he must be an archetype, the totality of certain collective aspirations, and therefore he must necessarily become immobilized in an emblematic and fixed nature which renders him easily recognizable (this is what happens to Superman); but, since he is marketed in the sphere of a "romantic" production for a public that consumes "romances," he must be subjected to a development which is typical, as we have seen, of novelistic characters.

2: The plot and the "consumption" of the character

A tragic plot, according to Aristotle, involves the character in a series of events, reversals, recognitions, pitiful and terrifying cases that culminate in a catastrophe; a novelistic plot, let us add, develops these dramatic units in a continuous and narrated series which, in the popular novel, becomes an end in itself. They must proliferate as much as possible ad infinitum. *The Three Musketeers*, whose adventures continue in *Twenty Years Later* and conclude finally in *The Vicomte de Bragelonne* (but here intervene parasitic narrators who continue to tell us about the adventures of the Musketeers' sons, or the clash between d'Artagnan and Cyrano de Bergerac, and so on), is an example of narrative plot which multiplies like a tapeworm; the greater its capacity to sustain itself through an indefinite series of contrasts, oppositions, crises, and solutions, the more vital it seems.

Superman, by definition the character whom nothing can impede, finds himself in the worrisome narrative situation of being a hero without an adversary and therefore without the possibility of any development. A further difficulty arises because his public, for precise psychological reasons, cannot keep together the various moments of a narrative process over the space of several days. Each story concludes within the limits of a few pages; or, rather, every weekly edition is composed of two or three complete stories in which a particular narrative episode is presented, developed, and resolved. Aesthetically and commercially deprived of the possibility of narrative development, Superman gives serious problems to his script writers. Little by little, varying formulae are offered to provoke and justify a contrast; Superman, for example, does have a weakness. He is rendered almost helpless by the radiation of Kryptonite, a metal of meteoric origin, which his adversaries naturally procure at any cost in order to neutralize their avenger. But a creature gifted with superhuman intellectual and physical powers easily finds a means to get out of such scrapes, and that is what Superman does. Furthermore, one must consider that as a narrative theme the attempt to weaken him through the employment of kryptonite does not offer a broad range of solutions, and it must be used sparingly.

There is nothing left to do except to put Superman to the test of several obstacles which are intriguing because they are unforeseen but which are, however, surmountable by the hero. In that case two effects are obtained. First, the reader is struck by the strangeness of the obstacles—diabolically conceived inventions, curiously equipped apparitions from outer space, machines that can transmit one through time, teratological results of new experiments, the cunning of evil scientists to overwhelm Superman with kryptonite, the hero's struggles with creatures endowed with powers equal to his, such as Mxyzptlk, the gnome, who comes from the fifth dimension and who can be countered only if Superman manages to make him pronounce his own name backwards (Kltpzyxm), and so on. Second, thanks to the hero's unquestionable superiority, the crisis is rapidly resolved and the account is maintained within the bounds of the short story.

But this resolves nothing. In fact, the obstacle once conquered (and within the space allotted by commercial requirements), Superman has still *accomplished something*. Consequently, the character has made a gesture which is inscribed in his past and which weighs on his future. He has taken a step toward death, he has gotten older, if only by an hour; his storehouse of personal experiences has irreversibly enlarged. *To act*, then, for Superman, as for any other character (or for each of us), means to "consume" himself.

Now, Superman cannot "consume" himself, since a myth is "inconsumable." The hero of the classical myth became "inconsumable" precisely because he was already "consumed" in some exemplary action. Or else he had the possibility of a continuing rebirth or of symbolizing some vegetative cycle—or at least a certain circularity of events or even of life itself. But Superman is myth on condition of being a creature immersed in everyday life, in the present, apparently tied to our own conditions of life and death, even if endowed with superior faculties. An immortal would no longer be a man, but a god, and the public's identification with his double identity would fall by the wayside.

Superman, then, must remain "inconsumable" and at the same time be "consumed" according to the ways of everyday life. He possesses the characteristics of timeless myth, but is accepted only because his activities take place in our human and everyday world of time. The narrative paradox that Superman's scriptwriters must resolve somehow, even without being aware of it, demands a paradoxical solution with regard to time.

3: Temporality and "consumption"

The Aristotelian definition of time is "the amount of movement from before to after," and since antiquity time has implied the idea of *succession*; the Kantian analysis has established unequivocally that this idea must be associated with an idea of *causality*: "It is a necessary law of our sensibility and therefore a condition of all perception that preceding Time necessarily determines what follows."[1] This idea has been maintained even by relativistic physics, not in the study of the transcendental conditions of the perceptions, but in the definition of the nature of time in terms of cosmological objectivity, in such a way that time would appear as the *order of causal chains*. Reverting to these Einsteinian concepts, Reichenbach recently redefined the order of time as the order of causes, the order of open causal chains which we see verified in our universe, and the *direction* of time in terms of *growing entropy* (taking up in terms even of information theory the thermodynamic concept which had recurrently interested philosophers and which they adopted as their own in speaking of the irreversibility of time).[2]

Before causally determines *after*, and the series of these determinations cannot be traced back, at least in our universe (according to the epistemological model that explains the world in which we live), but is irreversible. That other cosmological models can foresee other solutions to this problem is well known; but, in the sphere of our daily understanding of events (and, consequently, in the structural sphere of a narrative character), this concept of time is what permits us to move around and to recognize events and their directions.

Expressing themselves in other words, but always on the basis of the order of *before* and *after* and of the causality of the before on the after (emphasizing variously the determination of the before on the after), existentialism and phenomenology have shifted the problem of time into the sphere of the structures of subjectivity, and

---

1. *Critique of Pure Reason*, "Analytic of Principles," chapter 2, section 3.
2. See in particular Hans Reichenbach, *The Direction of Time* (Berkeley and Los Angeles: University of California Press, 1956).

discussions about action, possibility, plan, and liberty have been based on time. Time as a *structure of possibility* is, in fact, the problem of our moving toward a future, having behind us a past, whether this past is seen as a block with respect to our freedom to plan (planning which forces us to choose necessarily what we have already been) or is understood as a basis of future possibilities and therefore possibilities of conserving or changing what has been, within certain limits of freedom, yet always within the terms of positive processes.

Sartre says that "the past is the ever-growing totality of the in-itself which we are." When I want to tend toward a possible future, I must be and cannot not be this past. My possibilities of choosing or not choosing a future depend upon acts already accomplished, and they constitute the point of departure for my possible decisions. And as soon as I make another decision, it, in turn, belongs to the past and modifies what I am and offers another platform for successive projects. If it is meaningful to put the problem of freedom and of the responsibility of our decisions in philosophical terms, the basis of the discussion and the point of departure for a phenomenology of these acts is always the structure of temporality.[3]

For Husserl, the "I" is free inasmuch as it is in the past. In effect, the past determines me and therefore also determines my future, but the future, in turn, "frees" the past. My temporality is my freedom, and on my freedom depends my "Being-having-been" which determines me. But, in its continuous synthesis with the future, the content of my "Being-having-been" depends on the future. Now, if the "I" is free because it is already determined together with the "I-that-should-be," there exists within this freedom (so encumbered by conditions, so burdened with what was and is hence irreversible) a "sorrowfulness" (*Schmerzhaftigkeit*) which is none other than "facticity." (Compare with Sartre: "I am my future in the continuous prospective of the possibility of not being it. In this is the suffering which we described before and which gives sense to my present; I am a being whose sense is always problematic.")[4] Each time I plan I notice the tragic nature of the condition in which I find myself, without being able to avoid it. Nevertheless, I plan to oppose the tragic elements with the possibility of something positive, which is a change from that which is and which I put into effect as I direct myself toward the future. Plan, freedom, and condition are articulated while I observe this connection of structures in my actions, according to a dimension of *responsibility*. This is what Husserl observes when he says that, in this

---

3. For the Sartrian discussion, see *Being and Nothingness*, chapter 2.
4. Ibid.

"directed" being of the "I" toward possible scopes, an ideal "teleology" is established and that the future as possible "having" with respect to the original futurity in which I already always *am* is the universal prefiguration of the aim of life.

In other words, the subject situated in a temporal dimension is aware of the gravity and difficulty of his decisions, but at the same time he is aware that he must decide, that it is he who must decide, and that this process is linked to an indefinite series of necessary decision making that involves all other men.

4: A plot which does not "consume" itself

If contemporary discussions which involve man in meditation upon his destiny and his condition are based on this concept of time, the narrative structure of Superman certainly evades it in order to save the situation which we have already discussed, In Superman it is the concept of time that breaks down. The very structure of time falls apart, not in the time *about which*, but, rather, in the time *in which the story is told*.

In Superman stories the time that breaks down is the *time of the story*, that is, the notion of time which ties one episode to another. In the sphere of a story, Superman accomplishes a given job (he routs a band of gangsters); at this point the story ends. In the same comic book, or in the edition of the following week, a new story begins. If it took Superman up again at the point where he left off, he would have taken a step toward death. On the other hand, to begin a story without showing that another had preceded it would manage, momentarily, to remove Superman from the law that leads from life to death through time. In the end (Superman has been around since 1938), the public would realize the comicality of the situation—as happened in the case of Little Orphan Annie, who prolonged her disaster-ridden childhood for decades.

Superman's scriptwriters have devised a solution which is much shrewder and undoubtedly more original. The stories develop in a kind of oneiric climate—of which the reader is not aware at all—where what has happened before and what has happened after appear extremely hazy. The narrator picks up the strand of the event again and again, as if he had forgotten to say something and wanted to add details to what had already been said.

It occurs, then, that along with Superman stories, Superboy stories are told, that is, stories of Superman when he was a boy, or a tiny child under the name of Superbaby. At a certain point, Supergirl appears on the scene. She is Superman's cousin, and she, too, escaped from the destruction of Krypton. All of the events concerning Superman are retold in one way or another in order to account for the presence of this new character (who has hitherto not been mentioned, because, it is explained, she has lived in disguise in a girls' school, awaiting puberty, at which time she could come out into the world; the narrator goes back in time to tell in how many and in which cases she, of whom nothing was said, participated during those many adventures where we saw Superman alone involved). One imagines, using the solution of travel through time, that Supergirl, Superman's contemporary, can encounter Superboy in the past and be his playmate; and even Superboy, having broken the time barrier by sheer accident, can encounter Superman, his own self of many years later.

But, since such a fact could comprise the character in a series of developments capable of influencing his future actions, the story ends here and insinuates that Superboy has dreamed, and one's approval of what has been said is deferred. Along these lines the most original solution is undoubtedly that of the *Imaginary Tales*. It happens, in fact, that the public will often request delightful new developments of the script-writers; for example, why doesn't Superman marry Lois Lane, the journalist, who has loved him for so long? If Superman married Lois Lane, it would of course be another step toward his death, as it would lay down another irreversible premise; nevertheless, it is necessary to find continually new narrative stimuli and to satisfy the "romantic" demands of the public. And so it is told "what would have happened *if* Superman had married Lois." The premise is developed in all of its dramatic implications, and at the end is the warning: Remember, this is an imaginary story which in truth has not taken place. (In this respect, note Roberto Giammanco's remarks about the consistently homosexual nature of characters like Superman or Batman— another variation on the theme of "superpowers." This aspect undoubtedly exists, particularly in Batman, and Giammanco offers reasons for it which we refer to later; but, in the specific case of Superman, it seems that we must speak not so much of homosexuality as of "parsifalism." In Superman the element of masculine societies is nearly absent, though it is quite evident in characters like Batman and Robin, Green Arrow and his partner, and so on. Even if he often collaborates with the Legion of Super Heroes of the Future—youngsters gifted with extraordinary powers, usually ephebic but of both sexes—Superman does not neglect working with his cousin, Supergirl, as well, nor can one say that Lois Lane's advances, or those of Lana Lang, an old schoolmate and rival of Lois, are received by Superman with the disgust of a misogynist. He shows, instead, the bashful embarrassment of an average young man in a matriarchal society. On the other hand, the most perceptive philologists have not overlooked his unhappy love for Lois Lemaris, who, being a mermaid, could offer him only an underwater *menage* corresponding to a paradisiacal exile which Superman must refuse because of his sense of duty and the indispensable nature of his mission. What characterizes Superman is, instead, the platonic dimension of his affections, the implicit vow of chastity which depends on his will than on the state of things, and the singularity of his situation. If we have to look for a structural reason for this narrative fact, we cannot but go back to our preceding observations: the "parsifalism" of Superman is one of the conditions that prevents his slowly "consuming" himself, and it protects him from the events, and therefore from the passing of time, connected with erotic ventures.)

The *Imaginary Tales* are numerous, and so are the *Untold Tales* or those stories that concern events already told but in which "something was left out," so they are told again from another point of view, and in the process lateral aspects come to the fore. In this massive bombardment of events which are no longer tied together by any strand of logic, whose interaction is ruled no longer by any necessity, the reader, without realizing it, of course, loses the notion of temporal progression. Superman happens to live in an imaginary universe in which, as opposed to ours, causal chains are not open (A provokes B, B provokes C, C provokes D, and soon, *ad infinitum*), but closed (A provokes B, B provokes C, C provokes D, and D provokes A), and it no longer makes sense to talk about temporal progression on the basis of which we usually describe the happenings of the macrocosm.[5]

One could observe that, apart from the mythopoeic and commercial necessities which together force such a situation, a similar structural assessment of Superman stories reflects, even though at a low level, a series of diffuse persuasions in our culture about the problem of concepts of causality, temporality, and the irreversibility of events; and, in fact, a great deal of contemporary art, from Joyce to Robbe-Grillet, or a film such as *Last Year at Marienbad*, reflects paradoxical temporal situations, whose models, nevertheless, exist in the epistemological discussions of our times. But it is a fact that, in works such as *Finnegans Wake* or Robbe-Grillet's *In the Labyrinth*, the breakdown of familiar temporal relations happens in a conscious manner, on the part both of the writer and of the one who derives aesthetic satisfaction from the operation. The disintegration of temporality has the function both of

---

5. Reichenbach, pp. 36–40.

quest and of denunciation and tends to furnish the reader with imaginative models capable of making him accept situations of the new science and of reconciling the activity of an imagination accustomed to old schemes with the activity of an intelligence which ventures to hypothesize or to describe universes that are not reducible to an image or a scheme. In consequence, these works (but here another problem opens up) carry out a mythopoeic function, offering the inhabitant of the contemporary world a kind of symbolic suggestion or allegorical diagram of that absolute which science has resolved, not so much in a metaphysical modality of the world, but in a possible way of establishing our relation with the world and, therefore, in a possible way of describing the world.[6]

The adventures of Superman, however, do not have this critical intention, and the temporal paradox on which they are sustained should not be obvious to the reader (just as the authors themselves are probably unaware of it), since a confused notion of time is the only condition which makes the story credible. Superman comes off as a myth only if the reader loses control of the temporal relationships and renounces the need to reason on their basis, thereby giving himself up to the uncontrollable flux of the stories which are accessible to him and, at the same time, holding on to the illusion of a continuous present. Since the myth is not isolated exemplarily in a dimension of eternity, but, in order to be assimilated must enter into the flux of the story in question, this same story is refuted as flux and seen instead as an immobile present.

In growing accustomed to the idea of events happening in an ever-continuing present, the reader loses track of the fact that they should develop according to the dictates of time. Losing consciousness of it, he forgets the problems which are at its base, that is, the existence of freedom, the possibility of planning, the necessity of carrying plans out, the sorrow that such planning entails, the responsibility that it implies, and, finally, the existence of an entire human community whose progressiveness is based on making plans.

5: Superman as a model of "heterodirection"

The proposed analysis would be greatly abstracted and could appear apocalyptic if the man who reads Superman, and for whom Superman is produced, were not

---

6. See Chapter 1 of *The Role of the Reader*.

that selfsame man with whom several sociological reports have dealt and who has been defined as "other directed man."

In advertising, as in propaganda, and in the area of human relations, the absence of the dimension of "planning" is essential to establishing a paternalistic pedagogy, which requires the hidden persuasion that the subject is not responsible for his past, nor master of his future, nor even subject to the laws of planning according to the three "ecstasies" of temporality (Heidegger). All of this would imply pain and labor, while society is capable of offering to the heterodirected man the results of projects already accomplished. Such are they as to respond to man's desires, which themselves have been introduced in man in order to make him recognize that what he is offered is precisely what he would have planned.

The analysis of temporal structures in Superman has offered us the image of a *way of telling* stories which would seem to be fundamentally tied to pedagogic principles that govern that type of society. Is it possible to establish connections between the two phenomena affirming that Superman is no other than one of the pedagogic instruments of this society and that the destruction of time that it pursues is part of a plan to make obsolete the idea of planning and of personal responsibility?

6: Defense of the iterative scheme

A series of events repeated according to a set scheme (iteratively, in such a way that each event takes up again from a sort of virtual beginning, ignoring where the preceding event left off) is nothing new in popular narrative. In fact, this scheme constitutes one of its more characteristic forms.

The device of iteration is one on which certain escape mechanisms are founded, particularly the types realized in television commercials: one distractedly watches the playing out of a sketch, then focuses one's attention on the punch line that reappears at the end of the episode. It is precisely on this foreseen and awaited reappearance that our modest but irrefutable pleasure is based.

This attitude does not belong only to the television spectator. The reader of detective stories can easily make an honest self-analysis to establish the modalities that explain his "consuming" them. First, from the beginning the reading of a traditional detective story presumes the enjoyment of following a scheme: from the crime to the discovery and the resolution through a chain of deductions. The scheme is so important that the most famous authors have founded their fortune on its very immutability. Nor are we dealing only with a schematism in the order of a "plot," but with a fixed schematism involving the same sentiments and the same psychological attitudes: in Simenon's Maigret or in Agatha Christie's Poirot, there is a recurrent movement of compassion to which the detective is led by his discovery of the facts and which merges into an empathy with the motives of the guilty party, an act of *caritas* which is combined with, if not opposed to, the act of justice that unveils and condemns.

Furthermore, the writer of stories then introduces a continuous series of connotations (for example, the characteristics of the policeman and of his immediate "entourage") to such an extent that their reappearance in each story is an essential condition of its reading pleasure. And so we have the by now historical "tics" of Sherlock Holmes, the punctilious vanity of Hercule Poirot, the pipe and the familiar fixes of Maigret, on up to the daily idiosyncrasies of the most unabashed heroes of postwar detective stories, such as the cologne water and Player's #6 of Peter Cheyney's Slim Callaghan or the cognac with a glass of cold water of Brett Halliday's Michael Shayne. Vices, gestures, nervous tics permit us to find an old friend in the character portrayed, and they are the principal conditions which allow us to "enter into" the event. Proof of this is when our favorite author writes a story in which the usual character does not appear and we are not even aware that the fundamental scheme of the book is still like the others: we read the book with a certain detachment and are immediately prone to judge it a "minor" work, a momentary phenomenon, or an interlocutory remark.

All this becomes very clear if we take a famous character such as Nero Wolfe, immortalized by Rex Stout. For sheer preterition and by way of caution, in the likelihood of one of our readers' being so "highbrow" as to have never encountered our character, let us briefly recall the elements which combine to form Nero Wolfe's "type" and his environment. Nero Wolfe, from Montenegro, a naturalized American from time immemorial, is outlandishly fat, so much so that his leather easy chair must be expressly designed for him. He is fearfully lazy. In fact, he never leaves the house and depends, for his investigations, on the open-minded Archie Goodwin, with whom he indulges in a continuous relationship of a sharp and tensely polemic nature, tempered somewhat by their mutual sense of humor. Nero Wolfe is an absolute glutton, and his cook, Fritz, is the vestal virgin in the pantry, devoted to the unending care of this highly cultivated palate and equally greedy stomach; but along with the pleasures of the table, Wolfe cultivates an all-absorbing and exclusive passion for orchids; he has a priceless collection of them in the greenhouse on the top floor of the villa where he lives. Quite possessed by gluttony and flowers, assailed by a series of accessory tics (love of scholarly literature, systematic misogyny, insatiable thirst for money), Nero Wolfe conducts his investigations, masterpieces of psychological penetration, sitting in his office, carefully weighing the information with which the enterprising Archie furnishes him, studying the protagonists of each event who are obliged to visit him in his office, arguing with Inspector Cramer (attention: he always holds a methodically extinguished cigar in his mouth), quarreling with the odious Sergeant Purley Stebbins; and, finally, in a fixed setting from which he never veers, he summons the protagonists of the case to a meeting in his studio, usually in the evening. There, with skillful dialectical subterfuges, almost always before he himself knows the truth, he drives the guilty one into a public demonstration of hysteria and thus into giving himself away.

Those who know Rex Stout's stories know that these details hardly scratch the surface of the repertoire of *topoi*, of recurrent stock situations which animate these stories. The gamut is much more ample: Archie's almost canonic arrest under suspicion of reticence and false testimony; the legal diatribes about the conditions on which Wolfe will take on a client; the hiring of part-time agents like Saul Panzer or Orrie Carther; the painting in the studio behind which Wolfe or Archie can watch, through a peephole, the behavior and reactions of a subject put to the test in the office itself; the scenes with Wolfe and an insincere client—one could go on forever; we realize, at the end, that the list of these *topoi* is such that it could exhaust almost every possibility of the events permitted within the number of pages allowed to each story. Nevertheless, there are infinite variations of the theme; each crime has new psychological and economic motivations, each time the author devises what appears as a new situation. We say "appear"; the fact is that the reader is never brought to verify the extent to which something new is told. The noteworthy moments are those when Wolfe repeats his usual gestures, when he goes up for the *n*th time to take care of his orchids while the case itself is reaching its dramatic climax, when Inspector Cramer threateningly enters with one foot between the door and the wall, pushing aside Goodwin and warning Wolfe with a shake of his finger that this time things will not go so smoothly. The attraction of the book, the sense of repose, of psychological extension which it is capable of conferring, lies in the fact that, plopped in an easy chair or in the seat of a train compartment, the reader continuously recovers, point by point, what he already knows, what he wants to know again: that is why he has purchased the book. He derives pleasure from the nonstory (if indeed a story is a development of events which should bring us from the point of departure to a point of arrival where we would never have dreamed of arriving); the distraction consists in the refutation of a development of events, in a withdrawal from the tension of past-present-future to the focus on an *instant*, which is loved because it is recurrent.

7: The iterative scheme as a redundant message

It is certain that mechanisms of this kind proliferate more widely in the popular narrative of today than in the eighteenth-century romantic *feuilleton*, where, as we have seen, the event was founded upon a *development* and where the character was required to "consume" himself through to death. Perhaps one of the first inexhaustible characters during the decline of the *feuilleton* and bridging the two centuries at the close of *la belle époque* is Fantomas. (Each episode of Fantomas closes with a kind of "unsuccessful catharsis"; Juve and Fandor finally come to get their hands on the elusive one when he, with an unforeseeable move, foils the arrest. Another singular fact: Fantomas—responsible for blackmail and sensational kidnappings—at the beginning of each episode finds himself inexplicably poor and in need of money and, therefore, also of new "action." In this way the cycle can keep going.) With him the epoch ends. It remains to be asked if modern iterative mechanisms do not answer some profound need in contemporary man and, therefore, do not seem more justifiable and better motivated than we are inclined to admit at first glance.

If we examine the iterative scheme from a structural point of view, we realize that we are in the presence of a typical *high-redundance message*. A novel by Souvestre and Allain or by Rex Stout is a message which in forms us very little and which, on the contrary, thanks to the use of redundant elements, keeps hammering away at the same meaning which we have peacefully acquired upon reading the first work of the series (in the case in point, the meaning is a certain mechanism of the action, due to the intervention of "topical" characters). The taste for the iterative scheme is presented then as a taste for redundance. The hunger for entertaining narrative based on these mechanisms is a *hunger for redundance*. From this viewpoint, the greater part of popular narrative is a narrative of redundance.

Paradoxically, the same detective story that one is tempted to ascribe to the products that satisfy the taste for the unforeseen or the sensational is, in fact, read for exactly the opposite reason, as an invitation to that which is taken for granted, familiar, expected. Not knowing who the guilty party is becomes an accessory element, almost a pretext; certainly, it is true that in the action detective story (where the iteration of the scheme triumphs as much as in the investigation detective story), the suspense surrounding the guilty one often does not even exist; it is not a matter of discovering who committed the crime, but, rather, of following certain "topical" gestures of "topical" characters whose stock behavior we already love. To explain this "hunger for redundance," extremely subtle hypotheses are not needed. The *feuilleton*, founded on the triumph of information, represented the preferred fare of a society that lived in the midst of messages loaded with redundance; the sense of tradition, the norms of associative living, moral principles, the valid rules of proper comportment in the environment of eighteenth-century bourgeois society, of the typical public which represented the consumers of the *feuilleton*—all this constituted a system of foreseeable communication that the social system provided for its members and which allowed life to flow smoothly without unexpected jolts and without upsets in its value system. In this a sphere the "informative" shock of a short story by Poe or the *coup de theatre* of Ponson du Terrail acquired a precise meaning. In a contemporary industrial society, instead, the alternation of standards, the dissolution of tradition, social mobility, the fact that models and principles are "consumable"—everything can be summed up under the sign of a continuous load of information which proceeds by way of massive jolts, implying a continual reassessment of sensibilities, adaptation of psychological assumptions, and requalification of intelligence. Narrative of a redundant nature would appear in this panorama as an indulgent invitation to repose, the only occasion of true relaxation offered to the consumer. Conversely, "superior" art only proposes schemes in evolution, grammars which mutually eliminate each other, and codes of continuous alternations.

Is it not also natural that the cultured person who in moments of intellectual tension seeks a stimulus in an action painting or in a piece of serial music should in moments of relaxation and escape (healthy and indispensable) tend toward triumphant infantile laziness and turn to the consumer product for pacification in an orgy of redundance?

As soon as we consider the problem from this angle, we are tempted to show more indulgence toward escape entertainments (among which is included our myth of Superman), reproving ourselves for having exercised an acid moralism on what is innocuous and perhaps even beneficial.

The problem changes according to the degree to which pleasure in redundance breaks the convulsed rhythm of an intellectual existence based upon the reception of information and becomes the *norm* of every imaginative activity.

The problem is not to ask ourselves if different ideological contents conveyed by the same narrative scheme can elicit different effects. Rather, an iterative scheme becomes and remains that *only* to the extent that the scheme sustains and expresses a world; we realize this even more, once we understand how the world has the same configuration as the structure which expressed it. The case of Superman reconfirms this hypothesis. If we examine the ideological contents of Superman stories, we realize that, on the one hand, that content sustains itself and functions communicatively thanks to the narrative structure; on the other hand, the stories help define their expressive structure as the circular, static conveyance of a pedagogic message which is substantially immobilistic.

8: Civic consciousness and political consciousness

Superman stories have a characteristic in common with a series of other adventures that hinge on heroes gifted with *superpowers*. In Superman the real elements blend into a more homogeneous totality, which justifies the fact that we have devoted special attention to him; and it is no accident that Superman is the most popular of the heroes we talk about: he not only represents the forerunner of the group (in 1938), but of all the characters he is still the one who is most carefully sketched, endowed with a recognizable personality, dug out of longstanding anecdote, and so he can be seen as the representative of all his similars. (In any case, the observation that follows can be applied to a whole series of superheroes, from Batman and Robin to Green Arrow, Flash, the Manhunter from Mars, Green Lantern, and Aquaman up to the more recent Fantastic Four, Daredevil, and Spider Man, where the literary "genre," however, has acquired a more sophisticated form of self-irony.)

Each of these heroes is gifted with such powers that he could actually take over the government, defeat the army, or alter the equilibrium of planetary politics. On the other hand, it is clear that each of these characters is profoundly kind, moral, faithful to human and natural laws, and therefore it is right (and it is nice) that he use his powers only to the end of good. In this sense the pedagogic message of these stories would be, at least on the plane of children's literature, highly acceptable, and the same episodes of violence with which the various stories are interspersed would appear directed toward this final indictment of evil and the triumph of honest people.

The ambiguity of the teaching appears when we ask ourselves, *What is Good?* It is enough to reexamine in depth the situation of Superman, who encompasses the others, at least in their fundamental structure.

Superman is practically omnipotent, as we have said, in his physical, mental, and technological capacities. His operative capacity extends to a cosmic scale. A being gifted with such capacities offered to the good of humanity (let us pose the problem with a maximum of candor and of responsibility, taking everything as probable) would have an enormous field of action in front of him. From a man who could produce work and wealth in astronomic dimensions in a few seconds, one could expect the most bewildering political, economic, and technological upheavals in the world. From the solution of hunger problems to the tilling of uninhabitable regions, from the destruction of inhuman systems (if we read Superman into the "spirit of Dallas," why does he not go to liberate six hundred million Chinese from the yoke of Mao?), Superman could exercise good on a cosmic level, or on a galactic level, and furnish us in the meantime with a definition that through fantastic amplification could clarify precise ethical lines everywhere.

Instead, Superman carries on his activity on the level of the small cornmunity where he lives (Smallville as a youth, Metropolis as an adult), and—as in the case of the medieval countryman who could have happened to visit the Sacred Land, but not the closed and separate community which flourished fifty kilometers from the center of his life—if he takes trips to other galaxies with ease, he practically ignores, not exactly the dimension of the "world," but that of the "United States" (only once, but in one of the *Imaginary Tales*, he becomes president of the United States).

In the sphere of his own little town, evil, the only evil to combat, is incarnate in a species which adheres to the underworld, that of organized crime. He is busy by preference, not against blackmarket drugs, nor, obviously, against corrupt administrators or politicians, but against bank and mail-truck robbers. In other words, *the only visible form that evil assumes is an attempt on private property.* Outerspace evil is added spice; it is casual, and it always assumes unforeseeable and transitory forms; the underworld is an endemic evil, like some kind of impure stream that pervades the course of human history, clearly divided into zones of Manichaean incontrovertibility—where each authority is fundamentally pure and good and where each wicked man is rotten to the core without hope of redemption.

As others have said, in Superman we have a perfect example of civic conscious-ness, completely spit from political consciousness. Superman's civic attitude is per-fect, but it is exercised and structured in the sphere of a small, closed community (A "brother" of Superman—as a model of absolute fidelity to establish values—might appear in someone such as the movie and television hero Dr. Kildare).

It is strange that Superman, devoting himself to good deeds, spends enormous amounts of energy organizing benefit performances in order to collect money for orphans and indigents. The paradoxical waste of means (the same energy could be employed to produce directly riches or to modify radically larger situations) never ceases to astound the reader who sees Superman forever employed in parochial performances. As evil assumes only the form of an offense to private property, *good is represented only as charity*. This simple equivalent is sufficient to characterize Superman's moral world. In fact, we realize that Superman is obliged to continue his activities in the sphere of small and infinitesimal modifications of the immedi-ately visible for the same motives noted in regard to the static nature of his plots: each general modification would draw the world, and Superman with it, toward final consumption.

On the other hand, it would be inexact to say that Superman's judicious and measured virtue depends only on the structure of the plot, that is, on the need to for-bid the release of excessive and irretrievable developments. The contrary is also true: the immobilizing metaphysics underlying this kind of conceptual plot is the direct, though not the desired, consequence of a total structural mechanism which seems to be the only one suited to communicate, through the themes discussed, a particu-lar kind of teaching. The plot must be static and must evade any development, because Superman *must* make virtue consist of many little activities on a small scale, never achieving a total awareness. Conversely, virtue must be characterized in the accomplishment of only partial acts, so that the plot can remain static. Again, the discussion does not take on the features of the authors' preferences as much as their adaptation to a concept of "order" which pervades the cultural model in which the authors live and where they construct on a small scale "analogous" models which mirror the larger one.

Essayists

RALPH BERGENGREN (1871–1947?)
The poet Ralph Bergengren wrote many volumes of light verse and familiar essays for both adults and children. His books include *Comforts of Home* (1918) and *The Perfect Gentleman* (1919).

EDWARD ESTLIN CUMMINGS (1894–1962)
A leading member of the distinguished generation of American modernists that emerged after the First World War, Cummings was widely celebrated for writing lyrical love poems that played with language. Always tinkering with the conventions of print, he preferred to be known as e. e. cummings. In addition to many volumes of poetry, he wrote a perceptive expose of Stalinism in his travel diary *Eimi* (1933). Like his Harvard classmate and friend Gilbert Seldes, Cummings was an early admirer of *Krazy Kat* and wrote the introduction to the first book-form reprinting of George Herriman's strip in 1946. Cumming's poetic oeuvre was collected in a single volume in 1972.

UMBERTO ECO (1932–)
Born in Alessandria, Italy, Eco has had a dual career as a scholar and novelist. In non-fiction books such as *A Theory of Semiotics* (Italy 1975; United States 1976), Eco pioneered the academic discipline of semiotics, which sought to systemize the study of cultural signs. Many of Eco's essays touch on popular fiction, so appropriately enough his 1980 novel *The Name of the Rose* was an international bestseller. A murder mystery set in a medieval monastery, Eco's novel grew out of his scholarly interest in the intellectual history of the Middle Ages.

MANNY FARBER (1917–)
As a film critic in the 1940s and 1950s, Manny Farber was among the first to celebrate the achievement of directors such as Howard Hawks and Chuck Jones, who managed to achieve a distinctive style even while doing commercial Hollywood genre films or animated short cartoons. Farber's early writings appeared in *The*

Nation and *The New Republic* and were later collected in *Negative Spaces* (1971; expanded edition 1998). Farber is also a well-regarded painter.

LESLIE FIEDLER (1917–2003)

Born in Newark, New Jersey, Leslie Fiedler was perhaps the most controversial of the mid-century intellectuals. His focus on the homoerotic subtext of nineteenth century American literature (pursued in a famous *Partisan Review* essay and the 1960 book *Love and Death in the American Novel*) caused immense anxiety in the field of American studies. In his book *What Was Literature?* (1982), Fiedler called for the breaking down of the barrier between high art and popular culture. In addition to his energetic and contentious non-fiction books and articles, Fiedler also wrote short stories and novels.

CLEMENT GREENBERG (1909–1994)

Along with Harold Rosenberg, Clement Greenberg was the foremost art critic among the New York intellectuals. Greenberg forcefully championed abstract expressionism as the logical heir to modernism, thereby helping legitimize the work of artists such as Jackson Pollock. Greenberg's emphasis on the formal properties of art, the way that good painting must make use of the qualities of paint, has been much challenged in recent years. However, few can deny that he fundamentally defined the language for discussing modern art. His collected essays were published in four volumes by the University of Chicago Press from 1986 to 1993.

IRVING HOWE (1920–1993)

The creative tension between art and politics lies at the heart of Irving Howe's writing. For many years in the 1930s and 1940s, he was a revolutionary Marxist, belonging to a remarkable cohort of young Americans influenced by Leon Trotsky and the Left Opposition. Yet during those years he also felt the tug of literary criticism, especially as practiced by the formalist New Critics. An attempt to balance the claims of politics and culture can be seen in many of Howe's books, notably *Politics and the Novel* (1957; with a new preface 1992) and in his *Selected Writings* (1990). Aside from helping launch *Dissent* magazine in 1953, Howe also found time to write a much-loved history of Jewish immigrant culture (*World of Our Fathers*, written with the assistance of Kenneth Libo in 1976) and a short biography of Trotsky (1978).

CYRIL LIONEL ROBERT JAMES (1901–1989)

A highly distinguished West Indian intellectual and historian, C. L. R. James was born in Trinidad and spent much of his life in Britain and the United States, where he worked as a writer and political activist. Some of his better known titles include *The Black Jacobins: Toussaint L'Ouverture and the San Domingo Revolution* (1938), *Mariners, Renegades, and Castaways: Herman Melville and the World We Live In* (1953), and *Beyond a Boundary* (1963). James wrote on popular culture in *American Civilization* (1950) and in essays and letters reprinted in *The C. L. R. James Reader* (1992).

GERSHON LEGMAN (1917–1999)

Born in Scranton, Pennsylvania, Legman was an autodidactic scholar who existed at the fringes of respectable academic life where he carried out many pioneering studies into the folk culture of modern society. During the early 1940s, he helped the Kinsey Institute collect erotica. From 1948 to 1951, he was editor of *Neurotica*, an immensely daring "lay journal" devoted to psychological issues. This magazine, published the early writings of Marshall McLuhan, Allen Ginsberg, and Anatole Broyard, as well as Legman's polemical essays on popular culture which were gathered together in *Love and Death: A Study in Censorship* (1949). Harassed by the United States government for publishing allegedly obscene material, Legman moved to France in 1953 and resided there until his death. His books include *The Limerick* (1953) and the two volume *Rationale of the Dirty Joke* (1968 and 1975).

MARSHALL McLUHAN (1911–1980)

Often stereotyped as a faddish 1960s "media guru," Marshall McLuhan was in fact a complicated thinker whose work fused together a unique combination of conservative Catholicism, modernism, and cultural studies. Born in Canada, he studied English literature in the 1930s with F. R. Leavis, a fierce proponent of close reading and high culture. In his mature work, McLuhan would apply Leavis's techniques to the artifacts of modern life, including advertising and comics. Fearful of the "chaos" of modern life, McLuhan converted to Catholicism in 1937. Yet once he became a Catholic, he attempted to re-orient his church to be more accepting of modern culture. McLuhan's principal books are *The Mechanical Bride* (1951), *The Gutenberg Galaxy* (1962), and *Understanding Media* (1964). A brilliant teacher, McLuhan profoundly shaped the world-view of many younger scholars, including Walter Ong and Hugh Kenner.

THOMAS MANN (1875–1955)

One of the giants of twentieth century literature, German-born writer Mann won the Nobel Prize in 1929. While dealing with a diverse array of milieus and time periods, his many novels are obsessed with the ideological and intellectual wars of modern life. Although an outspoken German nationalist in his youth, Mann became was deeply disturbed by the rise of Fascism in the 1920s and 1930s. He went into voluntary exile in Switzerland in 1933 and spent most of his remaining life in that country and in the United States. His novels include *Buddenbrooks* (1901) and *Doctor Faustus* (1947).

WALTER J. ONG (1912–2003)

A synoptic scholar who sought to link together the humanities with the social sciences, Walter Ong belonged to a cohort of Catholic intellectuals interested in the technological basis of cultural change. Ong joined the Society of Jesus in 1935 and was ordained as a priest in 1946. He received an extensive education, studying English literature under Marshall McLuhan at St. Louis University and American intellectual history under Perry Miller at Harvard. From McLuhan, Ong gained his lifelong interest in the impact of the mass media (especially print culture) on human culture. Miller taught Ong the importance of intellectual history, with a strong focus on early modern Europe and colonial America. In a series of books, Ong argued that print technology transformed human consciousness by allowing for the development of structured, linear thought. His books include *Ramus, Method, and the Decay of Dialogue: From the Art of Discourse to the Art of Reason* (1958) and *Orality and Literacy: The Technologizing of the World* (1982).

ANNIE RUSSELL MARBLE (1864–1936)

A literary critic and historian, Annie Russell Marble was particularly concerned about the heritage of New England. Her writings include *Women Who Came in the Mayflower* (1920) and *Builders and Books: The Romance of American History and Literature* (1931).

DOROTHY PARKER (1893–1967)

Celebrated for her sharp and sometimes cruel wit, Parker's writings existed at the cross-roads between journalism and literary modernism. Her early, biting theatre reviews appeared in *Vanity Fair* and she spent much of the 1920s reviewing fiction for the *New Yorker*, to whose pages she brought a metropolitan dash. Her short stories and poems continue to be admired for their verbal economy. In the early 1930s she moved to Hollywood, where she wrote many screenplays. While financially successful as a screenwriter, most of the movies she wrote were undistinguished Hollywood fare. A fine selection of her poems, stories, and reviews can be found in *The Portable Dorothy Parker* (revised and enlarged edition 1973).

DONALD PHELPS (1929–)

A working-class intellectual born in New York, Phelps started writing cultural essays in the late 1950s while working as a clerk for the New York State Department of Parole. In his early days as an essayist, Phelps belonged to a loose confederation of East Coast bohemian writers who wrote for small literary magazines such as *Kulchur* and *Second Coming*, a circle that included Susan Sontag, LeRoi Jones, and Gil Sorrentino. These writers were united by an attempt to articulate a new postmodern sensibility responsive to the post-World War II reality of mass culture. Phelps articulated the hidden aesthetic unity of these writers in his first essay collection *Covering Ground: Essays For Now* (1969). His more recent volume *Reading the Funnies* (2001) brings together his perceptive essays on early twentieth century comic strips.

HAROLD ROSENBERG (1906–1978)

Aside from being one of the most influential of modern art critics, Rosenberg was a characteristic New York intellectual in the range of his thoughts. For magazines like *Partisan Review*, *Dissent*, and the *New Yorker*, Rosenberg wrote on everything from political theory to pop art to the ideas of Marshall McLuhan. A gifted phrase maker, he coined the term "action painting" to describe the frenzied style of New York painters such as Willem de Kooning. Although dismissive of mass culture, Rosenberg did make a minor contribution to commercial folklore: as an advertising executive he helped create the character "Smoky the Bear" who warned of the dangers of forest fires. Among his many essay collections, two of the best are *The Tradition of the New* (1959) and *Discovering the Present* (1973).

DELMORE SCHWARTZ (1913–1966)

Both as a poet and short story writer, Schwartz won wide praise with his first book *In Dreams Begin Responsibilities* (1938). Schwartz's writings sought to marry together contrary tendencies, notably the vernacular diction of New York's Jewish culture with the high church seriousness of T. S. Eliot's poetry. In his personal life Schwartz struggled with mental illness, movingly recorded in James Atlas's 1977 biography and Saul Bellow's novel *Humboldt's Gift* (1975).

GILBERT SELDES (1893–1970)

Born in Alliance, New Jersey, Gilbert Seldes first achieved prominence as a critic with his 1924 book *The Seven Lively Arts*, which argued for greater critical acceptance of popular culture. An accomplished and facile journalist, he wrote many essays for such magazines as the *New Republic*, *Esquire*, and the *Saturday Evening Post*. Aside from his essays, he also wrote plays (for both theatre and radio) and served as the first program director for CBS Television.

ROBERT WARSHOW (1917–1955)

An editor at *Commentary*, Warshow wrote film criticism for that magazine and for *Partisan Review*. Viewing film as a social art, he tried to find the ideological and mythical subtext of genres such as the western and the gangster film. Like other New York intellectuals, his outlook was forged in the political wars over Stalinism in the 1930s and 1940s, which accounts for his often combative tone. Warshow's son Paul went on to attend Harvard University and donated his collection of early *Mad* comic books to that school. Robert Warshow's essays are collected in the volume *The Immediate Experience* (1962, released in an enlarged edition in 2001).

Index